# NEW YO

D0913403

## TRAVEL+SMART™ TRIP PLANNER

*Boldt Castle, Alexandria Bay*

# NEW YORK STATE

## TRAVEL✦SMART™ TRIP PLANNER

Deborah Williams

John Muir Publications
Santa Fe, New Mexico

**Acknowledgments**
With thanks to Holly Gang, a consumate traveler and map reader, and to New York State tourism representatives, who were always enthusiastic and professional.


John Muir Publications, P.O. Box 613, Santa Fe, New Mexico 87504

Printed in the United States of America.
First edition. First printing October 1997.

ISSN 1093-8486
ISBN 1-56261-356-1


Editors: Sarah Baldwin, Elizabeth Wolf
Graphics Editor: Stephen Dietz
Production: Janine Lehmann
Design: Janine Lehmann, Linda Braun
Typesetting: Kathleen Sparkes, White Hart Design, Albuquerque, NM
Map Style Development: American Custom Maps—Albuquerque, NM U.S.A.
Map Illustration: Kathleen Sparkes, White Hart Design, Albuquerque, NM
Printing: Publishers Press
Front cover photo: Leo de Wys Inc./J. Blank
Back cover photos: *top*—Marshall J. Brown
                   *bottom*—New York Convention and Visitors Bureau


Distributed to the book trade by
Publishers Group West
Emeryville, California

# HOW TO USE THIS BOOK

The *New York State Travel✦Smart Trip Planner* is organized in 17 destination chapters, each covering the best sights and activities, restaurants, and lodging available in that specific destination. Thanks to thorough research and experience, the author is able to bring you only the best options, saving you time and money in your travels. The chapters are presented in geographic sequence so you can follow an easy route from one place to the next. If you were to visit each destination in chapter order, you'd enjoy a complete tour of the best of New York State.

**Each chapter contains:**

- User-friendly maps of the area, showing all recommended sights, restaurants, and accommodations.
- "A Perfect Day" description—how the author would spend her time if she had just one day in that destination.
- Sightseeing highlights, each rated by degree of importance: ✯✯✯ Don't miss; ✯✯ Try hard to see; ✯ See if you have time; and No stars—Worth knowing about.
- Selected restaurant, lodging, and camping recommendations to suit a variety of budgets.
- Helpful hints, fitness and recreation ideas, insights, and random tidbits of information to enhance your trip.

**The Importance of Planning.** Developing an itinerary is the best way to get the most satisfaction from your travels, and this guidebook makes it easy. First, read through the book and choose the places you'd most like to visit. Then, study the color map on the inside cover flap and the mileage chart (page 12) to determine which you can realistically see in the time you have available and at the travel pace you prefer. Using the Planning Map (pages 10–11), map out your route. Finally, use the lodging recommendations to determine your accommodations.

**Some Suggested Itineraries.** To get you started, six itineraries of varying lengths and based on specific interests follow. Mix and match according to your interests and time constraints, or follow a given itinerary from start to finish. The possibilities are endless. *Happy travels!*

# SUGGESTED ITINERARIES

With the *New York State Travel•Smart Trip Planner* you can plan a trip of any length—a one-day excursion, a getaway weekend, or a three-week vacation—around any special interest. To get you started, the following pages contain six suggested itineraries geared toward a variety of interests. For more information, refer to the chapters listed—chapter names are bolded, and chapter numbers appear inside black bullets. You can follow a suggested itinerary in its entirety, or shorten, lengthen, or combine parts of each, depending on your starting and ending points.

Discuss alternative routes and schedules with your travel companions—it's a great way to have fun, even before you leave home. And remember: don't hesitate to change your itinerary once you're on the road. Careful study and planning ahead will help you make informed decisions as you go, but spontaneity is the extra ingredient that will make your trip memorable.

© Joseph Pobereskin/NYCVB

*Central Park, Manhattan*

# New York State in One to Three Weeks

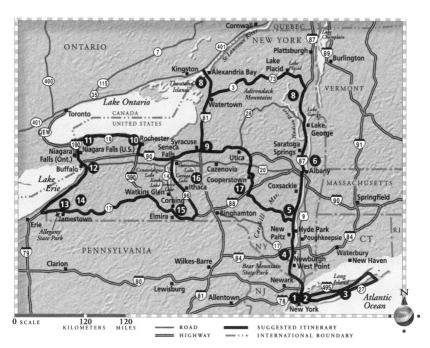

If you have one week to visit, see:
- ❶ **Manhattan**
- ❹ **The Hudson River Valley**
- ⓫ **Niagara Falls**

If you have two weeks to visit, add:
- ❸ **Long Island**
- ❽ **The Adirondacks**
- ⓭ **Chautauqua County**
- ⓯ **Corning and Elmira**
- ⓰ **The Finger Lakes**

If you have three or more weeks, add:
- ❷ **New York City's Outer Boroughs**
- ❺ **The Catskills**
- ❻ **Albany and Saratoga Springs**
- ❽ **The Thousand Islands**
- ❾ **Syracuse**
- ❿ **Rochester**
- ⓬ **Buffalo**
- ⓮ **Cattaraugus County**
- ⓱ **Central Leatherstocking**

# Nature Lover's Tour

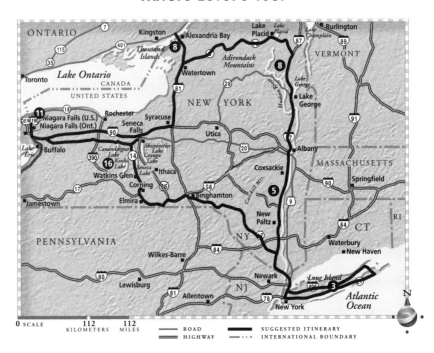

New York offers a tantalizing array of sights for nature lovers, from miles of Long Island beaches to the lakes and peaks of the Adirondacks and the Catskills, from the Finger Lakes to the Hudson River Valley, and from the shores of the Great Lakes to Niagara Falls.

❸ **Long Island** (Fire Island National Seashore, Jones Beach State Park)
❺ **The Catskills** (Ice Caves Mountain, Minnewaska State Park)
❽ **The Adirondacks** (Whiteface Mountain, Ausable Chasm, Mt. Van Hoevenberg)
❽ **The Thousand Islands** (Wellesley Island State Park)
⓫ **Niagara Falls** (Goat Island, Niagara Reservation State Park)
⓰ **The Finger Lakes** (Watkins Glen State Park, Montezuma National Wildlife Refuge)

Time needed: 2 to 3 weeks

# Arts and Culture Tour

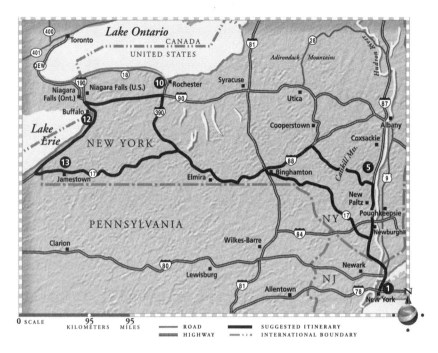

New York State has rich arts and cultural offerings, such as Chautauqua; Buffalo, well-known for its architectural treasures, art galleries, and lively theater scene; Rochester, home to world-famous museums; and the Catskills, popular with artists and host to a variety of cultural festivals. Manhattan is the theater and arts capital of the United States—some would say the world.

- **①** **Manhattan** (Museums, Lincoln Center, Carnegie Hall, Broadway)
- **⑤** **The Catskills** (Bronck Museum, Huguenot Street)
- **⑩** **Rochester** (George Eastman House and International Museum of Photography and Film, Strong Museum, Memorial Art Gallery)
- **⑫** **Buffalo** (Albright-Knox Art Gallery, Delaware Avenue, Buffalo Philharmonic Orchestra, Theater District)
- **⑬** **Chautauqua County** (Chautauqua Institution)

Time needed: 2 weeks

# Family Fun Tour

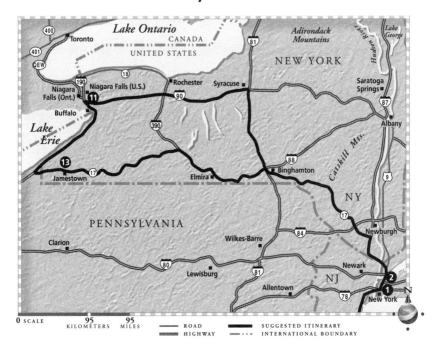

Everyone is amazed by Niagara Falls, but families will find a wealth of activities in Chautauqua County, too. Manhattan, of course, is home to a multitude of sights to dazzle and entertain people of all ages.

- ❶ **Manhattan** (American Museum of Natural History, Museum of Television and Radio, Statue of Liberty, Empire State Building)
- ❷ **New York City's Outer Boroughs** (Bronx Zoo)
- ⑪ **Niagara Falls** (*Maid of the Mist*)
- ⑬ **Chautauqua County** (Chautauqua Institution)

Time needed: 1 weeks

# Literary Tour

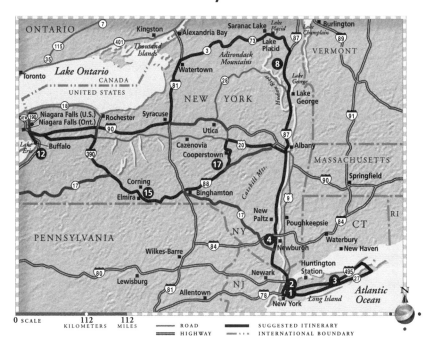

There's hardly any place in the state that doesn't have literary connections, but the places listed below have particularly strong literary ties. In parentheses are some of the area's famous writers, many of whose haunts, homes, and books can be visited and examined.

❶ **Manhattan** (O. Henry, Henry James, Eugene O'Neill, John Reed, Damon Runyon, Edith Wharton, Thomas Wolfe)

❷ **New York City's Outer Boroughs** (Truman Capote, Arthur Miller, Edgar Allen Poe, Walt Whitman)

❸ **Long Island** (Walt Whitman)

❹ **The Hudson River Valley** (Washington Irving)

❽ **The Adirondacks** (Robert Louis Stevenson, Laura Ingalls Wilder)

⓬ **Buffalo** (Mark Twain)

⓯ **Corning and Elmira** (Mark Twain)

⓱ **Central Leatherstocking** (James Fenimore Cooper)

Time needed: 2 to 3 weeks

# Outdoor Sports and Recreation Tour

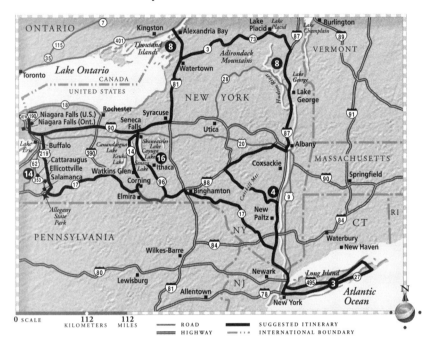

Whether you like hiking or golfing, skiing or fishing, camping or canoeing, New York has ample opportunities for outdoor enthusiasts.

❸ **Long Island** (Fire Island, Jones Beach, Greenbelt Trails; hiking, swimming)

❹ **The Catskills** (Mohonk Mountain House, Minnewaska State Park, Hunter Mountain, North Lake Area; trout fishing, hiking, camping)

❽ **The Adirondacks** (Whiteface Mountain, Mt. Van Hoevenberg Recreation Area; all snow sports, fishing, canoeing, hunting, camping)

❽ **The Thousand Islands** (Wellesley Island State Park, Selkirk Shores Park; golfing, fishing, camping)

⓮ **Cattaraugus County** (Allegany State Park, Holiday Valley; hiking, camping)

⓰ **The Finger Lakes** (Watkins Glen State Park, Taughannock Falls State Park, Finger Lakes Trail; hiking, skiing, boating, camping)

Time needed: 2 to 3 weeks

# USING THE PLANNING MAP

A major aspect of itinerary planning is determining your mode of transportation and the route you will follow as you travel from destination to destination. The Planning Map on the following pages will allow you to do just that.

First, read through the destination chapters carefully and note the sights that intrigue you. Then, photocopy the Planning Map so you can try out several different routes that will take you to these destinations. (The mileage chart that follows will help you to calculate your travel distances.) Decide where you will be starting your tour of New York State. Will you fly into New York City, Albany, or Buffalo, or will you start from somewhere in between? Will you be driving from place to place or flying into major transportation hubs and renting a car for day trips? The answers to these questions will form the basis for your travel route design.

Once you have a firm idea of where your travels will take you, copy your route onto the additional Planning Map in the Appendix. You won't have to worry about where your map is, and the information you need on each destination will always be close at hand.

New York Convention and Visitors Bureau

*Times Square, Manhattan*

# Planning Map: New York State

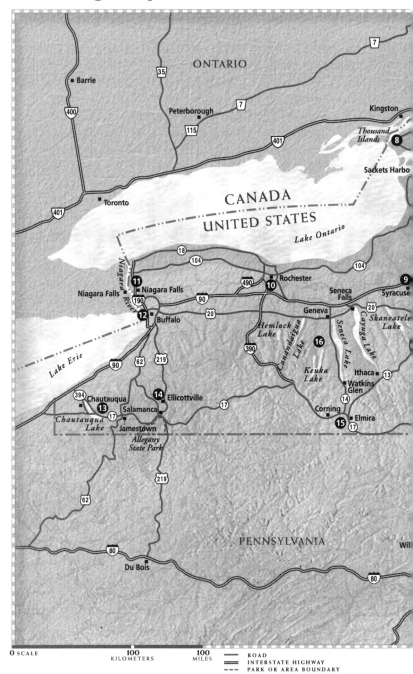

ONTARIO

Barrie

35

400

Peterborough

115

7

401

7

Kingston

Thousand
Islands

8

Sackets Harbo

Toronto

401

CANADA

UNITED STATES

Lake Ontario

Niagara River

18

104

104

490

Rochester

10

104

9

Niagara Falls

11

Niagara Falls

190

Seneca
Falls

Syracuse

90

20

20

Geneva

Skaneatele
Lake

12

Buffalo

20

Hemlock
Lake

Seneca Lake

Cayuga Lake

16

Lake Erie

390

Canandaigua Lake

Keuka
Lake

90

62

219

Ithaca

13

Watkins
Glen

14

Chautauqua

394

Ellicottville

17

Corning

14

13

Salamanca

15

Elmira

Chautauqua
Lake

17

Jamestown

17

Allegany
State Park

219

62

80

PENNSYLVANIA

Wil

Du Bois

80

0 SCALE     100 KILOMETERS     100 MILES

ROAD
INTERSTATE HIGHWAY
PARK OR AREA BOUNDARY

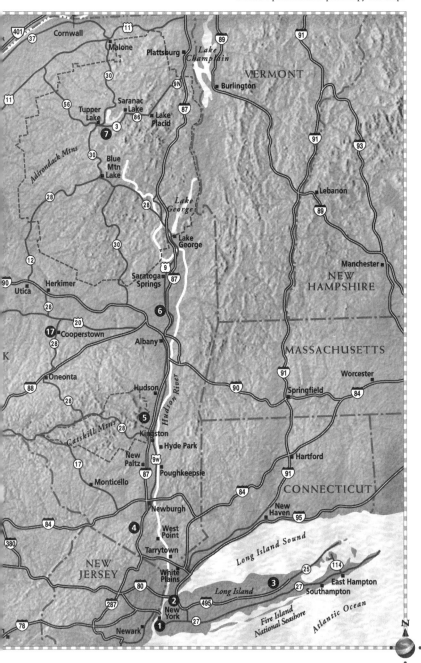

# NEW YORK STATE MILEAGE CHART

| | Albany | Binghamton | Buffalo | Elmira | Glens Falls | Ithaca | Jamestown | Kingston | New York City | Niagara | Rochester | Saranac Lake | Syracuse | Utica |
|---|---|---|---|---|---|---|---|---|---|---|---|---|---|---|
| Binghamton | 134 | | | | | | | | | | | | | |
| Buffalo | 295 | 200 | | | | | | | | | | | | |
| Elmira | 189 | 58 | 142 | | | | | | | | | | | |
| Glens Falls | 54 | 75 | 305 | 266 | | | | | | | | | | |
| Ithaca | 178 | 53 | 155 | 33 | 199 | | | | | | | | | |
| Jamestown | 354 | 219 | 71 | 163 | 369 | 188 | | | | | | | | |
| Kingston | 54 | 135 | 341 | 189 | 105 | 182 | 351 | | | | | | | |
| New York City | 159 | 195 | 393 | 251 | 212 | 246 | 414 | 107 | | | | | | |
| Niagara Falls | 302 | 217 | 21 | 164 | 317 | 167 | 92 | 353 | 437 | | | | | |
| Rochester | 231 | 166 | 78 | 119 | 240 | 90 | 140 | 276 | 373 | 85 | | | | |
| Saranac Lake | 159 | 239 | 330 | 272 | 108 | 239 | 394 | 210 | 307 | 339 | 254 | | | |
| Syracuse | 147 | 76 | 154 | 93 | 161 | 58 | 216 | 197 | 269 | 164 | 90 | 189 | | |
| Utica | 95 | 131 | 199 | 126 | 109 | 93 | 163 | 142 | 239 | 211 | 134 | 146 | 52 | |
| Watertown | 179 | 148 | 210 | 163 | 175 | 130 | 174 | 225 | 341 | 219 | 134 | 120 | 72 | 84 |

# WHY VISIT NEW YORK STATE?

It could be argued that there is more to see and do in New York State than in most countries. From the awesome beauty of the Adirondacks and Niagara Falls to the majesty of the Hudson River and the cultural and commercial explosion of Manhattan, New York is certainly one of the most diverse states in the nation. From its very beginnings, when George Washington proclaimed that it would be "the seat of our Empire," New York State has been known as the Empire State. It's still possible to dine, sleep, and even worship in some of the same places the Father of Our Country did while leading the new nation; the state is as rich in history as it is varied in landscape.

Though New York has lost its status as the nation's most populous state, the tiny island of Manhattan still makes it the artistic and economic capital of the country and, some would argue, the world. New York City inspires lists of superlatives in visitors and residents alike; its reputation as the biggest and the best in many things is well deserved. The city has long been a gateway for floods of immigrants and to this day is continually reenergized by waves of newcomers.

Psychologically, the city and the rest of the state abide in a love-hate relationship. The geographic diversity of the state creates distinct regional personalities, all worthy of exploration, yet some New Yorkers feel that the power and fame of New York City at times eclipses the glories of the rest of the state. Most non-residents of the state would probably be surprised to discover, for instance, that agriculture is one of the state's top industries. Orchards, vineyards, and vegetable and dairy farms dot the countryside. In fact, outside of New York City and a few other cities, New York State is predominantly rural, with open country filled with lakes, rivers and streams, rolling hills, mountains, gorges, and waterfalls to rival any in the world. Explorers will discover that mighty Manhattan's urban sublimities are matched by natural counterparts throughout the rest of the state.

## HISTORY

Two major Native American groups inhabited what is now New York State when Europeans began exploration of the area. The Algonquins occupied much of the Hudson Valley, Manhattan, and Long Island, while the Iroquois controlled most of the rest of the region.

The first European sighting of New York was made in 1524 by Giovanni da Verrazano, a Florentine merchant, who described the land he found as having a "commodiousness and beauty." An early tourist mini-boom occurred in 1609, when Samuel de Champlain and Henry Hudson visited. Champlain traveled south from Canada and named the lake that now forms the state's eastern border after himself. Henry Hudson, who was employed by the Dutch East India Company, sailed into New York harbor in 1609, on the *Half Moon* and up the river that was to become his namesake to what is now Albany. At that point he realized that, although it was a "mighty deep-throated river," it was not the Northwest Passage he had been searching for.

Because of Hudson's discoveries, the Dutch claimed the land and named it New Netherland. Peter Minuit, the first governor of the Dutch colony, bought Manhattan Island from the Algonquins in 1626 for 24 dollars' worth of tools and trinkets—surely one of the shrewdest buys in history. In 1664 Peter Stuyvesant, the peg-legged Dutch governor, surrendered beleaguered New Amsterdam to the British. The colony was renamed New York after the Duke of York, who later became King James II.

New York was Britain's most important outpost, and its location made it a key player in the century-long struggle between France and Britain for control of North America. Though it was still mostly wilderness at the outbreak of the Revolutionary War, nearly one-third of all the battles were fought in New York. At the war's end, General Washington bid an emotional farewell to his soldiers at Fraunces Tavern in New York City, the new nation's first capital. Just a few years later he served in New York City as the country's first president.

Under the leadership of Governor DeWitt Clinton, the Erie Canal was built between 1817 and 1825 to link New York City with Buffalo. Its completion opened up the state to development, commerce, and settlement. Fortunes were made in trade and commerce, and a new era of industrialization began. The state quickly became the economic center of the nation. During the nineteenth century, state residents founded a religion, launched the women's rights movement, invented the camera, and founded several important colleges and universities.

Following the Civil War, European immigrants flocked to New York City and spread across the state and the nation. As the population swelled, the nation's largest city began to take on the look it has today, with its towering skyscrapers, and it soon became the pacesetter for the nation. In this century the state sent two native sons, both Roosevelts (Theodore and Franklin D.) and both former governors, to the White House, where they made their mark on world history.

## CULTURES

All the major cities in the state have long traditions of ethnic diversity. Buffalo is home to large enclaves of Polish, Irish, and Italians, as well as African Americans who came north to work in the once-flourishing steel mills. More recently, Puerto Rican neighborhoods have sprung up in Buffalo and other upstate cities. Syracuse maintains a strong Irish neighborhood. The Native American presence is still felt in some areas of western and central New York, where several reservations are located; Salamanca, in Cattaraugus County, is the only city in the country on a Native American reservation.

New York City is the world's most ethnically diverse city, and immigrants from all over the globe continue to arrive daily seeking the American dream. One of the country's most enduring images is of immigrants entering the New World huddled on overcrowded ships with all their possessions in tattered cases, determined to make it in the Promised Land. Newcomers' first sight of America was the Statue of Liberty in New York's harbor. During the early nineteenth century, German and Irish immigrants began arriving. Chinese and Southern and Eastern Europeans followed in waves. Jews from Eastern Europe began arriving in the late nineteenth century, fleeing the pogroms in Russia. In the early part of this century, tens of thousands of African Americans fled the Deep South; many settled in Harlem, later to become home to Puerto Ricans as well.

Although the massive immigration period is history, immigration, legal and illegal, continues at a steady pace. Chinatown has grown dramatically in recent years. In the 1970s Russian immigrants transformed Brooklyn's Brighton Beach area. Greek residents have similarly made their mark on Astoria in Queens. East Indians, Koreans, West Indians, Filipinos, Latinos, Eastern Europeans, and Middle Easterners are prominent among the nearly 100,000 people who settle in New York each year. All these groups have influenced the city with their customs, languages, and cuisines. In fact, the ethnic composition of the city changes so rapidly, it's difficult to keep track of demographic effects.

The state's ethnic diversity is reflected in hundreds of annual festivals and parades, from the Pulaski Day Parade in Buffalo to the Keeper of the Western Door Pow-Wow in Salamanca; from German, Irish, Italian, and Native American festivals in the Catskills to Greek, Puerto Rican, Japanese, and Ukrainian parades in New York City.

## THE ARTS

New York has a laudable reputation for supporting the arts. In the southwestern corner of the state, Chautauqua Institution—a uniquely American summer enclave of arts, theater, music, sports, and religion—has attracted visitors since its founding in 1874. Buffalo is well known for its rich architectural treasures, designed by the likes of Louis Sullivan and Frank Lloyd Wright, and for the world-famous Albright-Knox Art Gallery. Artpark, in the village of Lewiston, north of Niagara Falls, is the only state park in the country devoted to the arts. In Rochester, the George Eastman House and the International Museum of Photography and Film showcase the world's finest collection of photography. Corning's Museum of Glass is the world's largest and finest glass museum.

The Adirondack Museum in Blue Mountain Lake is rated as one of the finest regional museums in the country. In Albany, the New York State Museum is the oldest state museum in the country. Sugar Loaf Art and Craft Village is a community of more than 60 artist-owned craft shops and galleries in the Hudson Valley, the area that inspired the nineteenth-century Hudson River School artists; the magnificent landscapes they painted helped make them the driving force in American art during the decades before the Civil War.

Last but hardly least on our list is New York City, unarguably one of the world capitals of theater, art, dance, and music. The theater scene alone is legendary: Back in the 1920s, George M. Cohan proclaimed, "When you are away from old Broadway you are only camping out." Many Manhattanites still believe this. Between Broadway, off-Broadway, and off-off-Broadway, there are hundreds of theaters in Manhattan. You can find just about any kind of production here, from lavish musicals to experimental productions in converted lofts. The musical and operatic life of the city plays out in such legendary houses as Carnegie Hall, Radio City Music Hall, and the Metropolitan Opera House in Lincoln Center. The greatest names in all musical genres have performed at Carnegie Hall, from Tchaikovsky and Toscanini to Gershwin and Billie Holiday. New York boasts five major ballet companies and dozens of modern dance troupes.

Some of the world's greatest museums are in New York City, including the Metropolitan Museum of Art, the Solomon R. Guggenheim Museum, the Whitney Museum of American Art, the American Museum of Natural History, and the Museum of Modern Art. Even the main branch of the New York Public Library, itself an architectural wonder, is filled with priceless collections. The museums, like everything else about the city, are on a grand scale. The city draws artists from all over the world, and there are hundreds of galleries showcasing their work.

## CUISINES

You'll find delectable meals in award-winning restaurants throughout the state. New York's many farms and vineyards supply excellent local produce and wines. The world-renowned Culinary Institute of America in Hyde Park has three restaurants where diners can sample innovative menus of great chefs–in–training. Name any country, even any region in any country, and "The City" (as modest Manhattanites generally refer to their town) will most likely have a selection of restaurants specializing in the cuisine of that area. The rule of thumb is, if it's edible, you can probably find it in New York City, where there are more restaurants per capita than anywhere else in the country. More than 17,000 dining establishments, from world-class temples of the culinary arts to corner pizza parlors, serve up an astounding range of cuisines at an equally astounding range of prices.

Even Manhattan's street food is varied, from the ubiquitous hot dog and soft pretzel to such delicacies as Chinese dumplings, Jewish knishes, Middle Eastern falafel, Jamaican *roti*, Italian sausages, Mexican tacos, and, in the summer, good old-fashioned ice cream. Beyond the multitude of street vendors, there are more delis than in any other city, and every New Yorker has a favorite. Whatever your appetites, you will surely find copious opportunities to satisy them here. On a humbler note, New York State gave the world Buffalo chicken wings, the potato chip, Thousand Island salad dressing, the hamburger, and, yes, the hot dog.

## FLORA AND FAUNA

New York has long led the nation in the preservation of natural resources. Niagara Falls Reservation State Park was the first state park in the country, and the Adirondacks is the largest park area in the Lower 48 states. Nature lovers owe much to New Yorker Theodore Roosevelt, one of the nation's earliest and most ardent conservationists, who created many national parks. His regard for the natural world undoubtedly was shaped during his summers in the wilds of the Adirondacks. Wild turkey and deer populations have increased dramatically in much of the state, and hunters flock here during the hunting seasons. So strongly do New Yorkers believe in the preservation of the forests of the Adirondacks and the Catskills as "forever wild" that it is specified in the State Constitution.

Trees cover about 60 percent of the state, and the Adirondack Park covers much of the northern third of the state. The Adirondack Forest Preserve was established in 1885 as the 42 percent of the park that is public land, to be forever preserved as wilderness. In the southeast part of the park, oaks are predominant, while in the higher Adirondacks, spruce and fir predominate. Northern hardwoods, including birch, sugar maple, basswood, ash, and yellow birch, comprise the majority of trees in the rest of the state. Oaks are mingled with northern hardwoods in the Finger Lakes region and along much of the Hudson River Valley.

Common animals are the fox, raccoon, opossum, woodchuck, muskrat, deer, rabbit, and squirrel. Bears can be found in the Adirondacks and areas of the Southern Tier. A wide variety of birds, including ducks and wild turkeys, inhabit most areas of the state. At the Montezuma National Wildlife Refuge in the Finger Lakes region, as well as in other parts of the state, there are bald eagles, Canada geese, snow geese, and many kinds of ducks, including mallards, American black ducks, blue-winged and green-winged teal, American widgeon, and wood ducks as well as canvasbacks, redheads, and common and hooded mergansers. Great blue herons and loons can sometimes be seen at Montezuma and on other waterways.

## THE LAY OF THE LAND

New York has some of the most varied topography in the country—from sandy beaches and salt marshes to alpine lakes and mountain peaks—and a unique range of natural habitats and ecosystems.

If water is a region's lifeblood, then New York is indeed blessed with a great circulatory system. The Erie Canal transformed the state and the nation when it opened in 1825. Now the 524-mile New York State Canal System—which links hundreds of miles of lakes and rivers across the state, from the Hudson River to Niagara, Lake Champlain, and beyond—has been turned into an adventure waterway for recreational boaters.

The lakes of the Finger Lakes region were created when Ice Age glaciers retreated about a million years ago. The intense pressure of those ice masses created the long, narrow lakes lying side by side, as well as the deep gorges with rushing falls and wide, fertile valleys that extend south for many miles. These features are found nowhere else in the world. The waters are deep and blue, yielding a bountiful harvest of fish.

In the northeastern part of the state, the Adirondack Park covers 6.1 million acres of public and private land. More than 40 mountains in the Adirondacks are more than 4,000 feet above sea level. The mountains were rounded off and smoothed down by the weight of glacial ice during the last Ice Age. Within the range are 2,200 glacier-formed ponds and lakes and 30,000 miles of rivers and streams.

To the south, the Catskill Mountains achieved their present form through eons of erosion. A succession of ice sheets covered the Catskills until some 15,000 years ago, leaving the region gouged and scraped, with sand and gravel heaped up and valleys turned into lakes. All this activity produced Slide Mountain, at 4,204 feet, the Catskills' highest summit. It also created a rocky wall 2,000 feet high facing miles of the Hudson River.

## OUTDOOR ACTIVITIES

It would be hard to find a place with more varied opportunities for outdoor activities than New York. Hikers, climbers, and walkers have hundreds of miles of trails to wander throughout the state. Explorers who want a guided wilderness trip can find licensed, professional guides, who continue the tradition begun in the nineteenth century, when Adirondack guides led "city sports" on canoe and hunting trips. There are more than 500 public and privately owned campgrounds, some deep in the wilderness, accessible only by boat or foot. Many hug the state's lakes and river as well as the Atlantic Ocean.

Beach lovers can explore some of the country's most expansive and beautiful beaches on Long Island and along the Great Lakes.

Fishing enthusiasts enjoy world-class freshwater fishing. Fishing records have been set on the state's many lakes and rivers as well as on the ocean waters off Long Island. Though the state is far from the tropics, there are unique wrecks awaiting scuba divers who like to explore the skeletons of sunken ships. Canoeists have miles of lakes and rivers to travel in the wilds of the Adirondacks and the Catskills. Whitewater rafting is popular on several rivers, especially during the high-water spring season.

In the winter, skiers can schuss down a multitude of ski hills and mountains. Ski resorts are close to all the state's metropolitan centers. Lake Placid was home to two Winter Olympics and continues as an Olympic training center. Whether your winter sport is skiing, bob-sledding, luging, or skating, you'll find excellent facilities here. Snow-mobiling attracts hundreds of thousands of fans, who come for the miles and miles of well-groomed trails and the snow—the Tug Hill area north of Syracuse boasts more snow than any area east of the Rockies.

The state's largest cities—New York, Buffalo, and Rochester—have Frederick Law Olmsted–designed parks that welcome joggers and walkers; a host of outdoor activities takes place during all seasons in the parks. America's first golf club was established in Yonkers in 1891, and today there are more than 400 public golf courses in the state. There's even a 19-hole course overlooking the St. Lawrence River.

# PRACTICAL TIPS

## HOW MUCH WILL IT COST?

The costs to travelers in New York State are as varied as the attractions. Upstate, budget travelers can expect to spend about $40 to $50 per night for a motel room. In the moderate range expect to pay about $60 to $70; upscale hotel rooms cost $80 and up. Bed and breakfasts can be as expensive as high-end hotels, depending on the accommodations and location. Campers can save the most money; there are more than 500 campgrounds in the state, with prices ranging from $10 to $25 per night. In areas of the Adirondack and Catskill Parks, it's possible to camp in lean-tos for free—although even in the wilds of the Adirondacks, there's a Great Camp where a night's stay can exceed $1,000!

As a rule, prices are higher in New York City. However, even in the city there are special weekend and other package rates for hotels that can reduce costs. A moderate city hotel room generally costs a little over $100 per night, while luxury hotels range from $200 to $400, and a luxurious suite in a top New York City hotel can set you back $3,000 or more. At the other end of the spectrum, hostels and some bed and breakfasts typically charge around $50 per night for two. Outside the city, lodging prices are lower; some people stay in the outlying areas and take a train or bus into the city for sightseeing. Be sure to factor in the extra transportation costs and the inconvenience if you are considering this approach.

Meal prices across the state also vary widely. You can expect to pay $30 to $40 for dinner for two at moderate places and $50 and up at higher-end restaurants. In New York City travelers can eat quite inexpensively at diners and ethnic eateries, where dinners average less than $25 for two. Of course, it's also possible to spend $200 or more for dinner in top city establishments. Some Long Island restaurants match or exceed Manhattan's more expensive spots.

Admission prices to parks, museums, and attractions run the gamut from free to expensive. Some attractions have free days, and others offer special discounts to seniors. Figure on an average of $5 to $8 per person. If you are a New York State resident 62 or older, you can obtain free vehicle access on any weekday (except holidays) to state parks and arboretums; free entrance to state historic sites; and fee reduction for state-operated swimming, golf, tennis, and boat rental.

Don't forget to add in New York State taxes. Sales taxes vary across the state, but they average 7 to 8.25 percent, plus bed taxes on hotel rooms in most areas of the state, including the major tourist destinations.

## WHEN TO GO

It's no exaggeration to say that the tourist season in New York State runs from January through December. The best time to visit depends upon where you are going and which activities you wish to pursue. The high season is generally June, July, and August. During these months, prices are the highest and crowds the largest at popular destinations such as Long Island and Niagara Falls. September can be lovely in these areas, and crowds tend to be smaller. However, the summer months usually offer the best weather—warm but not oppressively hot days. Of course, the winter months are the choice for winter sports enthusiasts. Skiing is usually available from late November through March in the Adirondacks, the Catskills, the Finger Lakes, and Cattaraugus County. April is usually considered mud season in the North Country. May is often an ideal choice for travelers, as spring is in full bloom throughout the countryside. Many attractions in upstate areas are open from May through Columbus Day.

Many people consider fall to be New York's most glorious season; the colors rival any New England state's. Weekend reservations are a must at many country inns during the leaf-peeping season. It's possible to follow the fall colors for a month or more from late September in the Adirondacks to late October in the New York City and Long Island areas.

Spring and fall are generally considered the best seasons to visit New York City. November and December are also quite popular visiting months because of the holiday shopping opportunities and the spectacular decorations, especially along Fifth Avenue. Summer can be quite hot and humid, and the concrete seems to magnify the temperatures.

## CLIMATE

The accompanying chart shows average high and low Fahrenheit temperatures for selected cities across the state, plus average precipitation, in inches. Temperatures are rounded to the nearest degree. "S" indicates snow and "R" indicates rain.

## NEW YORK STATE CLIMATE

Average daily high and low temperatures in degrees Fahrenheit, plus monthly precipitation in inches.

|       | Buffalo | Syracuse | Albany | New York |
|-------|---------|----------|--------|----------|
| Jan.  | 30/17   | 30/14    | 32/16  | 37/24    |
|       | 23.5 (S)| 29.8 (S) | 16 (S) | 7.6 (S)  |
| Mar.  | 42/26   | 43/25    | 43/27  | 45/30    |
|       | 11.5 (S)| 17.4 (S) | 11.9 (S)| 5.1 (S) |
| May   | 66/47   | 68/46    | 70/49  | 68/53    |
|       | 2.9 (R) | 3.3 (R)  | 3.3 (R)| 3.6 (R)  |
| July  | 80/62   | 82/59    | 83/63  | 82/66    |
|       | 2.9 (R) | 3.8 (R)  | 3.7 (R)| 4.2 (R)  |
| Sept. | 71/53   | 72/51    | 74/54  | 79/60    |
|       | 3.1 (R) | 3.8 (R)  | 3.2 (R)| 3.7 (R)  |
| Nov.  | 47/34   | 48/33    | 47/32  | 51/37    |
|       | 11.3 (S)| 9.7 (S)  | 4.2 (S)| .9 (S)   |

# TRANSPORTATION

Three major airports serve New York City: LaGuardia and John F. Kennedy in Queens and Newark in Newark, New Jersey. There are major airports in Albany, Syracuse, Rochester, and Buffalo (which serves Niagara Falls) as well as smaller airports in Ithaca, Jamestown, Saranac Lake, and White Plains.

Amtrak covers most of the state, including the cities and towns along the Hudson River and the cities along the Albany–Buffalo/Niagara Falls corridor. The Long Island Rail Road serves the entire island, from Manhattan to Montauk. Resort areas on Long Island, the Catskills, and the Hudson are geared to guests without cars, and transportation from the train or bus station to the hotel is not usually difficult to arrange.

For the rest of the state, car travel is the best way to go. The principal east-west highway is the New York State Thruway (or I-90), from the Pennsylvania border in the southwestern corner of the state to New York City. This is a toll highway, reputed to be the longest in the country (New York likes to be number one in everything, including tolls and taxes). Route 17 is a good (and free) alternative to the Thruway—it's a major four-lane highway that runs along the southern border of the state to New York City. Several major highways, all accessible from the Thruway, run north-south, including U.S. 87 from Albany to the Canadian border, U.S. 81 from Binghamton to the Thousand Islands and the Canadian border, and I-390 from the Pennsylvania border to Rochester. Many areas of the state, including the Adirondacks, Thousand Islands, Syracuse, Rochester, Buffalo, Chautauqua, and Cattaraugus, get ample snowfalls every winter. Road crews are experienced at clearing the roads, and driving is not usually a problem except in blizzard conditions.

## CAMPING, LODGING, AND DINING

This book includes a cross-section of restaurants and lodgings in an attempt to appeal to varied tastes and budgets. It is fair to say that some of the best dining in the country can be found in New York. Award-winning restaurants are scattered across the state, from Buffalo to Manhattan. The state also enjoys an incredible number and variety of ethnic restaurants. Because new restaurants are constantly opening while others are folding or reorganizing, in addition to using this book's recommendations, be sure to ask locals for dining suggestions.

The state has a wide variety of accommodations, including hostels, bed and breakfasts, budget motels, country inns, city hotels, resorts, dude ranches, and a number of historic properties. Special package or weekend rates can discount the official published rate. In addition, if you are a member of AAA or of the American Association of Retired Persons, you can usually receive a 10 percent discount. It is often possible to secure a corporate rate even if you are not traveling on business. Wheelchair accessibility has improved tremendously in recent years; most moderate and high-end hotels and motels, and most state park campgrounds, are wheelchair accessible.

Bed and breakfasts have grown in popularity across the state. Now found in major cities as well as rural and resort areas, some bed and breakfasts offer luxury and pampering with prices to match—$100 and up. However, many offer lower prices and comfortable, homey accommodations with the added bonus of a chance to make new friends.

New York is blessed with an extensive state park system that offers well-maintained campgrounds in spectacular natural settings across the state. Many state parks have cabins as well as campsites. Reservations are usually necessary during the high season at state campgrounds. If you can't get a campsite in your chosen park, be sure to check back because there are often no-shows.

## RECOMMENDED READING

Thousands of books have been written about or set in New York State. James Fenimore Cooper, author of 32 novels, including the Leatherstocking Tales (*The Pioneers, The Last of the Mohicans, The Prairie, The Pathfinder*, and *The Deerslayer*), devoted much of his writings to the frontier days in New York State. More recently, Pulitzer Prize–winning William Kennedy set a trio of novels in the state capital: *Legs, Billy Phelan's Greatest Game*, and *Ironweed*; he also wrote a nonfiction history of his hometown, *O Albany!* Prize-winning author Joyce Carol Oates is a native of Lockport in western New York. Her novel *A Bloodsmoor Romance* is set in the state.

The Adirondacks have inspired many works of literature. Foremost among the many books is William H. H. Murray's *Adventures in the Wilderness*, published in 1869. Twentieth-century titles include William Chapman White's *Adirondack Country* and Lincoln Bennett's *Ancient Adirondacks*. Barbara McMartin's detailed guide, *Fifty Hikes in the Adirondacks*, published by the Countryman Press, is a good choice for hikers.

For nonfiction about the state, Edmund Wilson's *Upstate: Records and Recollections* is a combination of family reminiscences, visits with literary figures, and sketches of local characters. An entertaining history of Niagara Falls, *Niagara: A History of the Falls*, by Pierre Berton, was recently published by Kodansha International.

New York City has been home to hundreds of writers who have drawn inspiration from their hometown. The city is also the publishing capital of the country. One of the city's earliest popular writers was Washington Irving, whose satirical *A History of New York* was written under the pseudonym of Diedrich Knickerbocker. Under his own name he wrote the classic *The Legend of Sleepy Hollow*. Walt Whitman wrote about Manhattan and the Brooklyn Bridge while living in Brooklyn, but every publisher in the city turned down *Leaves of Grass*, considered one of the greatest works of American poetry.

New York in the 1880s is the stage for Edith Wharton's *The Age of Innocence* and *The House of Mirth* and Henry James' *Washington Square*. The Louis Auchincloss classic, *The Book Class*, captured the lives of the city's wealthy elite. Irwin Shaw's two family sagas, *Rich Man, Poor Man* and *Beggarman, Thief*, are set primarily in New York.

The history of New York's Jewish community can be traced through novels such as *World of Our Fathers*, by Irving Howe; *The Promise*, by Chaim Potok; *Call It Sleep*, by Henry Roth; *The Assistant*, by Bernard Malamud; and *Enemies, A Love Story*, by Isaac Bashevis Singer.

E. L. Doctorow's *Ragtime*, a novel about the intertwined lives of an upper-middle-class New Rochelle family, a Jewish immigrant family, and a black musician during the early twentieth century, has gained new audiences after its transformation into a musical. F. Scott Fitzgerald's *The Great Gatsby* portrays the dark side of the Jazz Age in New York and on Long Island. Truman Capote was living in Brooklyn while he wrote *Breakfast at Tiffany's*, depicting New York's high life in 1950s. Tom Wolfe's *Bonfire of the Vanities* is a biting social satire of the city in the 1980s.

For a behind-the-scenes look into politics and business, read *Mayor*, by Edward I. Koch; *Trump*, by Donald H. Trump; and *The Power Broker*, by Robert A. Caro. For a guide to the city's architecture, read the *AIA Guide to New York City*, by Norval White, and *A Guide to New York City Landmarks*, published by the Landmark Preservation Committee.

## RESOURCES

### STATE TOURISM/VISITOR INFORMATION

**New York State Hospitality and Tourism Association:** (800) ENJOY-NY
**New York State Tourism Information:** (800) CALL-NYS
    or (518) 474-4116
**New York State Tourism Web Site:** //iloveny.state.ny.us

### CITY AND COUNTY TOURISM/VISITOR INFORMATION

**Adirondacks:** (800) 487-6867 or (518) 648-5239
**Albany:** (800) 732-8259 or (518) 434-1217
**Buffalo:** (800) BUFFALO or (716) 852-0511
**Catskills:** (800) 882-CATS, (914) 331-9300, (800) 355-CATS,
    or (518) 943-3223
**Cattaraugus:** (800) 331-0543 or (716) 938-9111

Chautauqua: (800) 242-4569 or (716) 753-4304
Corning: (800) 284-3352 or (607) 974-2066
Elmira: (800) 627-5892 or (607) 734-5131
Finger Lakes: (800) KIT 4 FUN or (315) 536-7488
Hudson River Valley: (800) 762-8687 or (914) 294-5151
Lake Placid: (800) 2PLACID or (518) 523-2445
Leatherstocking: (800) 233-8778 or (315) 866-1500
Long Island: (800) 441-4601 or (516) 951-3440
New York City: (800) NYC-VISIT or (212) 484-1200
Niagara Falls: (800) 338-7890 or (716) 439-7300
Rochester: (800) 677-7282 or (716) 546-3070
Saratoga Springs: (518) 584-3255
Syracuse: (800) 234-4SYR or (315) 470-1800
Thousand Islands: (800) 8-ISLAND or (315) 482-5906

## BED AND BREAKFAST ASSOCIATIONS

Adirondack Bed and Breakfast Reservation Service: (518) 891-1632
At Home in New York: (212) 956-3125
Bed and Breakfast Network of NY: (800) 900-8134 or (212) 645-8134
Cherry Valley Ventures: (315) 637-2836
Finger Lakes Bed and Breakfast Association: (800) 695-5590
International Bed and Breakfast Club: (800) 723-4262
       or (716) 873-4462
Leatherstocking Bed and Breakfast Association: (800) 941-BEDS
New World Bed and Breakfast: (800) 443-3800 or (212) 675-5600
Urban Ventures: (212) 594-5650

## TRANSPORTATION

Amtrak: (800) USA-RAIL
Long Island Railroad: (718) 217-LIRR or (516) 231-LIRR
New York City Subway and Bus Information: (718) 330-1234

## OTHER USEFUL NUMBERS

Hosteling International: (800) 909-4776
New York State Campgrounds Reservations: (800) 456-CAMP
New York State Canal System: (800) 4 CANAL 4
New York State Department of Environmental Conservation:
       (518) 457-2500
New York State Parks: (518) 474-0456

# 1

# MANHATTAN

What most people think of when they hear "New York" is really Manhattan, a narrow, 12-mile-long island—surely the most renowned island on earth. Manhattan is the oldest of New York City's five boroughs, and it's the heart and soul of the city. "Other cities are nouns," John F. Kennedy once said. "New York is a verb." It's hard to argue with his assessment. Manhattan's streets are teeming with people and an almost overwhelming energy. The nation's most populous city, New York attracts more visitors than any of the world's great cities. The Statue of Liberty, the Empire State Building, the World Trade Center, Times Square, Broadway, Fifth Avenue, Rockefeller Center, Grand Central Station, Wall Street, Central Park, Greenwich Village, Lincoln Center, Carnegie Hall, a bevy of world-class museums and galleries, thousands of restaurants and shops, the world's greatest concentration of theaters, countless nightclubs—it's no wonder this is "the city that never sleeps."

Manhattan was the nation's first capital, and remnants of the city's history can be found amidst the towering skyscrapers. The city remains the financial, publishing, and entertainment capital of the country, and waves of immigrants continue to make their mark here. Surely one of the world's best walking cities, the people-watching can't be beat; here, as nowhere else, just about anything goes.

H. G. Wells summed up New York's powerful role in world history: "To Europe, she was America, to America she was the gateway of the earth. But to tell the story of New York would be to write a social history of the world." ◼

# MANHATTAN

# Sights

- Ⓐ American Museum of Natural History
- Ⓑ Cathedral Church of St. John the Divine
- Ⓒ Chinatown
- Ⓓ Cloisters Museum
- Ⓔ Cooper Hewitt National Design Museum
- Ⓕ El Museo del Barrio
- Ⓖ Ellis Island National Monument
- Ⓗ Empire State Building
- Ⓘ Federal Hall National Monument
- Ⓙ Fraunces Tavern Museum
- Ⓚ Frick Collection
- Ⓛ Gracie Mansion
- Ⓜ Grand Central Terminal
- Ⓝ *Intrepid* Sea-Air-Space Museum
- Ⓞ Lower East Side Tenement Museum
- Ⓟ Metropolitan Museum of Art

- Ⓕ Museum of the City of New York
- Ⓠ Museum of Modern Art
- Ⓡ Museum of Television and Radio
- Ⓢ New Museum of Contemporary Art
- Ⓣ New York Public Library
- Ⓤ New York Stock Exchange
- Ⓥ Pierpont Morgan Library
- Ⓦ Rockefeller Center
- Ⓡ St. Patrick's Cathedral
- Ⓧ St. Paul's Chapel
- Ⓔ Solomon R. Guggenheim Museum
- Ⓨ South Street Seaport
- Ⓩ Statue of Liberty
- Ⓐ Theodore Roosevelt National Historic Site
- Ⓑ United Nations
- Ⓒ Whitney Museum of American Art
- Ⓥ World Trade Center

*Note: Items with the same letter are located in the same area of town.*

## A PERFECT DAY IN MANHATTAN

Start where the city did, at the South Street Seaport, a 12-block historic area filled with ships, restaurants, shops, and street entertainment on the tip of Manhattan. A short walk takes you to Battery Park, where you can catch the ferry to the Statue of Liberty, one of the city's most moving sights. The views of the World Trade Center and the other towering buildings from the island are among the best you'll find. Enjoy an outdoor lunch in the Seaport before heading uptown for an afternoon at the Museum of Natural History. Stop for tea at the elegant Plaza Hotel before enjoying a night at the theater. Eat an after-theater supper at the Algonquin Hotel. If the night is clear, have a drink at the Rainbow Room bar or take a late-night trip to the Empire State Building to view the dazzling lights of the city.

## GETTING AROUND THE CITY

Manhattan is one of the easiest major cities in which to get around, since most of it is laid out on a grid. Even-numbered one-way streets go east, while odd-numbered streets go west—known as going crosstown. The avenues run north and south. Buildings, houses, and offices are all numbered sequentially. When you get down to the SoHo, Greenwich Village, and Wall Street areas, however, it's not quite so easy. Bring a map along and ask questions; most New Yorkers are used to giving directions and are quite helpful.

### Public Transportation

You'll find it convenient to get subway and bus maps from the Convention and Visitors Bureau before you go to Manhattan; otherwise, pick them up at your hotel or at any subway booth once you arrive. Subways are efficient and increasingly safe—some 3.5 million people use them every day to commute to work or school. Nevertheless, don't use them very late at night or early in the morning. Street buses are air-conditioned and clean. They stop every few blocks, although many routes also have express buses stopping every ten blocks or so.

The price for both the subway and bus is $1.50, or half-price for seniors. On the bus you can use a token, the new plastic Metro Card, or exact change (but no pennies or bills); you must buy tokens or use the Metro Card for the subway. The Metro Card comes in various denominations ranging from $5 to $80 and can be purchased at subway stations and some retail outlets.

At your request, the bus driver will give you a paper transfer to a connecting bus; for $1.50 and that transfer you can go down Fifth Avenue, say from 57th Street to 23rd Street, get on the crosstown bus at 23rd Street, and ride all the way to the Chelsea Pier at the Hudson River.

### Taxis

Hail a taxi just about anywhere by raising your arm. It will cost you $2 just to get in, then 30 cents for ⅕-mile. Short rides reach $5 before you know it. Drivers can charge only one fare, no matter how many passengers there are. It's a good idea to note the driver's name and medallion number, so if you leave anything in the cab or have a problem with the driver, you'll have the correct information to give to the New York City Taxi and Limousine Commission, (212) 692-8294.

Never take a "gypsy" cab. Stick with yellow cabs with "NY City Taxi" on them; the drivers of those cabs are licensed, regulated by the city, and required to provide air conditioning in hot weather and to give you a receipt. There's no guarantee that all licensed taxi drivers are terrific, but most are quite nice.

## Tours

A bus tour offers the best way to see the most in the least amount of time. Several all-day tours visit the top tourist attractions. **Gray Line**, (212) 397-2620, and **Short Line**, (212) 397-2600, schedule a variety of tours. For more than 50 years **Circle Line Cruises**, (212) 563-3200, has offered narrated tours around Manhattan that provide up-close views of the docks and skyline. An evening cruise is also available. From the South Street Seaport, the 1885 schooner *Pioneer* makes 90-minute daytime and twilight trips around the harbor from May through September. Unreserved tickets are sold daily starting at 10 a.m. at Pier 16 or can be reserved by calling (212) 669-9400, ext. 6. **Seaport Liberty Cruises** has 60-minute harbor cruises from late March until December; tickets at Pier 16 or call (212) 630-8888. The **New York Waterways** "lunch boat" leaves South Street Seaport or the World Financial Center Marina several times a day. Bring your own picnic or buy lunch on board. (800) 533-3779.

The best bargain of all is a ride on the **Staten Island Ferry**, (718) 390-5253, from Battery Park to Staten Island. The pedestrian round-trip, which used to cost only 50 cents, is now free and provides grand views of the Lower Manhattan skyline and the Statue of Liberty. **World Yacht**, (212) 630-8100, schedules brunch and dinner cruises and tours of New York Harbor. If you wish to see Manhattan from on high, **Island Helicopters**, (212) 683-4575, gives tours by helicopter.

A walking tour is a great way to get a feel for the neighborhoods that make up Manhattan. **The New York Convention & Visitors Bureau**, 2 Columbus Circle, (212) 397-8222, offers brochures for self-guided walking tours. Guided tour companies include **Sidewalks of New York**, (212) 517-0201; **Adventures on a Shoestring**,

(212) 265-2663; **Citywalks**, (212) 989-2456; **Urban Exploration**, (718) 721-5254; and the **Big Apple Greeters**, (212) 669-2362.

## SIGHTSEEING HIGHLIGHTS

★★★ **American Museum of Natural History**—This grand museum holds more than 30 million specimens and artifacts exploring the American Indian, Asian, Pacific Islander, South American, and Aztec and Mayan cultures. Its world-famous fossil exhibits have been greatly enhanced by a recent $30-million renovation. This section's high points are the two **Dinosaur Halls** featuring magnificent skeletons of *Tyrannosaurus rex* and *Apatosaurus*. The **Hall of Human Biology and Evolution**, opened in 1993, explores the workings of the human body, traces our ancestors over the centuries, and features a computerized archeological dig. Above the **Hall of Ocean Life and Biology of Fishes** is a 10-ton replica of the world's largest mammal, the blue whale. The **Hall of Minerals and Gems** contains an awesome $80-million collection. The **Hayden Planetarium**, which adjoins the museum, offers state-of-the-art astronomy exhibitions and guided tours of the nighttime sky. However, the planetarium is closed for a large reconstruction project; it's scheduled to reopen in 2000. The **Naturemax Cinema** shows natural history films on a giant IMAX screen. Wheelchair accessible. Central Park West at W. 79th Street; (212) 769-5100; open daily 10 a.m. to 5:45 p.m., Friday and Saturday to 8:45 p.m. Admission $8 adults, $6 seniors and students, $4.50 children; theater $8 adults, $6 seniors, $4.50 children. (3 hours)

★★★ **Empire State Building**—From *King Kong* to *Sleepless in Seattle*, Hollywood has long paid homage to this landmark, probably New York's most enduring and best-loved emblem, rising 1,454 feet above Midtown. Completed in 1931 after only two years of construction, it held the title of the world's tallest building until the 1973 completion of the first World Trade Center tower. Elevators run to the outdoor observatory on the 86th floor. On a clear day you can see for more than 50 miles. Another elevator takes visitors to the glass-enclosed observation tower on the 102nd floor, but if the lines are long, it's hard to justify the second wait. The top 30 floors of the building are lit year-round from dusk to midnight, and the light colors change seasonally. Wheelchair accessible. 34th Street at Fifth Avenue; (212) 736-3100; observation tower open daily 9:30 a.m. to midnight (last ticket sold at 11:30 p.m.). Admission $4.50 adults, $2.25 seniors and children. (1 hour)

★★★ **Grand Central Terminal**—Once dubbed "the gateway to the nation," everything about this terminal is indeed grand. By 1939, as many people as lived in the entire United States passed through Grand Central Terminal each year. The huge scale of the Main Concourse, said to be the largest room in the world, is a monument to the heyday of train travel. The 12-story ceiling displays the constellations of the zodiac. The terminal was completed in 1913 after the ten-year construction of the New York Central and Hudson River Railroad, founded by Commodore Cornelius Vanderbilt. Outside, a bronze likeness of the Commodore faces south down Park Avenue, as do 48-foot-high figures of Mercury, Hercules, and Minerva. The lower levels provide access to the subway and a number of restaurants, including the legendary **Oyster Bar** (see Food in this chapter). 42nd Street between Lexington and Vanderbilt Avenues; open daily. Free guided tours on Wednesday, run by the Municipal Art Society, (212) 935-3960, begin at 12:30 p.m. outside the Chemical Bank branch on the Main Concourse. (1 hour)

★★★ **Metropolitan Museum of Art**—One of the world's great museums, there is no way to see everything here in one visit. Pick up a map at the entrance and plan your tour carefully. The best way to think of this museum is as a dozen or so separate museums. Among the collections are Egyptian, Greek, and Roman art; Near Eastern art and antiquities; European and Oriental paintings and sculpture; arms and armor; musical instruments; arts from Africa, Oceania, and the Americas; twentieth-century art; and European and American decorative arts. Some highlights include works by Winslow Homer, Manet, Monet, Cezanne, Gauguin, Renoir, van Gogh, Rembrandt, and Vermeer. Also of note: the **Costume Exhibition**, with 35,000 articles of fashion; and the entire **Temple of Dendur**, given to the people of the United States in appreciation for their help in saving monuments threatened when the Aswan Dam was built. The Met offers many concerts, fascinating lectures, and book and gift shops, said to be the largest of any museum. Several appealing dining options are also available. Wheelchair accessible. 1000 Fifth Avenue at 82nd Street; (212) 535-7710; open Tuesday through Sunday 9:30 a.m. to 5:15 p.m., Friday and Saturday until 8:45 p.m. Admission $8 adults, $4 seniors and students, children under 12 free. Admission includes the **Cloisters Museum** in Upper Manhattan. (3 hours)

★★★ **South Street Seaport**—This 12-block historic seaport district has cobblestone streets, waterfront piers, shops, restaurants, and a great view of the Brooklyn Bridge, Brooklyn, and the harbor. The bars and restaurants attract the Wall Street crowd. The **Fulton Fish Market** lends an air of authenticity to the area, which overflowed during the nineteenth century with the cargo and sailors from the tall ships docked at the piers. Robert Fulton once parked his steamboat in the area. The *1911 Peking*, a four-masted cargo vessel, is one of the more interesting ships open for touring. Visitors center at 12 Fulton Street; (212) 748-8600; ships and museum open daily 10 a.m. to 5 p.m. November through March; 10 a.m. to 6 p.m. April through October. Admission $6 adults, $5 seniors, $4 students, $3 children. No charge for visiting the area and enjoying the street entertainment. (3 hours)

★★★ **Statue of Liberty**—There is no greater symbol of the United States and of freedom for all than this statue, which has stood in New York Harbor since 1886. The statue was presented to the United States by France to commemorate the two countries' alliance during the American Revolution. Measuring 151 feet high, the statue has welcomed millions of immigrants in its hundred-year history. After the ferry ride from Battery Park, you have several choices: You can simply walk about and enjoy up-close views of Lady Liberty; you can climb the 354 steps to the crown (remember, you have to come back down); or you can visit the **American Museum of Immigration** in the statue's base, which traces the history of immigration into the United States. Wheelchair accessible. Liberty Island; (212) 269-5755; ferry operates daily 9:30 a.m. to 3:30 p.m. Return trips every 30 minutes. Admission to the statue free; ferry from Gangway S, Battery Park $7 adults, $5 seniors, $3 children. (2 hours)

★★ **Cathedral Church of St. John the Divine**—The cornerstone of this grand Episcopal church was laid in 1892, and it is still under construction. Spread across 11 acres, two football fields long and 17 stories high, it is the largest church in the country and the largest Gothic church in the world. The church is built entirely of stone, including Maine granite and Indiana limestone. The **Biblical Garden** contains more than 100 plants mentioned in the Bible. 1047 Amsterdam Avenue; (212) 316-7490; guided tours Tuesday through Saturday at 11 a.m.; Sunday at 1 p.m.; open daily 7 a.m. to 5 p.m. Services on Sunday and religious holidays. Admission $5. (1 hour)

★★ **Chinatown**—This 40-square-block area, between Little Italy and the Lower East Side, includes Canal, Mott, Pell, and Doyers Streets. Home to about half of New York's 300,000 Chinese population, it teems with shops, outdoor stalls, restaurants, noodle shops, and dim sum houses. Hong Kong banks have opened here, and shops and shopping malls plying jewelry and electrical goods have sprung up. You'll know when you've arrived—the shop signs and movie marquees are in Chinese, while the phone booths are built in pagoda style. The **Museum of Chinese in the Americas**, 70 Mulberry Street, (212) 619-4785, has unusual exhibits devoted to the Chinese experience in America; it also sponsors several walking tours. (2 hours)

★★ **Cloisters Museum**—Escape from the twentieth century for an afternoon and make the trek to this remote branch of the Metropolitan Museum of Art. Devoted to medieval art, it includes parts of five French cloisters, a Romanesque chapel, and extensive gardens. The tapestries are particularly lovely. Another outstanding collection includes six fifteenth-century stained-glass windows. The museum is set on a spectacular site above the Hudson River. The best view is in the **Herb Garden** within the Bonnefront Cloister; from there you can see across the Hudson to the Palisades in New Jersey. John D. Rockefeller protected this view by purchasing the land across the river. Wheelchair accessible. Fort Tryon Park, Washington Heights; (212) 923-3700; open daily 9:30 a.m. to 5:15 p.m. Admission $8 adults, $4 seniors and students, children under 12 free. Admission to the Cloisters includes the **Metropolitan Museum of Art**. (2 hours)

★★ **Ellis Island National Monument**—Located close to the Statue of Liberty and accessed by the same ferry that leaves Battery Park, this monument was the main point of entry for millions of immigrants from 1892 to 1924. Around 100 million present-day Americans have ancestors who passed through Ellis Island. After its closing it was neglected for years until a $160-million restoration reopened the major building as the **Ellis Island Immigration Museum** in 1990. Exhibits chronicle the history of the island and its processing station. An award-winning film about America's immigrants is shown at regular intervals. The future of many would-be Americans was determined in this building. About 2 percent of the new arrivals were deported for sickness or other reasons. Outside, near the ferry dock, the **American Immigrant Wall of Hono**r records nearly 400,000 names, just a small percentage of those who entered the United States here. Wheelchair accessible. Ellis Island; (212) 363-3200; open daily 9 a.m. to 5 p.m. Admission free; ferry $7 adults, $5 seniors, $3 children. (3 hours)

★★ **Frick Collection**—Nineteenth-century robber baron Henry Clay Frick built this French-style mansion to showcase his superb collection of fourteenth- to nineteenth-century European art. Part of this museum's beauty lies in its manageable size and intimate format—the collection is displayed as if it were still in a private home. The many masterpieces include works by Vermeer, Titian, El Greco, Rembrandt, Gainsborough, and Turner. 1 E. 70th Street; (212) 288-0700; open Tuesday through Saturday 10 a.m. to 6 p.m., Sunday 1 p.m. to 6 p.m. Admission $5 adults, $3 seniors and students; children under 10 not admitted. Call for a schedule of concerts. (1 hour)

★★ *Intrepid* **Sea-Air-Space Museum**—Permanently moored on the Hudson River, the *Intrepid* is an aircraft carrier that saw service during World War II and the Vietnam War. It is filled with exhibits from its own wartime exploits—its aircraft shot down 650 enemy planes and destroyed 289 ships—and from its peacetime role retrieving *Mercury* and *Gemini* space capsules. There are several dozen fighter and bomber planes on the flight deck. Alongside the carrier are a destroyer, the U.S.S. *Edson*, and the U.S.S. *Growler*, a guided missile submarine with a nuclear cruise missile inside. Pier 86 on W. 46th Street at Twelfth Avenue; (212) 245-2533; Memorial Day through Labor Day open daily 10 a.m. to 5 p.m.; Wednesday through Sunday 10 a.m. to 5 p.m. rest of year. Admission $10 adults, $7.50 seniors and ages 12–17, $5 ages 6–11. (3 hours)

★★ **Museum of the City of New York**—This museum chronicles the development of one of the world's great cities. A delight for urban history buffs, the museum has maps and drawings of New York from the mid-1600s, a wonderful collection of toys and dolls, and rooms from the mansion of John D. Rockefeller, Sr. (Rockefeller's amazing Moorish room is in the Brooklyn Museum). Fifth Avenue and 103rd to 104th Streets; (212) 534-1672; open Wednesday through Saturday 10 a.m. to 5 p.m., Sunday 1 p.m. to 5 p.m. Admission $5 adults, $3 seniors and students, $8 families. (2 hours)

★★ **Museum of Modern Art**—Considered by many to be the world's best museum of modern art, MOMA is filled with a remarkable collection of paintings, sculptures, drawings, prints, photographs, architectural models, films, and videotapes. One of the museum's most celebrated possessions is van Gogh's *Starry Night*. The **Abbey Aldrich Rockefeller Sculpture Garden** includes works by Henry Moore, Picasso, Rodin, and others. In the warm weather the Sculpture Garden has free outdoor concerts, usually on Friday and Saturday evenings. Wheelchair accessible. 11 W. 53rd Street; (212) 708-9480; open Saturday through Tuesday 11 a.m. to 6 p.m., Thursday and Friday noon to 8:30 p.m. Admission $8.50 adults, $5.50 seniors and students, children under 16 free. (3 hours)

★★ **Museum of Television and Radio**—This museum is a TV addict's dream. Over 40,000 television and radio broadcasts from the 1920s to the present are stored here and available to the public. Once you have made your choice (restricted to two hours of viewing time), the show will be set up for watching at one of 100 video consoles. There are also various special programs. Wheelchair accessible. 25 W. 52nd Street; (212) 621-6800; open Tuesday through Sunday noon to 6 p.m., until 8 p.m. on Thursday. Admission $6 adults, $4 students and seniors, $3 children. (2 hours)

★★ **New York Public Library**—You can't check out a book here, but you can do research and marvel at one of the city's finest architectural treasures and the wonders on display. You enter between two marble lions—dubbed "Patience" and "Fortitude" by the late Mayor Fiorello LaGuardia, who visited the facility "to read between the lions." The library houses more than 5 million volumes as well as changing exhibits of rare books and other materials, including a Gutenberg Bible, a 1493 Christopher Columbus letter describing his New World discoveries, the first full folio edition of Shakespeare's work, a handwritten copy of Washington's farewell address, and an early draft of Jefferson's Declaration of Independence. Free tours leave the information desk Monday through Saturday at 11 a.m. and 2 p.m. Wheelchair accessible. Fifth Avenue and 42nd Street; (212) 930-0800; open Tuesday and Wednesday 11 a.m. to 7:30 p.m., Thursday through Saturday and Monday 10 a.m. to 6 p.m. Admission free. (1 hour)

★★ **Rockefeller Center**—Perhaps most famous for its Christmas tree–lighting ceremony and ice-skating rink, Rockefeller Center is the world's largest commercial and entertainment complex. The site encompasses 14 buildings as well as numerous restaurants, cafés, shops, underground walkways, and plazas. The heart of the center is the sunken plaza that holds an open-air restaurant and ice rink and is presided over by Paul Manship's *Prometheus*. A self-guided tour brochure is available at the information desk. **NBC Studio Tours** gives one-hour behind-the-scenes tours of the production areas of several television shows. Not to be missed is the 6,000-seat **Radio City Music Hall**, which presents stage spectaculars with the Rockettes as well as live concerts. Tours offered. Fifth Avenue to Avenue of the Americas and 48th to 51st Streets; (212) 698-2950 or (212) 664-4000 for NBC, and (212) 247-4777 for Radio City. NBC tours Monday through Saturday 9:30 a.m. to 4:30 p.m. NBC tour admission $8.25 (children under 6 not permitted). (2 hours)

★★ **Solomon R. Guggenheim Museum**—The Frank Lloyd Wright spiral-shaped building is one of the city's outstanding architectural land-marks. The best way to see the collection is to take the elevator to the top and slowly work your way down the spiral ramp. Highlights of the permanent collections include works by Kandinsky, Modigliani, Klee, Mondrian, Braque, and Malevich. Wheelchair accessible. 1071 Fifth Avenue; (212) 423-3600; open Sunday through Wednesday 10 a.m. to 6 p.m., Friday and Saturday 10 a.m. to 8 p.m. Admission $7 adults, $4 seniors and students, children under 12 free. Friday, pay what you wish from 6 p.m. to 8 p.m. (2 hours)

★★ **St. Patrick's Cathedral**—This Roman Catholic cathedral is one of the country's largest and most famous churches, with a seating capacity of 2,400. Twin spires 330 feet high grace the Gothic-style church. Fifth Avenue at 50th Street; (212) 753-2261; open daily 6:30 a.m. to 8:45 p.m.; guided tours by appointment. Admission free. (½ hour)

★★ **Whitney Museum of American Art**—This museum is an outgrowth of sculptor Gertrude Vanderbilt Whitney's studio and gallery, and it continues to showcase contemporary artists. It displays a superb collection of twentieth-century American art, including works by Edward Hopper, John Sloan, Georgia O'Keeffe, Roy Lichtenstein, Andy Warhol, and Willem de Kooning. 945 Madison Avenue; (212) 570-3676; open Friday through Sunday and Wednesday 11 a.m. to 6 p.m., Thursday 1 p.m. to 8 p.m. Admission $8 adults, $6 seniors and students, children under 12 with adult free. Free to all Thursday 6 p.m. to 8 p.m. (2 hours)

★★ **World Trade Center**—The twin towers are New York's tallest buildings and among the world's tallest. The elevator whisks you to the Observation Deck on the 107th floor in just 58 seconds. Signs posted at the ticket booth disclose how far you can see—as far as 50 miles on a clear day. An escalator continues up to the open rooftop level on the 110th floor. At ground level the 5-acre plaza hosts free open-air concerts during the summer. Wheelchair accessible. Church Street between Liberty and Vesey Streets; (212) 323-2350; June through August open daily 9:30 a.m. to 11:30 p.m.; 9:30 a.m. to 9:30 p.m. rest of year. Observation deck admission $4.75 adults, $2.75 seniors, $2.50 children. (1 hour)

★ **Cooper Hewitt National Design Museum**—Andrew Carnegie was one of the world's richest men when he built this house, which has since been transformed into a well-regarded design museum. The 1901 Georgian mansion sits amid extensive gardens and boasts 64 rooms. Vaulted ceilings, Tiffany glass windows, and a Louis XVI music room furnished with French antiques and a set of bagpipes—a reminder of Carnegie's Scottish origins—provide a backdrop for the impressive collection of ceramics, wall coverings, textiles, and decorative arts. The museum is officially the Smithsonian Institution National Museum of Design and sponsors many special exhibitions. Fifth Avenue and 91st Street; (212) 860-6868; open Tuesday through Saturday 10 a.m. to 5 p.m., until 9 p.m. on Tuesday; Sunday noon to 5 p.m. Admission $3 adults, $1.50 seniors and students, children under 12 free; free to all Tuesday 5 p.m. to 9 p.m. (2 hours)

★ **Fraunces Tavern Museum**—This replica of the tavern that played host to George Washington and his revolutionary friends was the base of the Department of Foreign Affairs, the War Department, and the Treasury during the country's early years. Washington made his famous emotional farewell to his Continental Army officers in the tavern's Long Room, and the scene is re-created on the third floor. The restaurant on the first floor has wood-burning fireplaces and is popular with the Financial District crowd. 54 Pearl Street; (212) 425-1778; open Monday through Friday 10 a.m. to 4:45 p.m., Saturday and Sunday noon to 4 p.m. Admission $2.50 adults, $1 seniors and students. (½ hour)

★ **Gracie Mansion**—Gracie Mansion was built in 1799 as a country retreat for shipping magnate Archibald Gracie. The house has been the official residence of the mayor of New York City since 1942. Numerous renovations have been made, and the building is now considered a fine example of Federal architecture. East End Avenue at 88th Street; (212) 570-4751; open for tours Wednesday 10 a.m., 11 a.m., 1 p.m., and 2 p.m. by reservation only. Admission $4 adults, $3 seniors. (1 hour)

★ **Lower East Side Tenement Museum**—This museum was once a six-story tenement building, built in 1863, that housed 11,000 people over a 70-year period. The upper floors have been re-created to show the living conditions endured by the house's tenants, including Irish, German, Russian Jewish, and Italian immigrants. The museum organizes various walking tours, each concentrating on a theme, such as the lives of women and tenement architecture. 90 Orchard Street; (212) 431-0233; open Tuesday through Friday 12 p.m. to 5 p.m., Saturday and Sunday 11 a.m. to 5 p.m. Admission to museum $8 adults; $6 seniors, students, and children. Additional charge for walking tours and dramas. (1 hour)

★ **New York Stock Exchange**—The sight of the apparent chaos on the Stock Exchange floor might lead you to reconsider your stock investments. You can view the spot where the crash of 1929 plunged the nation into the Great Depression and watch the day's hectic but exciting trading. (You cannot go onto the floor of the Exchange unless you know a member; if you have a New York–based broker, it's worth a phone call to see if he or she can get you in.) Just outside the Observation Gallery, there are exhibits on the history of the exchange and short videos. Plan on time to go through a metal detector line. 20 Broad Street; (212) 656-5167; open Monday through Friday 9:15 a.m. to 4 p.m. Admission free, but tickets are required and numbers are limited. (1 hour)

★ **Pierpont Morgan Library**—The private library of financier J. Pierpont Morgan is one of the country's loveliest. It is filled with rare editions, over 1,000 illustrated manuscripts, art objects, paintings, sculpture, and a glass-enclosed garden court. Some of the gems of the library collection are three Gutenberg Bibles; a Shakespeare first folio; an autographed manuscript of Milton's *Paradise Lost*; original musical scores from Bach, Brahms, and Beethoven; and manuscripts and early editions of Rudyard Kipling, Oscar Wilde, and Gertrude Stein. Morgan's study, once described as the most beautiful room in America, is lined with Italian Renaissance paintings. The **Morgan Café**, a lovely atrium-style restaurant, serves lunch and afternoon tea. 29 E. 36th

Street; (212) 685-0610; open Tuesday through Friday 10:30 a.m. to
5 p.m., Saturday 10:30 a.m. to 6 p.m., Sunday noon to 6 p.m.
Admission $5 adults; $3 seniors, students, and children. (2 hours)

★ **United Nations**—The United Nations, designed by 12 world-
renowned architects, consists of the majestic **Secretariat Building**, the
domed **General Assembly Building**, the **Conference Building**, and the
**Hammarskjöld Library**. Various member states have donated artwork.
During its mid-September to mid-December sitting, the U.N. General
Assembly can be witnessed from the public gallery. Visitors center on
First Avenue and 46th Street; (212) 963-1234; open daily 9:15 a.m. to
4:15 p.m. Free tickets to the public gallery are issued from the information desk in the lobby on a first-come, first-served basis. Guided tours,
which last about 45 minutes, are given daily from 9:15 a.m. to 4:45 p.m.
$7.50 adults, $4.50 students, and $3.50 grades one through eight. (1 hour)

**El Museo del Barrio**—This is the city's only museum devoted to the
cultures of Latin America, particularly that of Puerto Rico. There's a
small collection of pre-Columbian art as well as various special exhibitions of paintings, sculpture, and videos exploring the past and present
of Latin America. The museum is just across from the **Museum of the
City of New York** in East Harlem. Fifth Avenue at 104th Street; (212)
831-7272; open Wednesday through Sunday 11 a.m. to 5 p.m. Admission suggested donation $4 adults, $2 seniors and students. (1 hour)

**Federal Hall National Monument**—Built in 1842 on the site of the
original Federal Hall, the museum shows a short film and features a
collection of exhibits relating to events that occured on this site. In
April 1789, George Washington was sworn in as the country's first
president here; a dignified statue of the father of our country marks the
spot. A glass-encased balcony railing section shows where Washington
leaned when he addressed the crowd after his inauguration. Wall and
Nassau Streets; (212) 825-6888; open Monday through Friday 9 a.m.
to 5 p.m. Admission free. (1 hour)

**New Museum of Contemporary Art**—Located in the heart of an area
filled with artists' lofts and galleries, this museum is the only one in the
city devoted exclusively to art of the past two decades. The museum
features solo and group exhibitions and a variety of public programs.
583 Broadway (between Houston and Prince); (212) 219-1222; open

Wednesday through Sunday noon to 6 p.m., Saturday to 8 p.m. Admission $4 adults; $3 artists, seniors, and students, children under 12 free. Free Saturday 6 p.m. to 8 p.m. (1 hour)

**St. Paul's Chapel**—This chapel, regularly visited by George Washington, still houses the pew where Washington sat during his inauguration service in 1789. Dedicated in 1766, the church is considered the oldest public building in continuous use in Manhattan. Classical concerts and church music performed at noon on some Mondays and Thursdays. Broadway and Fulton Streets; (212) 602-0800; open Monday through Friday 9 a.m. to 3 p.m., Sunday 8 a.m. to 4 p.m. Admission by donation. (½ hour)

**Theodore Roosevelt National Historic Site**—This is the reconstructed birthplace of Roosevelt, the only American president born in the city. The house is filled with original Roosevelt furnishings. The lower floor showcases an exhibition on Roosevelt's life, from his childhood struggles with illness, to the tragic same-day deaths of his wife and his mother, to his rise to become the nation's youngest president at age 42. The room full of his hunting trophies and outdoor memorabilia captures his energetic personality. 28 E. 20th Street; (212) 260-1616; open Wednesday through Sunday 9 a.m. to 5 p.m. Admission $2 adults, seniors and children free. (1½ hours)

## SHOPPING

For many visitors, shopping is a big reason to visit the city. It's possible to spend a fortune, but real bargains can also be found. Peter Minuit got the best trade in the city's history back in 1626, when he bought Manhattan Island for a box of tools and trinkets worth the equivalent of $24.

New York department stores are the stuff of legend. **Macy's**, 34th Street and Sixth Avenue, has been called the world's largest department store. **Bloomingdale's**, Third Avenue at 59th Street, is considered high-style New York—the food department has a whole section devoted to caviar. For men's clothing, **Brooks Brothers**, Madison Avenue at 44th Street, and **Paul Stuart**, Madison Avenue at 45th Street, are long-time institutions. There are dozens of jewelers in the "diamond district" on 47th Street, but the store that attracts the most visitors is the legendary **Tiffany & Co.**, Fifth Avenue between 56th and 57th Streets.

For those with expansive credit limits, there are world-famous haute couture names such as **Giorgio Armani**, Madison Avenue at 68th Street; **Gucci**, 685 and 689 Fifth Avenue; **Yves St. Laurent**, Madison Avenue at 71st Street; and **Polo/Ralph Lauren**, Madison Avenue at 72nd Street, in a French Renaissance–style mansion. **Trump Tower**, at Fifth Avenue and 56th Street, has an elegant collection of fashion and gift shops. For the young and the young-at-heart, **F.A.O. Schwarz**, Fifth Avenue and 58th Street, is filled with childhood delights at lofty prices.

For better deals, the **Lower East Side**, in the area of Orchard and Delancey Streets, is a bargain-hunter's paradise, with shops and stalls overflowing with clothing, shoes, accessories, and linens; closed on Saturday, open on Sunday. The **South Street Seaport** district is also loaded with interesting shops.

Manhattan has hundreds of bookstores. Numerous **Barnes and Noble** bookstores can be found around the city, the newest at Union Square. The many specialty bookstores include those for mysteries, travel, and biographies. The **Strand**, 828 Broadway at 12th Street, (212) 473-1452, has miles of books and thousands of review copies of new books at discounted prices. The **Gotham**, 41 West 47th Street, (212) 719-4448, like the Strand, will help you locate almost any title, new or old.

## FITNESS AND RECREATION

Manhattan's "backyard," the 843-acre **Central Park**, (212) 360-8111, is a popular spot for jogging, cycling, horseback riding, softball, ice skating, tennis, boating, skateboarding, and hiking. Although there have been well-publicized accounts of muggings and other crimes in the park, it is considered safe during the day (it's best avoided at night except for public concerts or similar activities). Park rangers conduct walking tours and provide information about park activities on Saturdays and Sundays. The visitors center at 65th Street, west of the Central Park Wildlife Conservation Center, is open Tuesday through Sunday 11 a.m. to 5 p.m.

On the Hudson River between 17th and 23rd Streets a 30-acre space has recently been turned into a fascinating recreation area, the **Chelsea Pier Sports and Entertainment Complex**, (212) 336-6666, with a 75 foot pool, in-line skating, ice skating, jogging (the world's largest indoor track), ice hockey, basketball, rock climbing, and even kayaking. Way downtown on the Hudson River, between Battery Park and Chambers Street, is **Battery Park City**, a complex of rental apartments and condominiums on a 92-acre landfill site. Its Esplanade runs between Liberty and West Thames Streets and is open from dawn to dusk. This park area, managed by a private, nonprofit group, is clean, safe, and perfect for jogging or watching the river traffic. Wheelchair accessible. **Riverside Park**, along the Hudson River, and **Washington Square Park**, in Greenwich Village, also attract joggers.

## FOOD

Manhattan's dining establishments are unmatched in number, culinary variety, and general excellence. Entire books have been written about New York's restaurants, and it's possible to provide only a very limited sample here. You can, of course, dine throughout the city at world-famous and ultra-chic restaurants, some of which are mentioned below. If you hanker to eat at a top-echelon restaurant, you might want to go for lunch instead of dinner; not only is it less expensive, but it's also usually easier to get reservations on short notice. If your budget or your mood dictates something more casual, you'll also find hundreds of appealing moderate to inexpensive options, especially in Chinatown and at the many excellent Indian, Greek, and other ethnic restaurants. Coffee shops are a good choice for breakfast; they provide an affordable alternative to the typical Manhattan hotel fare.

In the Financial District, **Windows on the World**, on the 107th floor at 1 World Trade Center, (212) 524-7011, offers a view of the city that even the most jaded New Yorkers love. Dig deep into your pockets—main courses start around $28. When reserving, ask for a table near or at a floor-to-ceiling window with a direct view uptown. Even the **McDonald's**, Broadway at Liberty Street, (212) 385-2063, is special, with a doorman, flowers, a pianist, and burgers on silver trays. At South Street Seaport, **Sloppy Louie's**, 92 South Street, (212) 509-9694, has attracted fish lovers since 1930.

In Chinatown, **Nice Restaurant**, 13 Doyers Street, (212) 962-6047, is a long-time favorite, and **20 Mott Street**, 20 Mott Street, (212) 964-0380, is one of the area's most celebrated establishments. Next door, the **Peking Duck House**, 22 Mott Street, (212) 227-1810, is a favorite of former mayor Ed Koch. Nearby, Little Italy's **Puglia**, 189 Hester Street, (212) 226-8912, offers low prices, live music, and pasta of every imaginable kind. You may wind up dining at a communal table and singing along with the waiters.

In the Lower East Side and East Village areas, **Katz's Delicatessen**, East Houston Street near Orchard Street, (212) 254-2246, was legendary for its corned beef and pastrami even before it gained fame in the movie *When Harry Met Sally*; **Mitali**, 6th Street between First and Second Avenues, (212) 533-2508, offers high-quality Indian cuisine; and **Second Avenue Kosher Deli**, Second Avenue at 10th Street, (212) 677-0606, is a landmark family-run Jewish deli. **Chanterelle**, 2 Harrison Street, (212) 966-6960, is one of the city's four-star restaurants, with four-star prices, refined food, and pampering service. **TriBeCa Grill**, 375 Greenwich Street at Franklin Street, (212) 941-3900, is co-owned by Robert de Niro and draws a star-spotting crowd who come for the fine food.

Greenwich Village's favorite spots include the **Gotham Bar and Grill**, 12 E. 12th Street, (212) 620-4020, which combines lovely surroundings and wonderful food in a converted warehouse; and **Ye Waverly Inn**, 16 Bank Street at Waverly Place, (212) 929-4377, an early American inn with several wood-burning fireplaces, charmingly odd-shaped rooms, and good standard American fare. **Asti**, 13 East 12th Street, (212) 741-9105, is suggested not so much for the cuisine but for its singing waiters and professional opera singers, who perform arias while you eat decent Italian food.

Gramercy Park has recently become a trendy neighborhood for restaurants, but some old standbys have better values and lower noise levels. **Pete's Tavern**, 18th Street and Irving Place, (212) 473-7676, is where O. Henry is said to have written "The Gift of the Magi." Two famous and sometimes difficult-to-get-into restaurants specializing in creative American cuisine are run by Danny Meyer: the **Union Square Café**, 21 East 16th Street, (212) 243-4020, and the newer **Gramercy Tavern**, 42 East 20th Street, (212) 477-0777. Whether you want a peanut butter sandwich, filet mignon, or lobster, you'll find it and much more at **America**, 9 East 18th Street, between Broadway and Fifth Avenue, (212) 505-2110. Coffee is served in giantic cups, and better mashed potatoes would be hard to find. Huge, noisy, lots of fun, and open late.

In Chelsea, the elegant **Chelsea Bistro & Bar**, 358 West 23rd Street between 8th and 9th Avenues, (212) 727-2026, has superb food and a long bar frequented by local artists and writers. If you want a meal at 2 a.m., the 1930s, art deco–style **Empire Diner**, 210 Tenth Avenue, between West 22nd and 23rd Streets, (212) 243-2736, is open 24 hours a day. Don't be put off by the stretch limos outside—the prices are reasonable, at least for Manhattan.

Behind the New York Public Library is the recently cleaned up

# MANHATTAN

# Food

| | | | |
|---|---|---|---|
| (A) | 20 Mott Street | (Q) | Mitali |
| (B) | America | (R) | Museum Café |
| (C) | American Festival Café | (A) | Nice Restaurant |
| (D) | Asti | (K) | Orso |
| (E) | Au Café | (S) | Oyster Bar & Restaurant |
| (F) | Boathouse Café | (A) | Peking Duck House |
| (G) | Bryant Park Grill | (T) | Pete's Tavern |
| (H) | Café des Artistes | (U) | Pierre au Tunnel |
| (I) | Chanterelle | (V) | Puglia |
| (J) | Chelsea Bistro & Bar | (C) | Rainbow Room |
| (K) | Chez Josephine | (W) | Royaton Hall |
| (L) | Empire Diner | (X) | Second Avenue Kosher Deli |
| (D) | Gotham Bar and Grill | (Y) | Sloppy Louie's |
| (M) | Gramercy Tavern | (H) | Tavern on the Green |
| (K) | Joe Allen | (Z) | TriBeCa Grill |
| (N) | Katz's Delicatessen | (A) | Union Square Café |
| (O) | La Bonne Soupe | (H) | Vince & Eddie's |
| (O) | Le Quercy | (B) | Windows on the World |
| (P) | McDonald's | (C) | Ye Waverly Inn |

*Note: Items with the same letter are located in the same town or area.*

Bryant Park and the **Bryant Park Grill**, (212) 840-6500, which offers lovely views of the park. The outdoor café, which serves only drinks, and the open-air terrace are less pricey. The **Oyster Bar & Restaurant** on the lower level of Grand Central Station, (212) 490-6650, serves every kind of seafood conceivable. The main dining room is huge, with more intimate surroundings available in the **Saloon**.

If you can't decide where to eat before or after the theater, just head for Restaurant Row, lit by gas lamps and stretching along West 46th Street from Eighth to Ninth Avenues. These restaurants pride themselves in getting you out in time for the 8 p.m. curtain, but be sure to make a reservation first. Among the best are **Orso**, 322 West 46th Street, (212) 489-7212, and **Joe Allen**, 326 West 46th Street, (212) 581-6464. A number of small, creative, and experimental theaters line 42nd Street. Nearby, **Chez Josephine**, 414 West 42nd Street, (212) 594-1925, is beautifully run by Jean-Claude, adopted son of the late Josephine Baker. Live music plays before and after the theater. **Pierre au Tunnel**, 250 West 47th Street between Broadway and Eighth Avenue, (212) 575-1220, is an old, family-run place with excellent French bistro dishes at bargain prices.

Around Midtown, the **American Festival Café**, Rockefeller Center, (212) 332-7620, has tables on what becomes the famous ice skating rink in the winter. A popular spot for "power breakfasts," the restaurant also serves lunch, dinner, and after-theater food in one of Manhattan's prettiest settings. At the top of 30 Rockefeller Plaza is the romantic **Rainbow Room**, (212) 632-5000, a pricey place to dine and dance but certainly worth it once in a lifetime. During the summer and from time to time throughout the year, the restaurant offers specially priced or pre-theater prix fixe dinners. **Le Quercy**, 52 West 55th Street, (212) 265-8141, has first-rate French fare that rivals that of better-known, four star restaurants. For inexpensive but excellent soups, omelettes, and fondues, try **La Bonne Soupe**, 45 West 55th Street, (212) 586-7650. Many of the tables are close together, so go early or late for more privacy.

Carnegie Hall, now more than 100 years old, has something new— its **Royaton Hall**, (212) 903-9689, offers a pre-concert buffet dinner on certain nights, making concert-going very convenient. Reservations required. On Broadway, **Au Café**, at 53rd Street, (212) 757-2233, is one of the few places serving New Orleans–style *beignets*, as well as superb sandwiches, soups, pastas, and burgers. A palm-lined outdoor patio adds atmosphere to this inexpensive restaurant, open for all meals.

Uptown, **Tavern on the Green**, Central Park West at 67th Street, (212) 873-3200, is a city institution with a magical feel. Outdoor dining is featured in warm weather, along with jazz nights and other live music. **Vince & Eddie's**, 70 West 68th Street, (212) 721-0068, is one of the city's best American bistros, with incredibly warm service that ends the myth that New Yorkers aren't friendly. **Café des Artistes**, 1 West 67th Street at Central Park West, (212) 877-3500, gets rave reviews from almost everybody. One of the city's most romantic dining spots and a favorite of Jackie O, the restaurant is frequented by the likes of former mayor Koch, President Clinton, and many of the rich and famous. Howard Christy Chandler murals and flowers are everywhere.

Near the Museum of Natural History is the casual **Museum Café**, 366 Columbus Avenue at 77th Street, (212) 799-0150, serving salads, burgers, and soup. The restaurant is open all night on Thanksgiving

Eve, when the Macy's Thanksgiving Day Parade floats are being inflated on the side streets nearby. During the warm weather, don't miss the **Boathouse Café** in Central Park near 72nd Street, (212) 988-0576. If you don't want to walk through the park, a free trolley will pick you up at 72nd Street and Fifth Avenue after 7 p.m. Go before sunset for a gondola ride, then dine overlooking the lake.

## LODGING

Manhattan's hotels can be very expensive, but bargains do exist, especially with weekend and package rates. There are several bed and breakfast registries, including **B&B Network of NY**, (212) 645-8134 or (800) 900-8134, and **New World B&B**, (212) 675-5600 or (800) 443-3800. In Lower Manhattan, **Best Western Seaport Inn**, 33 Peck Slip, (212) 766-6600, offers dazzling views of the Brooklyn Bridge, refrigerators in each room, and a comfortable, country inn atmosphere ($139 to $214 for a double). The 504-room **New York Marriott Financial Center**, 85 West Street, (212) 385-4900, has many rooms with harbor views ($119 to $169 for a double).

In Midtown, **The Plaza**, Fifth Avenue at Central Park South, (212) 759-3000 or (800) 759-3000, is probably the city's most famous hotel and has welcomed all manner of celebrities, from Teddy Roosevelt to F. Scott and Zelda Fitzgerald to the Beatles ($275 to $3,000 for a two-person suite). The **Waldorf-Astoria**, 301 Park Avenue, (212) 355-3000 or (800) HILTONS, is rich in history and another of the city's most famous hotels ($280 to $440 for a double). The 52-story **Four Seasons Hotel**, 57 E. 57th Street, (212) 758-5700 or (800) 332-3442, designed by celebrated architect I. M. Pei, is the city's tallest hotel and one of its most opulent ($470 to $550 for a double). The **Pierre**, Fifth Avenue at 61st Street, (212) 940-8101 or (800) PIERRE4, has enormous rooms and was artist Salvador Dali's favorite New York hotel ($415 to $580 for a double). **Essex House Hotel Nikko**, 160 Central Park South, (212) 247-0300 or (800) 654-5687, is a stylish hotel with a lovely view of Central Park ($198 to $340 for a double). The **Ritz Carlton Hotel**, 112 Central Park South, (212) 757-1900, is an elegant, European-style hotel opposite Central Park ($275 to $400 for a double).

**Manhattan East Suite Hotels** is a family-owned group of comfortable, moderately priced Midtown and Upper East Side suite hotels that all include fully equipped kitchens ($119 to $269 per suite); call (800) ME-SUITE or (212) 465-3600 for reservations at any of the

# MANHATTAN

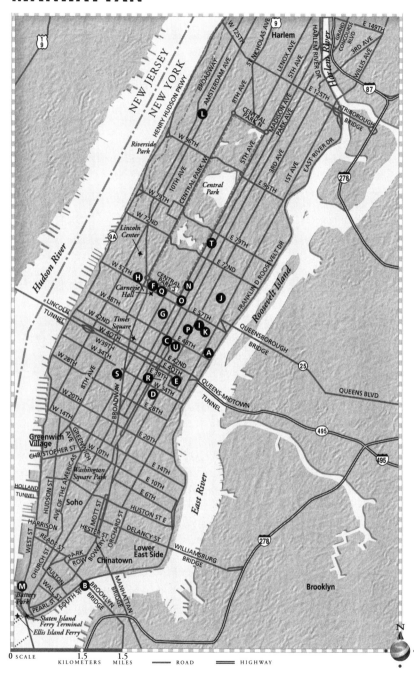

## Lodging

- **(A)** Beekman Tower
- **(B)** Best Western Seaport Inn
- **(C)** Beverly Hotel
- **(D)** Dumont Plaza
- **(E)** Eastgate Tower
- **(F)** Essex House Hotel Nikko
- **(G)** Four Seasons Hotel
- **(H)** Hotel Newton
- **(I)** Loews New York Hotel
- **(J)** Lyden Gardens
- **(K)** Lyden House
- **(L)** New York International Youth Hostel
- **(M)** New York Marriott Financial Center
- **(N)** Pierre
- **(O)** The Plaza
- **(P)** Plaza Fifty
- **(Q)** Ritz Carlton Hotel
- **(R)** Shelburne Murray Hill
- **(S)** Southgate Tower
- **(T)** Surrey Hotel
- **(U)** Waldorf-Astoria

following hotels: **Beekman Tower**, 3 Mitchell Place; **Dumont Plaza**, 150 E. 34th Street; **Eastgate Tower**, 222 E. 39th Street; **Lyden Gardens**, 215 E. 64th Street; **Lyden House**, 320 E. 53rd Street; **Plaza Fifty**, 155 E. 50th Street; **Shelburne Murray Hill**, 303 Lexington Avenue; **Southgate Tower**, 371 Seventh Avenue; and **Surrey Hotel**, 20 E. 76th Street. The centrally located **Beverly Hotel**, 125 E. 50th Street, (212) 753-2700 or (800) 223-0945, is great value for families, with kitchenettes in the one-bedroom suites ($149 to $169 for a double). **Loews New York Hotel**, 569 Lexington Avenue, is close to Rockefeller Center and the United Nations ($120 to $189 for a double). **Hotel Newton**, 2528 Broadway, (212) 678-6500 or (800) 643-5553, offers the most reasonably priced rooms close to theaters ($70 for a double). **New York International Youth Hostel**, 891 Amsterdam Avenue, (212) 932-2300 or (800) 909-4776, the largest youth hostel in the U.S., occupies an 1883 architectural landmark ($22 to $25 per person).

## NIGHTLIFE

In this city of big dreams, the range and quality of the nightlife are unparalleled. With nearly 40 Broadway theaters, three dozen off-Broadway theaters, and 200 off-off-Broadway houses, there is something for every theatrical taste. The principal differences between the three venues are size and price. Half-price day-of-performance tickets are sold from two branches of TKTS (cash only), on 47th Street between Broadway and Seventh Avenue and in the South Tower of the World Trade Center, between 3 p.m. and 8 p.m. for evening shows. During the summer, **Shakespeare in the Park** plays are staged in Central Park's Delacorte Theater. Tickets are free but are limited to two per person.

The spectacular **Lincoln Center**, 63rd Street and Columbus Avenue, is home to many world-renowned companies and performance venues: The **New York Philharmonic** plays in Avery Fisher Hall, (212) 875-5030; Alice Tully Hall, (212) 875-5050, is an important place for chamber music; the **New York City Ballet** is based in the New York State Theater, (212) 870-5570, where the **New York City Opera** also performs; the **Metropolitan Opera Company** performs at the Metropolitan Opera House, (212) 362-6000, as does the **American Ballet Theater**.

Other world-class venues in Manhattan include **Carnegie Hall**, (212) 247-7800, presenting visiting orchestras, recitals, chamber music, and pop concerts, and the **City Center**, (212) 239-6200, where the **Alvin Ailey American Dance Theater**, the **Dance Theater of Harlem**, and the **Merce Cunningham Dance Company** are based. If tickets for events at these venues are out of your price range, you can hear high quality classical music for free in the summer at concerts in the city's parks.

The Manhattan nightclub scene is constantly changing, and the action doesn't really begin until after midnight. To find out about the latest hot spots and upcoming acts, check out the weekly *Village Voice* and *Time Out New York*. Many of the jazz, blues, and folk clubs are in Greenwich Village. The **Village Vanguard**, Seventh Avenue at 11th Street, attracts top jazz stars. The legendary **Bitter End**, 147 Bleecker Street, and the **Speakeasy**, MacDougal and Bleecker Streets, feature folk acts on most nights. In Midtown **Michael's Pub**, 55th Street at Third Avenue, specializes in New Orleans–style jazz and sometimes finds Woody Allen playing a set on his clarinet on Monday evenings.

Manhattan's comedy clubs have given breaks to the likes of David Letterman, Eddie Murphy, and Robin Williams, among others. **Stand Up N.Y.**, 78th Street and Broadway; **Caroline's Comedy Club**, Broadway between 49th and 50th Streets; and **Dangerfield's**, 111 First Avenue, are some of most popular.

# 2

# NEW YORK CITY'S OUTER BOROUGHS

Brooklyn, Queens, Staten Island, and the Bronx—the four other boroughs that comprise the City of New York—offer a wide array of attractions and sights beyond the towering skyscrapers of Manhattan. The outer boroughs are easily reached from Manhattan by car, ferry, bus, or subway, depending on the borough. Most of the places described below provide clear directions on how to reach them from Manhattan and other nearby areas.

If Brooklyn were a separate city, which it was until 1898, it would be one of the largest in the United States, with over 75 square miles of land. Brooklyn's population represents an enormous cultural mix, including large enclaves of Russians in Brighton Beach, Italians in Bensonhurst, and Middle Easterners along Atlantic Avenue. Although in recent years more and more Manhattanites have moved to Brooklyn, bringing Manhattan-style urbanity with them, many neighborhoods maintain strong ethnic flavors. Brooklyn also has some beautiful and historic neighborhoods. The Park Slope area is distinguished by the elegant Victorian brownstones that line its broad streets and by its proximity to the Brooklyn Museum, the Brooklyn Botanical Garden, and Prospect Park. Brooklyn Heights is located right off the best known of the borough's many attractions, the spectacular Brooklyn Bridge.

Queens, a sprawling borough of stable residential villages and neighborhoods, is suburban in character. It, too, has a number of strong

# New York City's Outer Boroughs

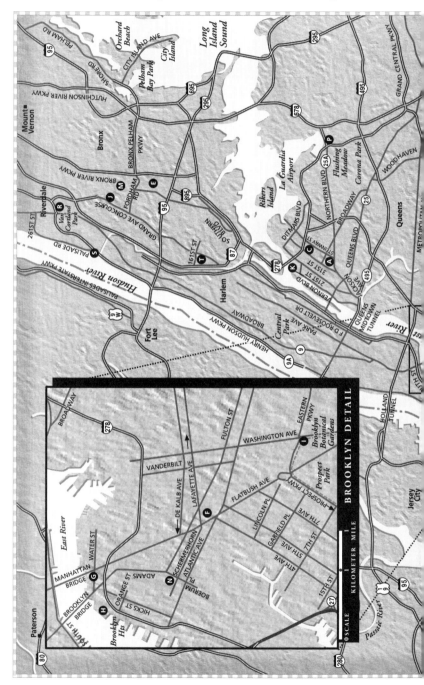

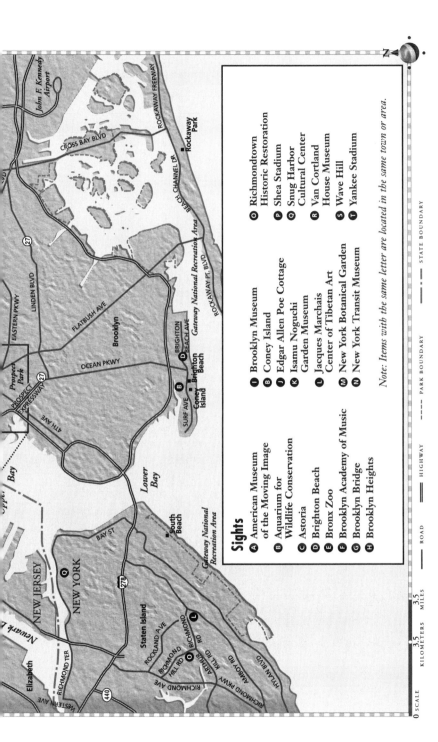

## Sights

Ⓐ American Museum
of the Moving Image

Ⓑ Aquarium for
Wildlife Conservation

Ⓒ Astoria

Ⓓ Brighton Beach

Ⓔ Bronx Zoo

Ⓕ Brooklyn Academy of Music

Ⓖ Brooklyn Bridge

Ⓗ Brooklyn Heights

Ⓘ Brooklyn Museum

Ⓙ Coney Island

Ⓙ Edgar Allen Poe Cottage

Ⓚ Isamu Noguchi
Garden Museum

Ⓛ Jacques Marchais
Center of Tibetan Art

Ⓜ New York Botanical Garden

Ⓝ New York Transit Museum

Ⓞ Richmondtown
Historic Restoration

Ⓟ Shea Stadium

Ⓠ Snug Harbor
Cultural Center

Ⓡ Van Cortland
House Museum

Ⓢ Wave Hill

Ⓣ Yankee Stadium

*Note: Items with the same letter are located in the same town or area.*

SCALE | 0 | 3.5 KILOMETERS | 3.5 MILES

ROAD — HIGHWAY — PARK BOUNDARY --- STATE BOUNDARY —·—

ethnic communities: Astoria is famously Greek, while Jackson Heights is known as "Little India," and Flushing as "Little Asia." The Rockaways, a 10-mile strip of beach on a peninsula, was once a popular summer vacation destination that still draws warm-weather visitors. Baseball fans associate Queens with Shea Stadium, home of the New York Mets. The borough is also the site of New York's two main airports, John F. Kennedy International and LaGuardia.

Staten Island, largely residential, is famous for the ferry connecting Lower Manhattan to the island—long one of the best bargains in the city, the beautiful round trip is now free to pedestrians (Staten Island is the only borough not connected to Manhattan by subway). The Richmond-town Historic Restoration shows the fruits of a half-century of restoring buildings from the seventeenth to the nineteenth centuries. The area encompasses beaches, boardwalks, walking trails, and even forests.

The Bronx is home to the world-renowned Bronx Zoo, the New York Botanical Garden, and Yankee Stadium, known as "the house that Ruth built" (Babe Ruth, that is), among other interesting spots. The Bronx is also the greenest of New York City's boroughs—nearly one-quarter of it is devoted to parks.

## A PERFECT DAY IN THE OUTER BOROUGHS

If you only have a day to explore the outer boroughs, spend it in the largest one, Brooklyn, starting at the oceanfront Aquarium for Wildlife Conservation. If you're hungry after seeing all those fish, try a hot dog at the original Nathan's Famous on Coney Island. An influx of thousands of Russian immigrants has revitalized the nearby Brighton Beach area, now filled with Russian shops and restaurants. Spend the afternoon in Brooklyn Heights, a National Historic Landmark area of nineteenth-century brownstones. Take a sunset stroll along the Promenade before enjoying dinner at one of the borough's outstanding restaurants, the River Café, virtually underneath the dramatic pylons of the Brooklyn Bridge. If you've got energy to spare, walk across the bridge and take in the glittering Manhattan skyline.

## SIGHTSEEING HIGHLIGHTS—BROOKLYN

★★★ **Brooklyn Bridge**—"All modern New York, heroic New York, started with the Brooklyn Bridge," wrote Kenneth Clark. One of the city's most celebrated sights, it was the world's first suspension bridge and, for 20 years, the longest bridge. Upon its completion in 1883, it formed the first fixed link between the then-separate cities of Manhattan and Brooklyn. The designers pioneered the use of steel wire cable to support the suspension bridge, and the criss-cross network gives the bridge a spider web effect, enhanced by two Gothic 272-foot-high stone arches. Both an engineering and an aesthetic marvel, it has long inspired writers, including the Brooklyn-based poet Walt Whitman. A walk across the mile-long pedestrian pathway affords incredible views of the city day or night. (½ hour)

★★★ **Brooklyn Heights**—Just off the Brooklyn Bridge are the tree-lined streets of Brooklyn Heights, set on the bluffs above the East River. The 30-block area of brownstone dwellings became a National Historic Landmark in 1965. These history-filled streets are ideal for strolling. The area was a major stopping point on the Underground Railroad; at the **Plymouth Church of the Pilgrims**, on Orange and Hicks Streets, Henry Ward Beecher delivered impassioned sermons against slavery before the Civil War. After the war he became the highest paid preacher in the nation, and thousands arrived in Brooklyn in "Beecher boats" every Sunday to hear him.

The Heights have been home to some of the country's most famous literary figures, from Walt Whitman to Thomas Wolfe. Whitman lived here for 40 years and set *Leaves of Grass* in type himself at a print shop while he served as editor of the *Brooklyn Eagle*. The ferry ride to Manhattan inspired one of his best-known poems, "Crossing Brooklyn Ferry." Novelists Bernard Malamud and Joseph Heller were born here. Truman Capote lived in a basement apartment on Willow Place while writing *Breakfast at Tiffany's* and *In Cold Blood*. Hart Crane conceived his masterpiece, *The Bridge*, in Columbia Heights, the area in which Norman Mailer now lives. Henry Miller set parts of *Tropic of Capricorn* in the neighborhood, and Arthur Miller wrote his Pulitzer Prize–winning play *Death of a Salesman* at 31 Grace Court. Thomas Wolfe wrote parts of *Of Time and the River* while living in the area.

The **Brooklyn Heights Promenade** with its breathtaking views of the Manhattan skyline, dominated by the twin towers of the World Trade Center and the tall ships of the South Street Seaport, has made many film appearances. (2 hours)

★★ **Aquarium for Wildlife Conservation**—Located just over the boardwalk from the Atlantic Ocean, this aquarium features a beluga whale; a sea cliffs exhibit that replicates the rocky Pacific coast, featuring walruses, sea otters, seals, and penguins; a Hudson River exhibit with local striped bass, bluegill, and carp; and outdoor and indoor pools, including a fascinating exhibit on the electric eel. Shows feature the electric eel, sea lions, and dolphins. Coney Island Broadwalk; (718) 265-FISH; open Monday through Friday 10 a.m. to 6 p.m.; Saturday, Sunday, and holidays 10 a.m. to 7 p.m. Admission $7.75 adults, $3.50 seniors and children. (2 hours)

★★ **Brighton Beach**—Now known as "Little Odessa" in honor of the many recent Russian settlers who arrived from that Black Sea port, this area has been revitalized by the more than 20,000 Russians who have settled here since the 1970s. Brighton Beach Avenue is currently home to riotous restaurants where Russians dance and drink vodka late into the night. Russian souvenirs are everywhere, and grocers and restaurants offer Russian food and delicacies such as caviar and smoked fish. (1 hour)

★★ **Brooklyn Academy of Music**—New Yorkers, regardless of the borough they live in, fondly refer to this organization as "BAM." It is noted for its innovative musical and dance programs, as well as first-rate

*The Brooklyn Bridge*

New York Convention and Visitors Bureau

theater and opera.  A shuttle bus leaves the Whitney Museum at Park
Avenue and 42nd Street in Manhattan one hour before curtain time and
returns after the performance, making a number of stops on both the east
and west sides of Manhattan.  The fare is $5 one way, and reservations
are a must.  The **BAM Café** serves dinner two hours before events. 30
Lafayette Avenue; (718) 636-4100. Ticket prices vary. (3–4 hours)

★★ **Brooklyn Museum**—This great museum is often overlooked by
visitors and New Yorkers alike because of Manhattan's more conveniently
clustered world-class museums. Housed in a magnificent McKim, Mead,
and White building, the museum's collection is particularly strong in
nineteenth-century American art, and the Egyptian collection is
considered one of the world's best. Highlights include American period
rooms and houses moved intact from elsewhere in Brooklyn; an American
and European picture gallery featuring a portrait of George Washington
by Gilbert Stuart; and paintings by artists of the Hudson River School,
including Thomas Cole and Frederick Church. Other noteworthy items
include the Moorish Room that once graced John D. Rockefeller's
Manhattan mansion, a 2,000-year-old Peruvian burial cloth, and a
collection of Native American crafts and artworks. If you have time before
or after your visit, take a stroll through the beautiful **Brooklyn Botanic
Garden**, (718) 622-4433, located next to the museum. The Garden's
**Terrace Café**, open year-round, serves lunch outdoors in warm weather.
Museum located at 200 Eastern Parkway; (718) 638-5000; open
Wednesday through Sunday 10 a.m. to 5 p.m. Admission $4 adults, $2
students, $1.50 seniors, children accompanied by adult free. (2 hours)

★ **New York Transit Museum**—Children of all ages and
transportation buffs enjoy this small museum that lets you travel back in
time.  It is filled with vintage cars, photographs, old turnstiles, and bus
and subway memorabilia. Boerum Place and Schermerhorn Street,
Brooklyn Heights; (718) 243-3060; open Tuesday  through Friday
10 a.m. to 4 p.m., Saturday and Sunday noon to 5 p.m. Admission $3
adults, $1.50 seniors and children under age 17. (1 hour)

**Coney Island**—The glory days of this amusement park, when
hundreds of thousands of people packed the park and the adjoining
Atlantic Ocean beach on a busy weekend, are long gone. However, if
visiting the aquarium next door, nostalgia and roller coaster buffs will
likely enjoy a stop here. The 1927 roller coaster known as the Cyclone

still attracts a loyal following. The park also features an even older
wooden Wonder Wheel, a 14-ride Kiddie Park, a water flume, and
various games. The original **Nathan's Famous**, home of the hot dog, is
still on the corner of Surf and Stillwell Avenues. Stillwell Avenue,
Coney Island; (718) 265-2100; mid-June through Labor Day open daily
noon to midnight; Palm Sunday to mid-June open weekends noon to
8 p.m. Admission $12.99 per person all-inclusive. Individual ride prices
available. Beach and boardwalk free. (3 hours)

## SIGHTSEEING HIGHLIGHTS—QUEENS

★★ **Astoria**—It has been said that only in Athens are there more Greeks
than in Astoria. The Greek Astoria stretches from Ditmars Boulevard in
the north down to Broadway, and from 31st Street across to Steinway
Street. Filled with Greek shops, cafés, and restaurants, the area draws
New Yorkers from other boroughs as well as out-of-towners. Greek
restaurants have long been famous for their ample portions and low
prices. Until the movie industry moved to the West Coast, Astoria was
the cinematic capital of the world. Recently, new film studios have
sprung up, and movies are again being made here. (2 hours)

★★ **Shea Stadium**—This 55,601-seat stadium is home to the New
York Mets baseball team. Though they're not the legendary Yankees,
the amazing Mets did win the World Series in 1986, and they continue
to thrill fans in their home stadium in Flushing Meadows. Flushing
Meadows was also the site of the 1939 and 1964 World's Fairs. 126th
Street and Roosevelt Avenue; (718) 507-8499; open April through
October. Admission $7 to $18. (3 hours)

★ **American Museum of the Moving Image**—Opened in 1988, this
museum is housed in an historic film studio complex that once hosted
Gloria Swanson, W. C. Fields, the Marx Brothers, and other early
movie stars. It is the only museum in the world providing a
comprehensive look at how moving images are made, marketed, and
shown. Interactive stations give visitors first-hand experience of jobs
such as sound editing, computer graphics design, bluescreen effects,
automatic dialogue replacement, and animation. The work of
cinematographers, TV directors, specific effects artists, screenwriters,
musical composers, and others is introduced through screenings of
documentaries and historic films and television shows played on

monitors and in mini-theaters. 35th Avenue and 36th Street, Astoria; (718) 784-0077; open Tuesday through Friday noon to 5 p.m., Saturday and Sunday noon to 6 p.m. Admission $5 adults, $4 seniors, $2.50 students and children. (1 hour)

★ **Isamu Noguchi Garden Museum**—This museum, which opened in 1985, is devoted entirely to the work of one artist, Isamu Noguchi (1904–1988). There are twelve galleries and an outdoor sculpture garden, with free films and tours offered regularly. On Saturday and Sunday, a shuttle bus runs from Park Avenue and 70th Street in Manhattan ($5 round trip). 3237 Vernon Boulevard at 33rd Road, Long Island City; (718) 204-7088; open April through October, Wednesday through Friday 10 a.m. to 5 p.m., Saturday and Sunday 11 a.m. to 6 p.m. Suggested donation $4 adults, $2 students and seniors. (1 hour)

## SIGHTSEEING HIGHLIGHTS—STATEN ISLAND

★★ **Richmondtown Historic Restoration**—This restored 100-acre village re-creates three centuries of local history. The buildings, moved from other areas of Staten Island and restored, range from a Dutch structure that doubled as a local church and schoolhouse to a general store packed with 1840s consumer goods. Guides dressed in period costumes provide insight into earlier times. 441 Clarke Avenue; (718) 351-1611. July and August: Wednesday through Friday 10 a.m. to 5 p.m., Saturday and Sunday 1 p.m. to 5 p.m. September through December and April through June: Wednesday through Sunday 1 p.m. to 5 p.m. Rest of year: Wednesday through Friday 1 p.m. to 5 p.m. Admission $4 adults; $2.50 seniors, students, and children. (2 hours)

★ **Jacques Marchais Center of Tibetan Art**—With the largest private collection of Tibetan art in the Western world, the center includes a wondrous stock of sculptured deities, ritual objects, incense burners, and other objects from the world's Buddhist cultures. The collection is housed in a stone cottage on Lighthouse Hill intended to replicate a Tibetan mountain temple. 338 Lighthouse Avenue; (718) 987-3500; April through November open Wednesday through Sunday 1 p.m. to 5 p.m.; by appointment Wednesday through Sunday 1 p.m. to 5 p.m. rest of the year. Admission $3 adults, $2.50 students and seniors, $1 children. Sunday programs $3 additional. (1 hour)

★ **Snug Harbor Cultural Center**—Considered the city's fastest growing center of the arts, this 80-acre National Landmark District park includes more than 25 restored and converted historic buildings. The hospital, founded in 1801 as the nation's first maritime hospital and home for "decrepit and worn-out sailors," was built in the classical style of the period. Jazz, classical, chamber, and folk music concerts are held in the **Newhouse Center for the Arts**. 1000 Richmond Terrace; (718) 448-2500; open Monday through Friday 9 a.m. to 5 p.m., Saturday and Sunday 10 a.m. to 6 p.m. Admission free except during concerts. (1 hour)

## SIGHTSEEING HIGHLIGHTS—THE BRONX

★★★ **Bronx Zoo**—Officially called the Bronx Zoo/Wildlife Conservation Park to emphasize its role as a refuge for endangered species, this is the largest city zoo in the nation. One of the first zoos to recognize that animals both looked and felt better out in the open, its 4,000 wild animals live in natural surroundings. Be sure to see the fascinating Wild Asia exhibit—nearly 40 acres of wilderness through which elephants, antelopes, rhinoceroses, and sika deer roam; it's viewable only on a narrated monorail ride. Visitors can explore the rest of the zoo by foot, aboard the Safari train, or via the aerial tramway. At the Children's Zoo, kids learn about animals by acting as they do—climbing spider webs or crawling through prairie dog tunnels. They can also pet and feed domestic animals. Fordham Road and Bronx River Parkway; (718) 367-1010; April through October open Monday through Friday 10 a.m. to 5 p.m., Saturday and Sunday 10 a.m. to 5:30 p.m.; open daily 10 a.m. to 4:30 p.m. rest of year. Admission April through October $6.75 adults, $3 seniors and children. Wednesday free to all. November through March $2.50 adults, $1 seniors and children. (3 hours)

★★ **New York Botanical Garden**—There's a wonderful mixture of formal gardens, rock gardens, and even a 40-acre virgin hemlock forest here. Within the last remaining primeval forest in the city is the Bronx River Gorge, best reached from its arched stone footbridge. The **Enid A. Haupt Conservatory**, a crystal palace of grand proportions, is full of glorious floral delights, banana plants, palm trees, and cacti. This National Historic Landmark, which recently underwent a $25 million restoration, is modeled after the Palm House at the Royal Botanic Gardens in Kew, England. A 350-foot scenic pathway along the Bronx

River offers majestic views of a waterfall. Special tours include those in foreign languages and the Baby Botanist Stroller Tour, in which guides lead little ones and their adult caregivers through a kid's-eye view of the gardens. Zoo Street and Southern Boulevard; (718) 817-8700; April through October open Tuesday through Sunday 10 a.m. to 6 p.m.; open 10 a.m. to 4 p.m. rest of year. Admission $3 adults, $1 seniors and children. (2 hours)

★★ **Yankee Stadium**—This 57,545-seat stadium is home to the New York Yankees, one of baseball's more successful teams. Many traditions were born in this stadium, including the original Bronx cheer. You can still feel the excitement created by legendary baseball greats Babe Ruth, Lou Gehrig, Joe DiMaggio, Mickey Mantle, and Roger Maris. 161st Street and River Avenue; (718) 293-6000; open April through October. Admission $12 to $21. (3 hours)

★ **Wave Hill**—This 28-acre Hudson River estate, where by turns Mark Twain, Theodore Roosevelt, and Arturo Toscanini lived, was given to New York by financier George Perkins in 1965. The nineteenth-century mansion now hosts a wide variety of cultural activities, all of which are reasonably priced: chamber music concerts, gardening and cooking workshops, botany lectures, tours of the extensive plant collection, a children's storytelling hour, an art program, and more. The gardens and greenhouses are extraordinary. This is a convenient stop if you're traveling up to Westchester or upstate New York. 249th Street and Independence Avenue, Riverdale; (718) 549-2055 or (718) 549-3200; grounds open Tuesday through Sunday 10 a.m. to 4:30 p.m., mid-May through mid-October open to 5:30 p.m. and to dusk on Fridays. Admission $4 adults, $2 students and seniors, free to children under age 6. Free to all on Tuesday and Saturday morning and from mid-November through mid-March. (2 hours)

**Edgar Allen Poe Cottage**—This 1812 house was occupied by the writer Edgar Allan Poe from 1846 to 1849. He moved here hoping that the country air would improve his wife's health. Sadly, she died of tuberculosis in the first winter, and Poe himself died three years later. He did, however, write some of his finest works here, including "Annabel Lee," "Ulalume," "The Bells," and "Eureka." The cottage contains a few of the couple's furnishings. An audiovisual presentation is shown. E. Kingsbridge Road at Grand Concourse; (718) 881-8900;

open Wednesday through Friday 9 a.m. to 5 p.m., Saturday 10 a.m. to
4 p.m., Sunday 1 p.m. to 5 p.m. Admission $2 adults, children under
age 12 free. (½ hour)

**Van Cortlandt House Museum**—This Colonial mansion in the
heart of Van Cortlandt Park was the military headquarters for
George Washington at various times. Built in 1748, it has been
accurately restored and filled with period antiques. Broadway and W.
246th Street, Riverdale; (718) 543-3344; open Tuesday through
Friday 10 a.m. to 3 p.m., Saturday and Sunday 11 a.m. to 4 p.m.
Admission $2 adults, $1.50 seniors and students; children under age
12 free. (½ hour)

## FITNESS AND RECREATION

A number of parks in the outer boroughs are playgrounds for joggers,
hikers, swimmers, and even golfers. In Brooklyn, **Prospect Park** was laid
out by the designers of Central Park, and many consider this their true
masterpiece. Near Fort Hamilton is **Dyker Beach Park**. In Queens,
**Flushing Meadow Park**, home to two New York World's Fairs, is
popular with joggers and walkers. **The Rockaways** is a 10-mile strip of
beach. **Breezy Point Park** is a nature preserve, and nearby **Jacob Riis
Park** includes beaches, handball courts, and a boardwalk.

On Staten Island, **South Beach** is popular for swimming and
walking along the 2.5-mile **Franklin D. Roosevelt Boardwalk**. The
2,500-acre **Greenbelt** includes two major trails: the 8.5-mile **Blue Trail**
and the **White Trail**. At the **Gateway National Recreation Area**, park
rangers lead nature tours. The Bronx is the greenest borough in the city,
with a surprising 23 percent devoted to parks. **Pelham Bay Park** is the
largest in the city and has two golf courses, many trails, and **Orchard
Beach**. **Van Cortlandt Park** is also popular with joggers.

## FOOD

Perhaps the most talked about (and elegant) Brooklyn restaurant is the
**River Café**, 1 Water Street, (718) 522-5200. Perfectly situated almost
under the Brooklyn Bridge, it provides dramatic views of the
Manhattan skyline and fine food to match. A great favorite with those
who like historic restaurants is **Peter Luger Steak House**, 178
Broadway, (718) 387-7400. Located at the foot of the Williamsburg

Bridge, it serves excellent porterhouse and other cuts of steak (credit cards not accepted).

Two Park Slope picks: **Cucina**, 256 Fifth Avenue at Garfield Place, (718) 230-0711, a favorite with locals, offers traditional Italian dishes in a rustic Tuscan atmosphere; and **Lemongrass Grill**, 61A Seventh Avenue at Lincoln Place, (718) 399-7100, boasts authentic Thai cooking.

If you want to dance on the tabletops, head for Brighton Beach and **Odessa**, 1113 Brighton Beach Avenue between 13th and 14th Streets, (718) 332-3223. This Russian restaurant has live music nightly and is an extraordinary experience even though the food is not. At **National Restaurant**, also on Brighton Beach Avenue, (718) 646-1225, $55 plus a 10 percent service charge will get you three drinks, dinner, a live show, and dancing on Saturday.

There are two old stand-bys for which Brooklyn is famous: **Lundy's**, 1901 Emmons Avenue at Ocean Avenue, Sheepshead Bay, (718) 743-0022, is a 400-seat restaurant noted for its huge portions of all-American fare. Ask about the shore dinner, which includes chowder, steamed lobster, grilled chicken, veggies, potatoes, pie, and coffee— all for about $25; and **Juniors**, 386 Flatbush Avenue at DeKalb, (718) 852-5257, is world-famous for its pastrami sandwiches and cheesecake.

Queens' many good restaurants include **Water's Edge**, 44th Drive at the East River, Long Island City, (718) 482-0033, which comes with wonderful views of the Manhattan skyline; plan time for drinks on the outside deck. **Taverna Astoria Park**, 19-06 Ditmars Boulevard, Astoria, (718) 626-9035, is a favorite Greek establishment. **Niederstein's**, 69-16 Metropolitan Avenue, (718) 326-0717, serves up traditional German dishes.

On Staten Island, a popular choice for Italian food is **La Fontana**, 2879 Amboy Road, (718) 667-4343. More representative of the Staten Island feeling is the rustic **Aesop's Tables**, 1233 Bay Street just south of Hylan Boulevard, (718) 720-2005, which has a patio for warm-weather dining and fresh fish, chicken, and chops.

In the Bronx, you can watch the boats sail by while dining at the **Lobster Box**, City Island Avenue near Rochelle Street, (718) 885-1952; the restaurant is in a small white 1800s house, where generations of the same family have been served lobster some ten different ways, along with other fresh seafood. **Lieberman's Kosher Deli**, 552 W. 235th Street, (718) 548-4534, is a popular Riverdale deli. **Il Boschetto**, 1660 E. Gun Hill Road,(718) 379-9335, is a fine choice for Italian food. In

# New York City's Outer Boroughs

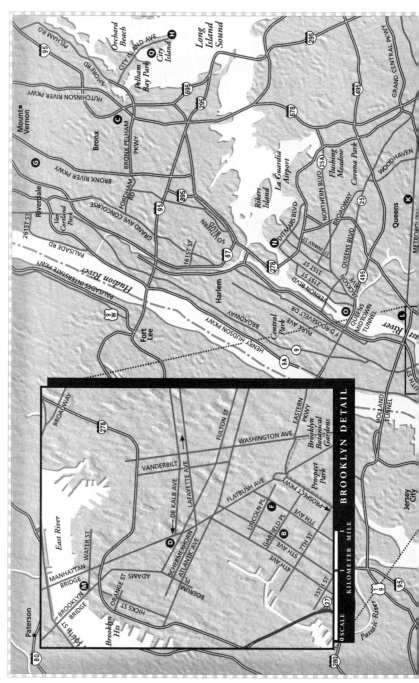

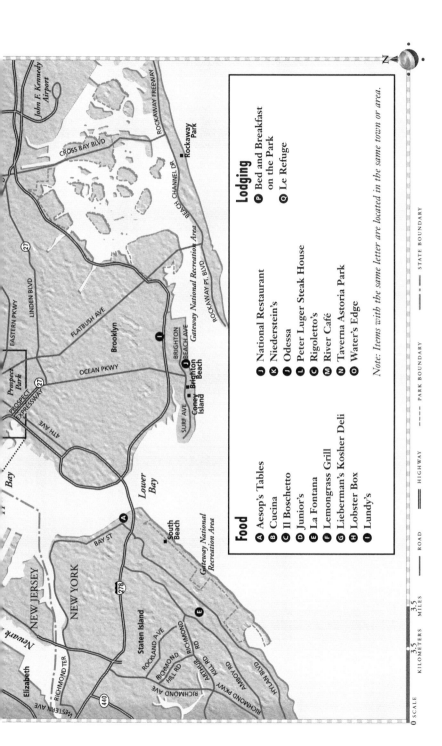

**Food**

- Ⓐ Aesop's Tables
- Ⓑ Cucina
- Ⓒ Il Boschetto
- Ⓓ Junior's
- Ⓔ La Fontana
- Ⓕ Lemongrass Grill
- Ⓖ Lieberman's Kosher Deli
- Ⓗ Lobster Box
- Ⓘ Lundy's

- Ⓙ National Restaurant
- Ⓚ Niederstein's
- Ⓛ Odessa
- Ⓜ Peter Luger Steak House
- Ⓖ Rigoletto's
- Ⓜ River Café
- Ⓝ Taverna Astoria Park
- Ⓞ Water's Edge

**Lodging**

- Ⓟ Bed and Breakfast on the Park
- Ⓠ Le Refuge

*Note: Items with the same letter are located in the same town or area.*

| | | | |
|---|---|---|---|
| O SCALE | | | |
| 0 | 3.5 KILOMETERS | | 3.5 MILES |
| ROAD | HIGHWAY | PARK BOUNDARY | STATE BOUNDARY |

the Little Italy area, **Rigoletto's**, 2311 Arthur Avenue, (718) 365-6644, is another favorite Italian restaurant.

## LODGING

The vast majority of New York City visitors stay in Manhattan. However, a number of chain hotels do exist around LaGuardia and John F. Kennedy Airports. For a taste of historic Brooklyn, **Bed and Breakfast on the Park**, 113 Prospect Park West, (718) 499-6115, is a lovingly restored nineteenth-century house with six spacious guest rooms. You'll find wood-burning fireplaces, canopied beds, Oriental rugs, and a delicious breakfast. Double rooms range from $110 to $250; some have shared baths. In the Bronx, **Le Refuge**, 620 City Island near City Island Bridge, (718) 885-2478, is a charming eight-room inn in what was once a sea captain's house. About a 30-minute subway ride from Manhattan, the inn is owned by the proprietor of Manhattan's popular restaurant of the same name. A double room with shared bath is $85; a suite for two with a private bath, $142; prices include breakfast.

For more information about bed and breakfasts in the outer boroughs, contact **B&B Network of NY**, (212) 645-8134 or (800) 900-8134; and **New World B&B**, (212) 675-5600 or (800) 443-3800.

# 3

# LONG ISLAND

Long Island is the largest and most varied island adjoining the continental United States. Technically, two of New York City's boroughs, Brooklyn and Queens, occupy Long Island's western section. However, the real Long Island begins only after leaving the city behind and crossing into Nassau County. East of Nassau is the more rural Suffolk County, with its two forks, north and south. From the Nassau/Queens border to the tip of Montauk Point, Long Island is 103 miles long.

There are many different Long Islands: the island of suburban sprawl and the notoriously congested Long Island Expressway; the rural island of farms and vineyards; the island of historic seaside villages; and the island of the rich and famous, on the North and South Shores in the string of beachside villages known collectively as "the Hamptons," also called the "New York Riviera." The North Shore, home to a number of estates built by real-life Great Gatsbys, is lapped by Long Island Sound, which F. Scott Fitzgerald dubbed "the most domesticated body of salt water in the Western Hemisphere." Teddy Roosevelt's summer home at Sagamore Hill and Walt Whitman's birthplace are North Shore attractions. Many of the South Shore attractions are beaches—at the grand oceanside Jones Beach State Park, on Fire Island, at the Hamptons, and at the end of the island at Montauk Point, where the state's oldest lighthouse looks out to the Atlantic Ocean. Despite the monied summer visitors, most of the island's finest beaches are part of national, state, or county parks and are open to all. Many fishing world records have been set in the waters around Long Island.

# LONG ISLAND

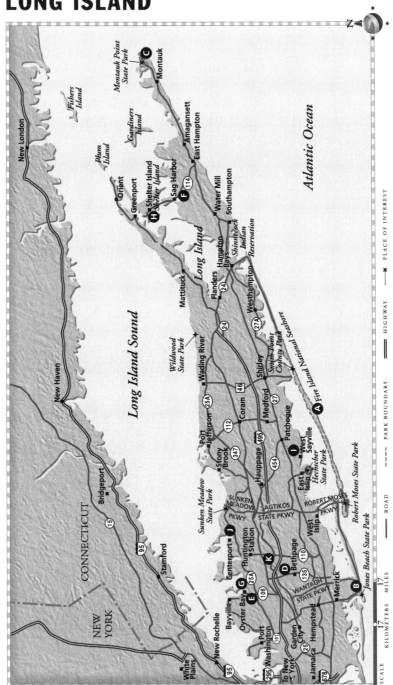

N

Montauk Point State Park
C — Montauk

Fishers Island

Gardiners Island

Amagansett
East Hampton

Plum Island

Orient
Greenport
Shelter Island
H — Shelter Island
Sag Harbor
F — (114)
Water Mill
Southampton

Long Island

Atlantic Ocean

Mattituck
Flanders
Hampton Bays — (24)
Shinnecock Indian Reservation
Westhampton — (27)

Long Island Sound

Wildwood State Park
Wading River
(24)

Shirley
Coram — (46)
Medford — (27)
Smith Point County Park
Patchogue
A — Fire Island National Seashore

New Haven

Port Jefferson — (25A)
(112)
Stony Brook — (347)
Hauppauge — (495)
(454)
West Sayville
I
East Islip
Heckscher State Park

Bridgeport
(15)

Sunken Meadow State Park
SUNKEN MEADOW
SAGTIKOS STATE PKWY
ROBERT MOSES
West Islip
ROBERT MOSES PKWY
Robert Moses State Park

Stamford

CONNECTICUT

J — Centerport
Huntington Station
K
D — Bethpage
(135)
(110)
WANTAGH STATE PKWY
Merrick
B
Jones Beach State Park

NEW ROCHELLE

G — (25A)
E — Oyster Bay — (106)
Bayville

NEW YORK

Port Washington — (101)
Garden City
Hempstead — (25)
Jamaica — (678)

White Plains
To New York
(295)
(95)

0 SCALE    17    17    MILES

0    17    17    KILOMETERS

● PLACE OF INTEREST    ✈ HIGHWAY    ---- PARK BOUNDARY    — ROAD

## Sights

- **Ⓐ** Fire Island National Seashore
- **Ⓑ** Jones Beach State Park
- **Ⓒ** Montauk Point Lighthouse
- **Ⓓ** Old Bethpage Village Restoration
- **Ⓔ** Planting Fields Arboretum and Coe Hall
- **Ⓕ** Sag Harbor

- **Ⓕ** Sag Harbor Whaling Museum
- **Ⓖ** Sagamore Hill National Historic Site
- **Ⓗ** Shelter Island
- **Ⓘ** Suffolk Marine Museum
- **Ⓙ** Vanderbilt Museum
- **Ⓚ** Walt Whitman Birthplace

*Note: Items with the same letter are located in the same town or area.*

## A PERFECT DAY ON LONG ISLAND

Beach lovers have a wealth of choices on Long Island, and one of my favorites is Montauk Point. At the very tip of the island, it is bathed in a delicious feeling of remoteness. There are miles of beaches in Montauk to explore. For a breathtaking view of the sea, climb to the top of Montauk Point Lighthouse, the oldest in the state. This is also one of the prime areas for fishing, whether from the shore, on a party boat, or on a deep-sea fishing charter boat. Top off your day of fishing and beachcombing with fresh seafood at Gosman's Restaurant, overlooking the harbor.

## SIGHTSEEING HIGHLIGHTS

★★★ **Fire Island National Seashore**—The National Seashore consists of four separate areas on Fire Island, comprising 32 miles of superb public beaches. Access to the Lighthouse area in the west and the Smith Point area in the east is by car. The National Seashore areas in the heart of the island, **Watch Hill** and **Sailors Haven**, can be reached only by water taxi, private boat, or ferry from Long Island in season. In between are clusters of small communities, but no roads. The National Park Service offers regular interpretive walks and programs ranging from lighthouse history to sing-alongs of old sea chanteys. There are Interpretive Centers at Sailors Haven, Watch Hill, and Smith Point.

The **Sunken Forest** in the Sailors Haven area of the seashore is the jewel of Fire Island. This is a forest unlike any you have experienced. Imagine entering an eerie woodland of gnarled branches—a forest primeval and a botanical wonderland at the same time. A network of well-maintained broadwalks extends for a mile and a half through the forest. Ocean salt kills vegetation, so when the foliage reaches the height of the dunes, it begins to grow horizontally instead of vertically. The result is a lovely, delicate canopy that forms a dark, cool respite from the hot sun. Elevated spots on the trail provide glimpses of ocean and bay, and from here there's a trail to the beach. Farther east is **Smith Point**, the only federally designated wilderness area in the state. With the exception of a broadwalk trail for those with disabilities at Smith Point West, the wilderness is accessible only by foot. Wheelchair accessible. National Seashore Headquarters, 120 Laurel Street, Patchogue; (516) 289-4810. Admission free, but there is a charge for parking and for the ferries, which run May through October. (6 hours)

★★★ **Jones Beach State Park**—From its opening in 1929, everything about Jones Beach has been grand. It was the dream of Robert Moses, a man who loved to build and create. What can you say about a park with parking fields for 23,000 cars, a landmark water tower that holds 300,000 gallons of water, eight ocean bathing areas, 250 lifeguards, and two Olympic sized pools? Five miles of ocean beach frontage and a ½-mile of bay frontage have been developed for swimming. There are nearly 12,000 lockers and dressing rooms in the two bathhouses, 17 cafeterias and refreshment stands, three restaurants, and nearly 2 miles of boardwalk. Fishing is also popular here. The 8,206-seat Jones Beach Theatre opened in 1952. The park can be very crowded on summer weekends, so arrive before 9 a.m. if possible. Otherwise, May and September can be beautiful and relatively uncrowded. Wheelchair accessible. Ocean Drive, Wantagh; (516) 785-1600 or (516) 221-1000 for concert schedules; open daily throughout the year. Admission $5 per car Memorial Day through Labor Day, weekends through mid-October; free otherwise. (6 hours)

★★ **Montauk Point Lighthouse**—This is the oldest lighthouse in the state, completed in 1796 on a spot where the British Royal Navy had maintained signal bonfires for its ships during the American Revolution. President George Washington authorized its construction. On November 5, 1797, Jacob Hand lit the wicks of 13 whale oil lamps, and a light shone from the Montauk Point Lighthouse for the first time.

In 1987 the Coast Guard automated and leased the lighthouse to the Montauk Historical Society. The society maintains the lighthouse and the surrounding property, fighting an ongoing battle against erosion. Visitors can climb the 137 iron steps to the top of the old keeper's quarters. On a clear day the view of the East End, the distant shore of Connecticut, and Block Island off the coast of Rhode Island is breathtaking. Route 27, Montauk; (516) 668-2544; Memorial Day through Columbus Day open daily 10:30 a.m. to 6 p.m., Columbus Day through November open weekends 10:30 a.m. to 5 p.m., Friday and Monday 10:30 a.m. to 4:30 p.m. Admission $3 adults, $2.75 seniors, $1 children; parking $3 Memorial Day through Labor Day, free otherwise. (1 hour)

★★ **Planting Fields Arboretum and Coe Hall**—This was the home of William Robertson Coe, a British-born insurance magnate, from 1913 to 1955. The Arboretum encompasses 409 landscaped acres of greenhouses, gardens, and natural habitat. The **Synoptic Garden**'s ornamental shrubs and small trees are arranged alphabetically and identified by botanical and common names and by family and country of origin. In the last years of his life, Coe planted the rhododendron park, one of the outstanding features of Planting Fields. Coe Hall at Planting Fields, built in 1919, is one of the finest examples of Tudor Revival architecture in America. The home is furnished with sixteenth- and seventeenth-century pieces. The **Buffalo Room** contains murals of buffalo and Native Americans set against a Western landscape. Wheelchair accessible. Planting Fields Road, Oyster Bay; (516) 922-9201; Arboretum open daily 9 a.m. to 5 p.m.; Coe Hall open daily 12:30 p.m. to 3:30 p.m. April through October. Admission to Arboretum $4 per car; Coe Hall admission $3.50 adults, $2 seniors, $1 children. (2 hours)

★★ **Sag Harbor**—The village of Sag Harbor retains the charm of its glory years in the 1800s, when it was one of the most productive whaling ports in the world. Its sheltered position between the North and South Forks of Long Island made it important from its earliest days. In 1789 President George Washington signed the Act of Congress that created two ports of entry for the new nation. The first port was Sag Harbor; the second, New York City. James Fenimore Cooper began his first novel here in 1824. The stately homes of whaling merchants line Main Street, which terminates in the 1,000-foot Long Wharf. Antique hunters have long since replaced whale hunters. Park your car and stroll down the back lanes. Sag Harbor Chamber of Commerce, 459 Main Street, Sag Harbor; (516) 725-0011. (1 hour)

★★ **Sagamore Hill National Historic Site**—This 23-room rambling Victorian home was built by Theodore Roosevelt in 1884–85. It was here he raised his six children. "There could be no healthier and pleasanter place in which to bring up children than in that nook of old-time America around Sagamore Hill," he reflected. After overcoming childhood sickness, he loved tough physical challenges and joined his children in playing games, riding horseback, and hiking in the woods.

This was the summer White House during the Roosevelt presidential years and his permanent home from 1887 to his death in 1919. Roosevelt received his nomination for governor of New York, for vice president, and for president of the United States on the piazza of the home. In the library he met with ambassadors from two warring countries, Russia and Japan. When they came out, they had agreed on a treaty ending the war. Roosevelt won the Nobel Prize for his role in the peace process. The house is filled with family possessions, including animal trophies shot during his world travels; the famous original teddy bear is in a place of honor in the nursery. The **Orchard Museum**, on the grounds, showcases family photos and shows a film about Roosevelt's life. 20 Sagamore Hill Road, Oyster Bay; (516) 922-4447; May 1 through the day before Columbus Day open daily 9:30 a.m. to 5 p.m.; rest of the year Wednesday through Sunday 9:30 a.m. to 5 p.m. Admission $2 adults, seniors and children free. (1½ hours)

★ **Old Bethpage Village Restoration**—This is a living history museum that re-creates eighteenth- and nineteenth-century rural life. Homes, barns, stores, and other buildings from that period have been moved here from their original sites and restored. The buildings are populated with costumed interpreters who familiarize visitors with the domestic habits, social customs, and work styles of an earlier time. When you enter the village you can exchange modern-day money for nineteenth-century paper scrip, which you can use to buy such old-fashioned items as birch beer, apple cider, pretzels, and penny candy in the tavern. Seasonal and holiday events are held throughout the year, including political campaigning, balloting, and victory celebrations for the 1848 elections in November. Wheelchair accessible. Round Swamp Road, Old Bethpage; (516) 572-8400; March through November 15 open Wednesday through Sunday 10 a.m. to 5 p.m.; Wednesday through Sunday 10 a.m. to 4 p.m. rest of year. Admission $5 adults, $3 seniors and children. (3 hours)

★ **Sag Harbor Whaling Museum**—To get into this museum, visitors pass through the jawbones of a right whale. Once through the jaw, there are exhibits of whaling equipment, scrimshaw, oil paintings, ship models, fishing gear, logbooks, and other objects connected with Colonial eastern Long Island. Wheelchair accessible. Main Street, Sag Harbor; (516) 725-0770; open May through September Monday through Saturday 10 a.m. to 5 p.m., Sunday 1 p.m. to 5 p.m. Admission $3 adults, $2 seniors, $1 children. (½ hour)

★ **Shelter Island**—Nestled in the bay between Long Island's North and South Forks, Shelter Island has managed to remain sheltered from much of the development to the west. The island maintains a New England atmosphere and was one of the first areas of Long Island settled by the English. It was a haunt of eighteenth-century pirates and, during Prohibition, a favorite landing point for bootleggers. It is accessible by a ten-minute auto/passenger ferry ride from either Greenport to the north or from North Haven near Sag Harbor to the south. You can use the island as a scenic stepping stone to pass from one fork to another. There are white sandy beaches and protected harbors for boaters. The 2,000-acre Mashomack Nature Preserve, with 12 miles of wild shoreline, occupies the entire southeast section of the island. Shelter Island Chamber of Commerce, (516) 749-0399 or (800) 9-SHELTER. (3 hours)

★ **Vanderbilt Museum**—The summer estate of William K. Vanderbilt II, the great-grandson of Commodore Cornelius Vanderbilt, is an ornate 24-room Spanish Revival mansion overlooking Northport Harbor and Long Island Sound. The **Vanderbilt Museum** is filled with specimens collected by Vanderbilt on three world cruises from 1926 to 1932, when he visited all of the world's seas and oceans. The planetarium, one of the largest in the country, is open to the public; its skyshows change three or four times a year. Wheelchair accessible. 180 Little Neck Road, Centerport; (516) 854-5555; open Tuesday through Sunday noon to 5 p.m. Memorial Day through Labor Day; noon to 4 p.m. rest of year. Admission $8 adults, $6 seniors and students, $4 children. (2 hours)

★ **Walt Whitman Birthplace State Historic Site**—Whitman, one of America's greatest poets, was born in 1819 in this humble farmhouse built by his father in 1810. He spent his early childhood here. Guided tours feature an audiovisual presentation. There's a good collection of nineteenth-century furnishings as well as changing exhibits of Whitman memorabilia, photographs, books, and excerpts from his writings and letters. 246 Old Walt Whitman Road, Huntington Station; (516) 427-5240; open Wednesday through Friday 1 p.m. to 4 p.m., Saturday and Sunday 10 a.m. to 4 p.m. Admission free. (1 hour)

**Suffolk Marine Museum**—Although the purpose of this museum is to protect and preserve the entire maritime heritage of Long Island, it highlights the history and lore of the oysterman. In an actual vintage oyster house, visitors can look at the gritty world of the Great South Bay oysterman, who culled and packed oysters along the bay from the late 1800s to the 1940s. There's a wonderful collection of small craft including oyster vessels, South Bay sailboats, and ice scooters. There's also an exhibit on the U.S. Life Saving Service, forerunner of the Coast Guard. Route 27A, West Sayville, on the ground of Suffolk County Park; (516) 567-1733; open Wednesday through Saturday 10 a.m. to 3 p.m., Sunday noon to 4 p.m. Admission by donation. (1 hour)

## FITNESS AND RECREATION

Many sports can be enjoyed on the island, including surfing, scuba diving, canoeing, and kayaking. The miles of beaches beckon swimmers, runners, and walkers. The most challenging hiking trails are Long Island's two Greenbelt Trails. The **Suffolk Greenbelt Trail** snakes 34 miles along the shores of the Nissequogue and Connetquot Rivers, from Sunken Meadow State Park on Long Island Sound southward to Heckscher State Park on the Great Sound Bay. The **Nassau Greenbelt Trail** extends 22 miles from Cold Spring Harbor to Massapequa. On Fire Island, a 20-mile beachfront trail runs from Davis Park eastward to Smith Point. Known to hikers as the **Fire Island Seashore Trail**, local residents affectionately refer to this dirt road/sand trail as "the Burma Road."

## FOOD

Long Island has restaurants that rival Manhattan's. More than 4,000 dining establishments provide a wealth of choices. Many restaurants boast some of the freshest fish, oysters, and clams, and award-winning local wines. In Montauk, at the tip of the island, **Gosman's Dock Restaurant**, at the entrance to Montauk Harbor, (516) 668-5330, offers a wide array of fish. On the road to Montauk, stop at the **Lobster Roll Restaurant** (locally known as LUNCH), Montauk Highway, Amagansett, (516) 267-3740, for great seafood, including the lobster roll. **Mirko's Restaurant**, Montauk Highway, Water Mill, (516) 726-4444, is one of best in the Hamptons. **Claudio's Restaurant**, Mina Street, Greenport, (516) 477-0627, in an 1840 National Historic Landmark building overlooking the waterfront, bills itself as the country's oldest same-family-run restaurant. **The Barge**, 86 Orchard Beach Boulevard, Port Washington, (516) 944-9403, is located on a converted World War II munitions barge and offers great water views and food to match. Long Island duckling and other Continental fare are good choices at the **Ram's Head Inn**, Shelter Island Heights, (516) 749-0811, which is also a lovely country inn. **Danford's Inn**, 25 E. Broadway, Port Jefferson, (516) 928-5200, adjacent to the ferry dock, offers fine dining overlooking the harbor. **Gasho**, 356 Vanderbilt Motor Parkway, Hauppauge, (516) 231-3400, features Japanese hibachi cooking at your table in a 400-year-old Japanese farmhouse. **Three Village Inn**, 150 Main Street, Stony Brook, (516) 751-0555, in a lovely Colonial inn overlooking the Stony Brook Harbor, features New England specialities. **Steve's Pier I**, 33 Bayville Avenue, Bayville, (516) 628-2153, in the heart of Oyster Bay, specializes in fish and beef.

## LODGING

In resort communities, a two-night minimum stay is frequently required during summer weekends, and rates are usually higher during the summer season. Hotel, motel, bed and breakfast, and resort accommodations are plentiful throughout the island. In Montauk, **Gurney's Inn Resort & Spa**, 290 Old Montauk Highway, (516) 668-2345, offers a full spa and a magnificent oceanfront location ($200 to $350 for a double, breakfast and dinner included). **Montauk Yacht Club Resort & Marina**, Star Island, Montauk, (516) 668-3100, boasts a full marina, resort facilities, and fine dining ($119 to $299 for a double). The **1770 House**, 143 Main Street, East Hampton, (516) 324-1770, is a gem of a small hotel, with a fine restaurant ($125 to $250 for a double). **Colonial Shores Resort**, 83 W. Tiana Road, Hampton Bays, (516) 728-0011, has pool or waterfront cottages and suites with full kitchens ($55 to $140 for a double). The **Shelter**

# LONG ISLAND

New London

Fishers Island

Montauk Point State Park

**E**

**R** Montauk

Amagansett

Plum Island

Gardiners Island

**F** East Hampton

New Haven

Orient

Shelter Island
Shelter Island

Sag Harbor

**K**

**L** 114

Water Mill

**B** Greenport

**H**

Southampton

Bridgeport

**G**

Shinnecock Indian Reservation

Long Island

Mattituck

Hampton Bays

**M** Westhampton

Flanders

24

New Haven

Long Island Sound

24

27A

Wildwood State Park

Wading River

**T**

Smith Point County Park

Shirley

46

Medford

27

Coram

Fire Island National Seashore

**S**

25A

112

**95**

Patchogue

Port Jefferson

**C** Stony Brook

347

Hauppage

454

West Sayville

Heckscher State Park

**J**

**D**

**Q** East Islip

Sunken Meadow State Park

SUNKEN MEADOW

SAGTIKOS STATE PKWY

ROBERT MOSES PKWY

Robert Moses State Park

PKWY

West Islip

CONNECTICUT

Centerport

Huntington Station

25A

**I**

Bayville

Oyster Bay

106

Bethpage

135

110

WANTAGH STATE PKWY

Merrick

**O**

15

95

Stamford

New Rochelle

Port Washington

**A**

101

Garden City

25

Hempstead

**N**

Jones Beach State Park

NEW YORK

White Plains

95

295

To New York

Jamaica

678

New Haven

Atlantic Ocean

Z

## Food

- Ⓐ The Barge
- Ⓑ Claudio's Restaurant
- Ⓒ Danford's Inn
- Ⓓ Gasho
- Ⓔ Gosman's Dock Restaurant
- Ⓕ Lobster Roll Restaurant
- Ⓖ Mirko's Restaurant
- Ⓗ Ram's Head Inn
- Ⓘ Steve's Pier I
- Ⓙ Three Village Inn

## Lodging

- Ⓚ 1770 House
- Ⓛ Baron's Cove Inn

## Lodging (continued)

- Ⓜ Colonial Shores Resort
- Ⓝ Garden City Hotel
- Ⓞ Gateway Inn
- Ⓟ Gurney's Inn Resort & Spa
- Ⓟ Inn at Medford
- Ⓔ Montauk Yacht Club Resort & Marina
- Ⓗ Shelter Island Resort

## Camping

- Ⓠ Hechscher State Park
- Ⓡ Hither Hills State Park
- Ⓢ Watch Hill
- Ⓣ Wildwood State Park

*Note: Items with the same letter are located in the same town or area.*

**Island Resort**, 35 Shore Road, Shelter Island, (516) 749-2001, offers fine water views and a beach ($69 to $210 for a double). **Baron's Cove Inn**, West Water Street, Sag Harbor, (516) 725-2100, has its own marina ($69 to $135 for a double). The **Garden City Hotel**, 45 Seventh Street, Garden City, (516) 747-3000 or (800) 547-0400, is one of the most opulent on the island ($185 to $255 for a double). The **Gateway Inn**, Sunrise Highway, Merrick, (516) 378-7100, is just minutes from Jones Beach and the Nassau Coliseum ($75 to $90 for a double). The comfortable **Inn at Medford**, 2695 Route 112, Medford, (516) 654-3000, is just five minutes from the Fire Island Ferries ($75 to $119 for a double).

## CAMPING

Most Long Island campgrounds beckon campers with the lure of the sea. **Hither Hills State Park**, Route 27, Montauk, (516) 668-2554, boasts 165 campsites just over the sand dunes from 2 miles of perfect white-sand beach ($12 per night). The 26-site **Watch Hill** campground on Fire Island, (516) 597-6633, is accessible only by boat or ferry ($5 per night); contact Superintendent, Fire Island National Seashore, 120 Laurel Street, Patchogue, (516) 289-4810, for summer camping applications. The 69-site **Hechscher State Park**, East Islip, (516) 581-4433 or (800) 456-CAMP, promises more than 3 miles of frontage on Great Sound Bay ($12 per night). The 737-acre **Wildwood State Park**, Route 25A, Wading River, (516) 929-4314 or (800) 456-CAMP, has 322 sites, more than a mile of beach on Long Island Sound, and 10 miles of hiking trails ($12 per night).

## FERRIES

Car ferry service is available year-round between Connecticut and Rhode Island. **Cross Sound Ferry, Inc.**, Orient Point, (516) 323-2743, provides service to New London, Connecticut. **Bridgeport & Port Jefferson Ferry Company**, Port Jefferson, (516) 473-0286, provides service to Bridgeport, Connecticut. **Viking Ferry**, Montauk, (516) 668-5709, provides passenger service to Block Island and Newport, Rhode Island, and to New London and Mystic, Connecticut.

Service to and from Shelter Island is available year-round for cars and passengers. **North Ferry Company**, Shelter Island, (516) 749-0139, travels to Greenport. **South Ferry, Inc.**, Shelter Island, (516) 749-1200, travels to North Haven, near Sag Harbor.

Several ferry companies travel to Fire Island—most during the April through October season. **Davis Park Ferry Co.**, Patchogue, (516) 475-1665, travels to Davis Park, Watch Hill, and Fire Island Seashore. **Fire Island Ferries**, Bay Shore, (516) 665-3600, travels to Saltaire, Ocean Beach, Atlantique, Kismet, Dunewood, Fair Harbor, Seaview, and Ocean Bay Park. **Sayville Ferry Service**, Sayville, (516) 589-0810, provides service to Fire Island Pines, Cherry Grove, Fire Island National Seashore, and Sailor's Haven.

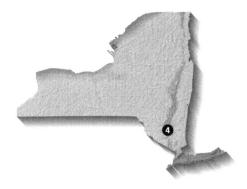

# 4

# THE HUDSON RIVER VALLEY

T he river that Native Americans called "the water that runs two ways" has always exerted a powerful influence on people who live near it or travel along it. No other river in America, with the possible exception of the Mississippi, has played such a major role in the country's history. It formed the backdrop for critical battles of the Revolutionary War; it served as a major industrial waterway; it gave its name to an American school of landscape painting; it led to the birth of the first effective steamboat; and the river valley has probably inspired more ghost stories than any other part of the country.

Native Americans had been thriving in this fertile valley for more than a thousand years when Henry Hudson sailed the *Half Moon* up the river in 1609 for the Dutch East India Company. From the early Colonial days, the river's banks have been a setting for the display of wealth. Dutch patrons divided the valley into great estates. Later, other Europeans settled the area. The U.S. Military Academy was built at West Point in 1802 to train American Army officers. The Vanderbilts, Rockefellers, Harrimans, and other moguls built massive country homes on the banks of the river. Much of this history is still visible today; visitors are invited to tour the grand estates of the "American aristocracy," to experience the special light that captivated artist Frederick Church, and to wander through the sleepy villages that inspired writer Washington Irving. ◣

# THE HUDSON RIVER VALLEY

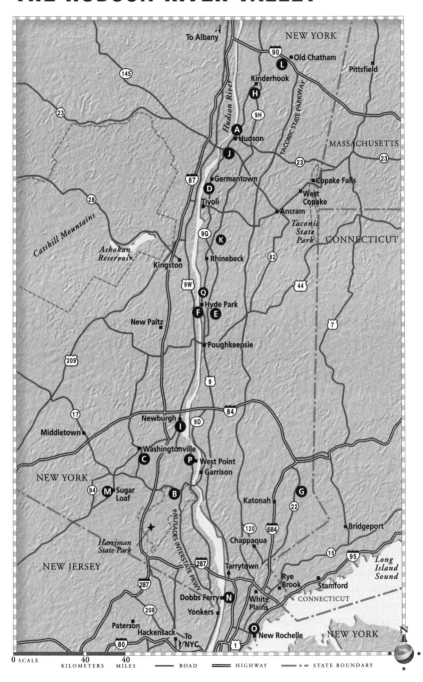

To Albany

NEW YORK

90 **L** Old Chatham

Pittsfield

Kinderhook

**H**

9H

Hudson River

**A** Hudson

MASSACHUSETTS

**J**

87

23

23

Germantown

Copake Falls

**D**

West
Copake

Tivoli

28

Ancram

*Taconic
State
Park*

CONNECTICUT

9G

**K**

*Ashokan
Reservoir*

82

*Catskill Mountains*

Rhinebeck

Kingston

8W

44

Q

Hyde Park

**F** **E**

7

New Paltz

Poughkeepsie

209

9

17

84

Newburgh **I** 9D

Middletown

Washingtonville

**C**

West Point

**P**

Garrison

NEW YORK

94 **M** Sugar
Loaf

**B**

Katonah

**G**

22

*Harriman
State Park*

120

684

Bridgeport

NEW JERSEY

Chappaqua

15

95

*Long
Island
Sound*

287

Tarrytown

Rye
Brook

Stamford

287

Dobbs Ferry **N**

White
Plains

CONNECTICUT

208

Yonkers

Paterson

Hackensack

To
NYC

**O** New Rochelle

NEW YORK

80

1

N

0 SCALE  40  40
KILOMETERS  MILES  — ROAD  ═ HIGHWAY  – – STATE BOUNDARY

# Sights

Ⓐ American Museum
of Fire Fighting

Ⓑ Bear Mountain State Park

Ⓒ Brotherhood Winery

Ⓓ Clermont

Ⓔ Eleanor Roosevelt
National Historic Site

Ⓕ Franklin D. Roosevelt
National Historic Site

Ⓖ John Jay Homestead

Ⓗ Martin Van Buren
National Historic Site

Ⓘ New Windsor Cantonment
State Historic Site

Ⓙ Olana State Historic Site

Ⓚ Old Rhinebeck Aerodome

Ⓛ Shaker Museum

Ⓜ Sugar Loaf Art and Craft
Village

Ⓝ Sunnyside

Ⓞ Thomas Paine Cottage

Ⓟ U.S. Military Academy

Ⓠ Vanderbilt Mansion

## A PERFECT DAY IN THE HUDSON RIVER VALLEY

Start your day with a hike in Bear Mountain State Park. If the day is clear, walk or drive to the top of the mountain for spectacular river and mountain views. As you drive north there are a number of mansions and historic sites to visit—history buffs will enjoy Franklin D. Roosevelt's home at Hyde Park; those who want to revel in what wealth could buy in the late nineteenth century should be sure to see the nearby Vanderbilt Mansion. Stop for lunch at the Culinary Institute of America in Hyde Park. The Rhinebeck Aerodome stages wonderful shows on the weekends. Before or after the shows you can become a barnstormer yourself and take a ride in a 1929 open-cockpit biplane. The best choice for dinner and overnight is the Beekman Arms Hotel, which has welcomed travelers since 1766 and bills itself as America's oldest hotel.

## SIGHTSEEING HIGHLIGHTS

★★★ **Franklin D. Roosevelt National Historic Site**—Better known as Hyde Park, this is the 1826 home where Roosevelt was born and raised and later lived while he was president. FDR's home reveals much about this complex man. His bedroom is large and impressive, with sweeping views of the Hudson River and the distant Catskill Mountains. Reading material from his last days still rests on a desk in his bedroom. Within easy reach are two telephones, one secretly coded with a direct line to the

White House. It was used many times during the dark days of World War II. The museum houses the original desk and chair used by FDR in the White House as well as drafts of some of his most famous addresses, including the "date which will live in infamy" speech after the Japanese attack on Pearl Harbor. The estate contains a walking trail and the graves of Franklin and Eleanor Roosevelt. U.S. 9, Hyde Park; (914) 229-9115; May through October open daily 9 a.m. to 5 p.m.; November through April, Thursday through Monday 9 a.m. to 5 p.m. Admission $8 adults, $7 seniors, children under 17 free. (1½ hours)

★★★ **U.S. Military Academy**—West Point is America's oldest and most distinguished military academy. Situated on the bluffs overlooking the Hudson River, West Point has been the training ground for U.S. Army officers since 1802. Here you can walk the paths of Patton, Eisenhower, MacArthur, and Schwarzkopf. George Washington ordered a massive iron chain to be placed across the river at West Point to thwart the British during the American Revolution. Links of the Great Chain are preserved and on view at **Trophy Point**. Here also are cannons and relics of all American wars dating back to the Revolutionary War.

The best place to begin your visit to West Point is the visitors center, which includes displays on cadet life, a model cadet room (extremely neat), and a theater showing movies covering a cadet's four-year stay at the academy and the history of West Point. Just behind the visitors center is the **West Point Museum**, which contains an astounding collection of sixteenth- through twentieth-century arms, uniforms, flags, military art, and West Point memorabilia. A poster sums up the West Point experience: "At West Point, much of the history we teach was made by people we taught." The 4,500-seat **Eisenhower Theatre** is the second-largest theater in the East. Cadet parades are held throughout the spring and fall. Route 9W, West Point; (914) 938-2638; museum open daily 10:30 a.m. to 4:15 p.m., visitors center open daily 9 a.m. to 4:45 p.m. Admission free. (2 hours)

★★ **American Museum of Fire Fighting**—Your guide here will be one of the residents of the Volunteer Firemen's Home, on whose grounds this museum sits. The museum is filled with an amazing collection of firefighting equipment and paraphernalia, including the oldest piece of firefighting machinery in the U.S.: the Newsham engine, built in London in 1725. This contraption of wooden wheels and leather pipes arrived in New York in 1731 and served the people of Manhattan for 154 years. 125 Harry Howard Avenue, Hudson; (518) 828-7695; open daily 9 a.m. to 4:30 p.m. Admission free. (1 hour)

★★ **Bear Mountain State Park**—The large statue of Walt Whitman alongside the park's nature trail was erected to please Mrs. E. H. Harriman, who rescued Bear Mountain and the surrounding lands from one of the most dunderheaded ideas ever: the state wanted to build a prison on top of Bear Mountain. Thankfully, the park was created instead, and the view has been preserved for all. Standing atop Bear Mountain on a very clear day, you can see Manhattan's skyline 45 miles to the south. Even if your view doesn't include Manhattan, it will include the Hudson River, Bear Mountain Bridge, and neighboring mountains and valleys. There's an extensive trail system here. Part of the Appalachian Trail passes through the **Bear Mountain Nature Trail** and **Trailside Museum**. The self-guided Bear Mountain Trail is the oldest continuously run trail in the country. Other attractions include a lake with boats for rent, fishing, a zoo, a huge swimming pool set amidst gigantic boulders, sledding, ice skating, festivals, crafts shows, and a lovely country inn. Bear Mountain, (914) 786-2731; open daily 8 a.m. to dusk. Admission $4 per car. (3 hours)

★★ **Eleanor Roosevelt National Historic Site**—This is a converted factory off a dirt road, on the Hyde Park grounds. Even while her husband was president, Eleanor Roosevelt usually stayed overnight here rather than in FDR's home. Named Val-Kill for "valley stream," the building was converted into two apartments, one for Eleanor and the other for her secretary. After FDR's death she lived here full-time. Begin your visit by viewing the film *First Lady of the World*. Although the building is plain and simple on the outside, it is warm and comfortable inside. Here Eleanor entertained friends, family, and heads of state. Route 9G, Hyde Park; (914) 229-9115; May through October open daily 9 a.m. to 5 p.m.; March, April, November, and December open weekends 9 a.m. to 5 p.m.; closed January and February. Admission $5 adults, children under 17 free. (1 hour)

★★ **New Windsor Cantonment State Historic Site**—This was the final encampment of Washington's army. More than 10,000 soldiers, cooks, blacksmiths, and other camp followers constructed the log cabins, outbuildings, and the meeting hall where Washington quelled a mutiny by troops who were upset over the slow payment of wages. The site features a visitors center, exhibits, artillery displays, and military demonstrations. Temple Hill Road, Vail's Gate; (914) 561-1765; April through October open Wednesday through Saturday 10 a.m. to 5 p.m., Sunday 1 p.m. to 5 p.m. Admission free. (2 hours)

★★ **Olana State Historic Site**—Olana is the dream home of Frederick Church, the most famous of the Hudson River School artists. It is also a fantastical 1870s Persian-style mansion on 250 acres. With his artist's eye Church pronounced "the views (from Olana) most beautiful and wonderful." Olana is derived from an Arabic word meaning "our place on high." Many of Church's best works are on display. Route 9G, Hudson; (518) 828-0135; grounds open daily 8 a.m. to dusk. House open for tours April 2 through November 2 Wednesday through Sunday 10 a.m. to 4 p.m. Admission $3 adults, $2 seniors, $1 children, grounds free. (1½ hours)

★★ **Old Rhinebeck Aerodome**—Aviation buffs will love this place, which is filled with old planes dating back to the earliest days of aviation. If you visit the Aerodome on the weekends, you can do more than admire the old planes. Air shows are held every Saturday and Sunday afternoon. Aircraft from the pioneer and Lindbergh eras show their stuff on some days, and on others, Percy Goodfellow and the Black Baron engage in a mock dogfight and bombing raid in World War I aircraft. After the show the public is invited to take a ride in a 1929 open-cockpit biplane for a 15-minute spin over the Hudson Valley and a flashy series of wing-overs and dives. 42 Stone Church Road, Rhinebeck; (914) 758-8610; open daily 10 a.m. to 5 p.m. May 15 to October 31. Admission $4 adults, $2 children; $10 adults for air show, $5 children. (3 hours for air show)

★★ **Sunnyside**—The was the home of *The Legend of Sleepy Hollow* writer Washington Irving from 1835 to 1859. He called it his "little snuggery." The house was built in the late seventeenth century as a tenant farmer's cottage. Irving added Dutch-style stepped gables to the main part of the house, attached a Romanesque tower, and planted wisteria and ivy vines. The interior has features far advanced for their day, such as a bathtub with running water and a hot water tank in the kitchen. Costumed guides explain the house and its furnishings, which include the author's library. Irving planted the trees and flowers on the grounds; picnicking is permitted. West Sunnyside Lane, Tarrytown; (914) 591-8763; April through December open Wednesday through Monday 10 a.m. to 5 p.m. Admission $8 adults, $7 seniors, $4 students and children. (1 hour)

★★ **Vanderbilt Mansion**—European royalty would feel at home in this "cottage" of Frederick William Vanderbilt, grandson of Commodore Cornelius Vanderbilt. The 54-room mansion, designed by Stanford White in 1895, was once described by the *New York Times* as "the finest place on the Hudson between New York and Albany." Like most prominent Hudson River families, the Vanderbilts used their retreat only for a few weeks in the spring and fall. Vanderbilt had a passion for tapestries, many of which adorn the walls. Mrs. Vanderbilt's bedroom is modeled after a French queen's bedroom of the Louis XV period. The white and gold railing around the bed recalls the custom of French queens and ladies of nobility, who would hold receptions in the morning while still in bed. The grounds provide sweeping views of the Hudson River. Route 9, Hyde Park; (914) 229-9115; May through October open daily 9 a.m. to 5 p.m.; November through April Thursday through Monday 9 a.m. to 5 p.m.; Admission $8 adults, kids under 17 free. (1 hour)

★ **Clermont**—This is the home of Robert Livingston, an early leader and the first chancellor of New York State. It is the focal point of a 450-acre state historic site. Originally built in 1730, the house was burned by the British during the Revolution and later rebuilt. This is probably the only mansion to have a steamboat named after it—the very first steamboat that Robert Fulton docked at the chancellor's dock on its maiden voyage up the Hudson River in 1807. (Livingston and Fulton were partners in the steamboat business.) Seven generations of Livingstons lived here. There are formal gardens, and you can picnic along the banks of the river. 1 Clermont Avenue, Germantown; (518) 537-4240; April through October open Tuesday through Sunday 11 a.m. to 4 p.m.; November through December 14 open weekends 11 a.m. to 4 p.m. Admission $3 adults, $2 seniors, $1 children. (1 hour)

★ **John Jay Homestead**—The Federal-style residence of the famous statesman and first Chief Justice of the U.S. Supreme Court is a State Historic Site. The restored period rooms tell the story of Jay, his family, and lifestyles in the new republic. 400 Jay Street, Katonah; (914) 232-5651; open April 15 through October Wednesday through Saturday 10 a.m. to 4 p.m., Sunday and Monday holidays noon to 4 p.m. Admission $3 adults, $2 seniors, $1 children. (1 hour)

★ **Shaker Museum**—This museum displays the diversity of the Shaker genius. The vast majority of the collection was acquired by John S. Williams Sr. between 1935 and 1965, with the help of the Shaker leadership. The goal was to provide a complete picture of Shaker life and culture from as many Shaker communities as possible. On display are furniture, oval boxes, baskets, buckets, stoves, and machinery. Ann Lee, spiritual founder of the Shakers, directed her believers to "do all your work as though you had a thousand years to live on earth, and as you would if you knew you must die tomorrow." 88 Shaker Museum Road, Old Chatham; (518) 794-9100; May through October open daily except Wednesday 10 a.m. to 5 p.m. Admission $6 adults, $5 seniors, $3 children, $14 family. (2 hours)

★ **Sugar Loaf Art and Craft Village**—This tiny village, founded in 1749, is a community of craftspeople. More than 65 shops, galleries, and restaurants, in buildings dating back to the 1700s and 1800s, line Main Street. Many craftspeople work in their shops, so visitors can watch works of art being created. Throughout the year there are special seasonal events, including concerts, a spring and fall festival, and a Christmas caroling and candle-lighting service complete with Santa. Most shops are open Tuesday through Sunday. (914) 469-9181. (2 hours)

★ **Thomas Paine Cottage**—In 1784, the year after the end of the American Revolution, New York State granted Thomas Paine 300 acres of land as a reward for his role in the war. The author of *Common Sense* was famous for his statement, "These are the times that try men's souls." The Thomas Paine Cottage was built in 1793 and originally stood atop a hill, but it was relocated to its current site. Several authentic Franklin stoves are on display, which were presented to Paine by Ben himself. 983 North Avenue, New Rochelle; (914) 632-5376; open Friday through Sunday 2 p.m. to 5 p.m.; closed December through March. Admission (suggested) $3 adults, $1 seniors and children. (1 hour)

**Brotherhood Winery**—More than 160 years old, this winery bills itself as America's oldest. Guided tours of its cavernous underground cellars end in a wine-tasting; hors d'oeuvres are also served. Brotherhood Plaza Drive, Washingtonville; (914) 496-9101; winery outlet open daily 11 a.m. to 6 p.m.; tours May through October 11 a.m. to

5 p.m.; January through April and November and December weekends noon to 5 p.m. Admission $4 adults, children free. (1 hour)

**Martin Van Buren National Historic Site**—Van Buren, the nation's eighth president, was born in the tiny village of Kinderhook and retired to Lindenwald, his home after his defeat for a second term. He has the distinction of being the first president born under the U.S. flag. The mansion was built in 1797, and Van Buren enjoyed making home improvements. He was proudest of the indoor plumbing, complete with a Wedgwood porcelain toilet bowl. Route 9H, Kinderhook; (518) 758-9689; mid-May through October 31 open daily 9 a.m. to 4:30 p.m.; November 1 through December 5 open Wednesday through Sunday 9 a.m. to 4:30 p.m. Admission $2 adults, children free. (1 hour)

## FITNESS AND RECREATION

Runners who need inspiration should head for the **U.S. Military Academy** at West Point, where all the cadets seem to run rather than walk. Visitors can jog along the campus paths and trails. **Bear Mountain State Park** and adjoining **Harriman State Park** are good choices for hiking, running, cross-country skiing, snowshoeing, and swimming. **Lake Taghkanic State Park** is popular for hiking, swimming, and boating. **Stony Kill Farm Environmental Education Center** is a 756-acre center with a variety of programs as well as hiking and ski touring trails.

## FOOD

There is a wealth of fine dining establishments in this region. Two of the best are at the Culinary Institute of America, 433 Albany Post Road, Hyde Park: the **American Bounty**, (914) 471-6608; and **Escoffier**, (914) 471-6608. **Crabtree's Kittle House**, Kittle Road, Chappaqua, (914) 666-8044, in a 200-year-old country house, is a delightful restaurant with an award-winning wine cellar of 10,000 bottles. **Gasho of Japan**, 2 Saw Mill River Road, Hawthorne, (914) 592-5900, is a Japanese restaurant housed in an authentic 400-year-old Japanese farmhouse surrounded by lush Oriental gardens. In Sugar Loaf, the **Barnsider Tavern**, Kings Highway, (914) 469-9810, offers a simple menu in a rustic taproom with a glass-enclosed patio overlooking the crafts community. The historic **Beekman Arms**, 4 Mill Street, Rhinebeck, (914) 876-7077, has four dining areas, including the 1766 Tap Room where Washington and

# THE HUDSON RIVER VALLEY

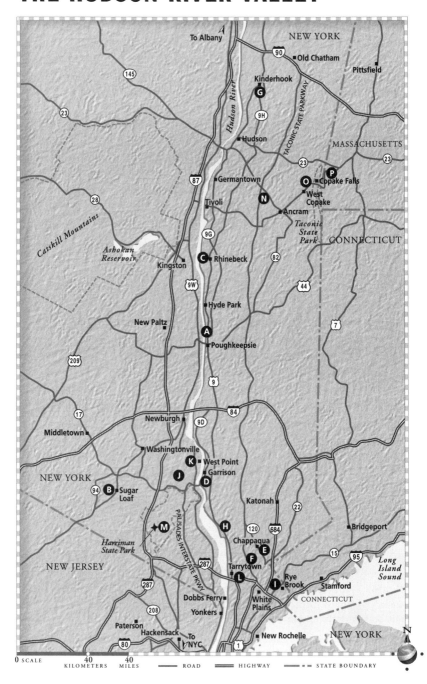

To Albany

NEW YORK

90 ■ Old Chatham

Pittsfield

145

Kinderhook

G

23

9H

Hudson River

■ Hudson

MASSACHUSETTS

87

■ Germantown

23

23

P

O ■ Copake Falls

Tivoli

N

■ West Copake

28

Ancram

Taconic State Park

CONNECTICUT

Catskill Mountains

Ashokan Reservoir

9G

Kingston

C ■ Rhinebeck

82

9W

44

New Paltz ■

■ Hyde Park

7

A

■ Poughkeepsie

209

9

17

Newburgh ■

9D

84

Middletown ■

■ Washingtonville

K ■ West Point

NEW YORK

J

D ■ Garrison

94 B ■ Sugar Loaf

Katonah ■

22

■ Bridgeport

M

H

120

684

Harriman State Park

Chappaqua

E

NEW JERSEY

287

F

15

95

Long Island Sound

PALISADES INTERSTATE PKWY

Tarrytown

L

I

Rye Brook

■ Stamford

NEW JERSEY

287

Dobbs Ferry ■

White Plains

CONNECTICUT

208

Yonkers ■

Paterson ■

Hackensack ■

To NYC

■ New Rochelle

NEW YORK

80

1

N

0 SCALE        40        40
KILOMETERS    MILES    ———— ROAD    ════ HIGHWAY    —·—· STATE BOUNDARY

## Food

- **A** American Bounty
- **B** Barnsider Tavern
- **C** Beekman Arms
- **D** Bird and Bottle Inn
- **E** Crabtree's Kittle House
- **A** Escoffier
- **F** Gasho of Japan
- **G** Old Dutch Inn

## Lodging

- **H** Alexander Hamilton House
- **I** Arrowwood

## Lodging (continued)

- **J** Bear Mountain Inn
- **C** Beekman Arms Hotel
- **K** Hotel Thayer
- **O** Tarrytown Hilton
- **L** Tarrytown House

## Camping

- **M** Beaver Pond Campground, Harriman State Park
- **N** Lake Taghkanic State Park
- **O** Oleana Campground
- **P** Taconic State Park

*Note: Items with the same letter are located in the same town or area.*

Jefferson dined; American regional fare dominates the menu. In Kinderhook, the **Old Dutch Inn**, 8 Broad Street, (518) 758-1676, is in the heart of the village in an old-fashioned country inn. The **Bird and Bottle Inn**, Old Albany Post Road, Garrison, (914) 424-3000, is another historic inn and dining room. All meals are five courses and fixed price.

## LODGING

The Hudson River Valley offers a wide variety of accommodations, including many historic inns and hotels. The **Beekman Arms Hotel**, 4 Mill Street, Rhinebeck, (914) 876-7077, built in 1766, bills itself as "America's oldest hotel"—Washington really did sleep here, and so did Thomas Jefferson and Franklin D. Roosevelt. Guests can stay in the original inn as well as in rooms in motel units, a house, a carriage house, and a restored townhouse ($80 to $140 for a double). The **Hotel Thayer**, on the grounds of West Point, Route 9W, West Point, (914) 446-4731 or (800) 247-5047, is an elegant historic hotel steeped in tradition. Many rooms have views of the Hudson River ($80 to $165 for a double; wheelchair accessible). Nearby is the **Bear Mountain Inn**, in Bear Mountain State Park, Route 9W, Bear

Mountain, (914) 786-2731. There are rooms in the original chalet-style main inn overlooking Hessian Lake and in five newer lodges on the opposite side of the lake ($89 for a double). **Arrowwood**, Anderson Hill Road, Rye Brook, (914) 939-5500 or (800) 633-6569, is in a country-club setting on 114 wooded acres with full resort facilities, including indoor and outdoor pools and tennis courts ($125 to $200 for a double; wheelchair accessible). The **Tarrytown Hilton**, 455 S. Broadway, Tarrytown, (914) 631-5700 or (800) HILTONS, is in a 10-acre garden setting with full resort facilities including a jogging trail ($105 to $175; wheelchair accessible). In Croton-on-Hudson, the **Alexander Hamilton House**, 49 Van Wyck Street, (914) 271-6737, is an historic bed and breakfast ($95 to $250 for a double). The **Tarrytown House**, East Sunnyside Lane, Tarrytown, (914) 591-8200 or (800) 678-8946, is a member of Historic Hotels of America and has complete meeting and resort facilities ($129 to $325 for a double).

## CAMPING

A number of state and private campgrounds dot the Hudson River Valley; call (800) 456-CAMP for reservations for state campgrounds. The **Beaver Pond Campground** at Harriman State Park, Route 106, Bear Mountain, (914) 947-2792, has 200 campsites and boating, swimming, and fishing ($11 per night). **Lake Taghkanic State Park**, Route 82, Ancram, (518) 851-3631, has 60 campsites, swimming, fishing, and boating ($11 per night). **Taconic State Park**, Route 22, Copake Falls, (518) 329-3993, offers 112 campsites, swimming, and fishing ($11 per night). **Oleana Campground**, Route 22, West Copake, (518) 329-2811, features 325 campsites, swimming, and fishing ($15 per night).

## BOAT TOURS

The best way to appreciate the Hudson River is to take a ride on it. **Half Moon Cruises** offers river cruises daily from June through October from Verplanck, (914) 736-0500. **Riverboat Tours** schedules sightseeing and dinner cruises from Poughkeepsie, (914) 473-5211. **Commander/Hudson Highlands Cruises and Tours** offers cruises from West Point, (914) 446-7171. **Hudson River Adventures'** two-hour cruises leave from Newburgh Landing, (914) 782-0685.

# 5

# THE CATSKILLS

Although the Catskills are not the highest of American mountain ranges, they are the most visited, painted, and written about. Much of their fame is a result of their proximity to New York City and to the millions of people who leave the city looking for a nearby respite.

The Catskills have many faces: the "Borscht Belt" Catskills, home to enormous Jewish resorts where many stars, including Danny Kaye, Sid Caesar, and Jerry Lewis, got their first breaks; the fly-fishing Catskills, home to some of the country's most renowned trout streams; the hiking Catskills; and the Catskills of old, filled with history and romance. Washington Irving brought the romance of the mountain region to the world in his 1819 *Tale of Rip Van Winkle*. "These fairy mountains," as Irving called them, took on a new image because of his story. Rock 'n' roll fans and the '60s generation still make pilgrimages to Bethel, home of the world-famous Woodstock Festival.

Like the Adirondacks, part of the Catskills are "forever wild," and, since 1885, they have been maintained as the Catskill Forest Preserve. Today the Catskill Park encompasses 705,500 acres and includes the Forest Preserve and towns and villages within the park boundaries. South of the Catskill Mountains are the Shawangunk Mountains, commonly called "the 'Gunks." Five lakes are hidden here, along with hundreds of miles of hiking trails. Geologically, the Shawangunks are not part of the Catskills—they are 100 million years older. But the 'Gunks are one with the region. ◼

# THE CATSKILLS

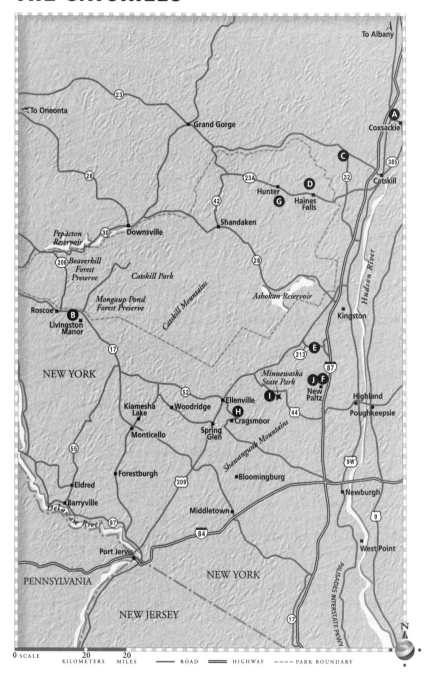

To Albany

Coxsackie **A**

Grand Gorge

To Oneonta

**C**

385

32

Catskill

23A

Hunter

**D**

**G** Haines Falls

42

Shandaken

Pepacton Reservoir

Downsville

30

Ashokan Reservoir

Hudson River

206 Beaverkill Forest Preserve

Catskill Park

28

Mongaup Pond Forest Preserve

Catskill Mountains

Kingston

Roscoe

**B** Livingston Manor

17

213 **E**

87

NEW YORK

Minnewaska State Park

**J** **F**

New Paltz

52

Ellenville

**I**

Highland

Kiamesha Lake

Woodridge

**H** Cragsmoor

44

Poughkeepsie

Monticello

Spring Glen

55

Shawangunk Mountains

9W

Forestburgh

209

Bloomingburg

Newburgh

Eldred

Barryville

Delaware River

97

Middletown

9

84

Port Jervis

West Point

PENNSYLVANIA

NEW YORK

PALISADES INTERSTATE PKWY

NEW JERSEY

17

N

0 SCALE   20        20
KILOMETERS   MILES   ——— ROAD   ═══ HIGHWAY   ---- PARK BOUNDARY

# Sights

- Ⓐ Bronck Museum
- Ⓑ Catskill Fly Fishing
  Center and Museum
- Ⓒ Catskill Game Farm
- Ⓓ Catskill Mountain House Site
- Ⓔ Delaware and
  Hudson Canal Museum
- Ⓕ Huguenot Street
- Ⓖ Hunter Mountain
- Ⓗ Ice Caves Mountain
- Ⓘ Minnewaska State Park
- Ⓙ Mohonk Mountain House

## A PERFECT DAY IN THE CATSKILLS

Fly-fishing enthusiasts will surely want to start their day at one of the many famed Catskill trout streams. On a clear day head for one of the celebrated lookout points; Ice Caves Mountain is certainly spectacular. The Mohonk Mountain House is like a fairy-tale castle and befits the romantic aura of the Catskills. It's a favorite with most everyone who has seen it. The miles and miles of trails at Mohonk offer wondrous views around almost every turn. Nearby Huguenot Street in New Paltz is a testament to the seventeenth-century settlers of the region and their ability to create homes for the ages.

## SIGHTSEEING HIGHLIGHTS

★★★ **Catskill Mountain House Site**—One of the most spectacular views in all the Catskills is from this site, a hotel that is no more. James Fenimore Cooper called it "the greatest wonder of all creation." Artist Thomas Cole, founder of the Hudson River School, felt that this "grand diorama" was far too sublime for him to paint. They were talking about the view from the then world-famous Catskill Mountain House, one of the most beloved hotels in nineteenth-century America. Everyone who was anyone stayed here. The hotel lasted into the twentieth century but then fell into slow decline and was burned to the ground by the state in 1963. Today all that is left is a commemorative marker on the site. But the view remains. Walk along the escarpment to enjoy the different vistas and to watch the changes in the light patterns. At Haines Falls take a right on State 18 at the sign for North Lake State Campsite. There you can get a map to the Mountain House Site. (1 hour)

★★★ **Ice Caves Mountain**—If heights unnerve you, stay away from the edges at Sam's Point on Ice Caves Mountain in the Shawangunks. But the view is definitely breathtaking, and on a clear day you can see five states. Sam's Point, a registered national landmark, is a little less than a ½-mile above sea level on Ice Caves Mountain, a privately operated park. You get there by taking a road to the top of the mountain, then hiking the well-marked trail down the Stairway of Stone, past the River of Mystery, and through crevices created by the glacial ice millions of years ago, ending at the Ice Cave, which is well-lit with remarkable mineral formations. Tours are self-guided. Be sure to wear sturdy shoes or sneakers. Route 52, Ellenville; (914) 647-7989; May to November open daily 9 a.m. to dusk. Admission $6 adults, $4 children. (2 hours)

★★ **Bronck Museum**—This was once home to nine generations of the Bronck family, who gave their name to the Bronx. The original structure is a 1663 stone house. The 1738 Brick House is connected to the stone house and is now used to display paintings by eighteenth- and nineteenth-century artists including Frederic Church and Thomas Cole. The three barns each represent a different era. A walk through the family cemeteries can bring you closer to the people who made the Bronck complex a working farm. Pieter Bronck Road, Coxsackie; (518) 731-8862; open last Sunday in June to the Sunday before Labor Day Tuesday through Saturday 10 a.m. to 5 p.m., Sunday 2 p.m. to 6 p.m.; Labor Day through October 15 open Tuesday, Saturday, and Sunday noon to 4 p.m. Admission $4 adults, $3.50 seniors, $2 children ages 12–15, $1 children ages 5–11. (1 hour)

★★ **Catskill Game Farm**—One of the oldest and most popular game farms in the country, the farm is home to more than 2,000 animals, including lions, tigers, and bears. Special shows feature pigs, elephants, and monkeys. The petting zoo is a popular area for younger children. There is a small train that transports visitors from one section to another, along with an amusement park and picnic and play area. Game Farm Road, Catskill; (518) 678-9595; May through October open daily 9 a.m. to 6 p.m. Admission $13 adults, $9 children, free under 4. (3 hours)

★★ **Huguenot Street**—Considered the oldest street in America with its original houses, Huguenot Street's stone houses were built between 1692 and 1712. The Huguenots were French Protestants who were persecuted in their native country by the Catholic majority. They came here in pursuit of freedom and tolerance. In 1677, 12 of their number purchased these lands from the Esopus Indians and built log huts. As they prospered they decided to build more permanent dwellings. And permanent they were. The six houses and the 1717 stone church are owned by the Huguenot Historical Society. The dark rooms of the 1692 **Abraham Hasbrouck House** include a cellar kitchen and a built-in Dutch bed. The **Jean Hasbrouck House** once served as a store and tavern. Four of the six homes are wheelchair accessible. 18 Broadhead Avenue, New Paltz; (914) 255-1889; June through October open for tours Wednesday through Sunday 9:30 a.m. to 4 p.m. Admission $7 adults, $6 seniors, $3.50 children. (2 hours)

★★ **Hunter Mountain**—Hunter Mountain bills itself as the "snow-making capital of the world." The ski resort was born January 9, 1960, defying expert advice that the mountain would never become a major ski center. Despite these dire predictions, the average ski season here is 162 days, with skiing on 47 slopes and trails. Hunter Mountain is a multiple-season center of activity, hosting the Patriot Festival, the German Alps Festival, the Hunter Country Music Festival, Rockstalgia, the International Celtic Festival, the National Polka Festival, the Mountain Eagle Indian Festival, and Oktoberfest during the summer/fall season. The **Skyride**, the longest and highest chair lift in the Catskills, operates from spring through the fall to offer splendid views. Route 23A, Hunter; (518) 263-4223, (800) FOR-SNOW, or (800) 367-7669; open daily 9 a.m. to 4 p.m. Admission $42 adult ski lift ticket on weekends, $34 adult ski lift ticket mid-week. (7 hours)

★★ **Mohonk Mountain House**—Twins Alfred and Albert Smiley established the Mohonk Mountain House in 1869. More than 7,500 acres in the heart of the Shawangunk Mountains surrounding the fairy-tale castle-hotel have been preserved. The property has numerous skiing/hiking routes that are open to non–hotel guests on a day-pass basis. Cross-country skis can be rented. The sprawling Victorian hotel sits on trout-stocked **Lake Mohonk**, a ½-mile-long lake. From the observation point known as Sky Top Tower, there are stunning panoramic views. The hotel and surrounding lands were named a National Historic Landmark in 1986. Lake Mohonk, New Paltz; (914) 256-2197; open 7 a.m. to one hour before dusk. Admission $6 adults ($9 weekends and holidays), $4 children ($5 weekends/holidays). (5 hours)

★ **Catskill Fly Fishing Center and Museum**—This is the place for fly fishermen and -women. At the library and **Hall of Fame of Fly Fishing**, learn about the people who made Catskill dry fly fishing famous. The art gallery showcases the many paintings of fly fishing scenes, rods, reels, and examples of hand-tied flies. Special appearances by well-known anglers and craftspeople take place during the season. Wheelchair accessible. Main Street, Livingston Manor; (914) 439-4810; April through September open daily 10 a.m. to 4 p.m.; October through March open Monday through Friday 10 a.m. to 1 p.m. Admission free. (1 hour)

★ **Minnewaska State Park**—This is an 11,000-acre preserve in the heart of the Shawangunk Mountains. There's a superb network of 50 miles of walking and hiking trails. Just a few minutes from the park's information booth is **Awosting Falls**, where the foaming waters of the Peters Kill tumble over a sheer cliff into a deep pool. **Lake Minnewaska** itself is surrounded by a network of woodland trails and carriageways that are excellent for hiking, horseback riding, and cross-country skiing. The paved carriageways are great for biking. Swimming is permitted at the sandy beach area of the lake and also on Lake Awosting. Route 44, Minnewaska; (914) 255-0752; open daily 9 a.m. to dusk. Admission $5 per car from late June through Labor Day; $4 per car during spring and fall. During the winter charges are per person for skiers: $4 adults, $3 children, $2 seniors. On weekends and holidays, charges are $5 adults and seniors, $4 for children. (4 hours)

**Delaware and Hudson Canal Museum**—This museum is dedicated to the history and lore of the 108-mile Delaware and Hudson Canal, built in the early nineteenth century. The canal was used to ship coal from the mines of Pennsylvania to the factories of New York. Conceived by the designer of the Erie Canal, the locks were an engineering wonder of their day. Exhibits depict life along the canal and activity on the canal boats. A self-guided tour of the locks is available. Mohonk Road, High Falls; (914) 687-9311; May 30 through Labor Day open Monday and Thursday through Saturday 11 a.m. to 5 p.m., Sunday 1 p.m. to 5 p.m.; May 1–29 and the day after Labor Day through October open Saturday 11 a.m. to 5 p.m. and Sunday 1 p.m. to 5 p.m. Admission $2 adults, $1 children. (1 hour)

## FITNESS AND RECREATION

The Catksills offer a rich array of hiking, walking, and skiing opportunities. The **Mohonk Mountain House** has 128 miles of paths and carriage roads to hike and cross-country ski. **Minnewaska State Park** also has many miles of excellent trails. The trails in the **North Lake** area in Greene County are renowned for their fantastic views of the Hudson Valley. **Kaaterskill Falls** and the **Catskill Mountain House** are particularly scenic hiking trails. More experienced hikers enjoy **Devil's Path**, named for its steepness. The path passes over rugged terrain, particularly **Indian Head Mountain** and the **West Kill Mountain Range Trail**. At 4,040 feet **Hunter Mountain** is the second-highest peak in the Catskills and has good hiking trails.

## FOOD

Dining opportunities are plentiful in the this region. Hotels that operate on all-inclusive plans also welcome meal guests. The **Roscoe Diner**, Old Route 17, Roscoe, (607) 498-4405, is a long-time favorite that offers Greek specialties and wondrous home-made desserts. **Eldred Preserve Restaurant**, Route 55, Eldred, (914) 557-8316 or (800) 557-FISH, open daily June through August and limited days off-season, specializes in fresh trout. The **Inn at Lake Joseph**, 400 St. Joseph Road, Forestburgh, (914) 791-9506, offers fine dining in a lovely setting. **Eagle's Nest Hotel**, Mountain Road, Bloomingburg, (914) 733-4561, specializes in German and Continental cuisines. The **Bridge Restaurant**, Route 97, Barryville, (914) 557-6088, overlooks the Delaware River at Roebling's Bridge. The **Old Schoolhouse Restaurant**, Main Street, Downsville, (607)363-7814, serves traditional fare in a former schoolhouse. The bar is in the former first-grade classroom. **Auberge des 4 Saisons**, Route 42, Shandaken, (914) 688-2223, serves fine French country cuisine.

## LODGING

From small rustic inns to dude ranches to huge sprawling resorts, the Catskills have it all. It's hard to match the wonder of the **Mohonk Mountain House**, Lake Mohonk, New Paltz, (914) 255-1000 or (800) 772-6646, which is a mountaintop Victorian castle and National Historic Landmark ($280 to $490 for two persons including all meals;

# THE CATSKILLS

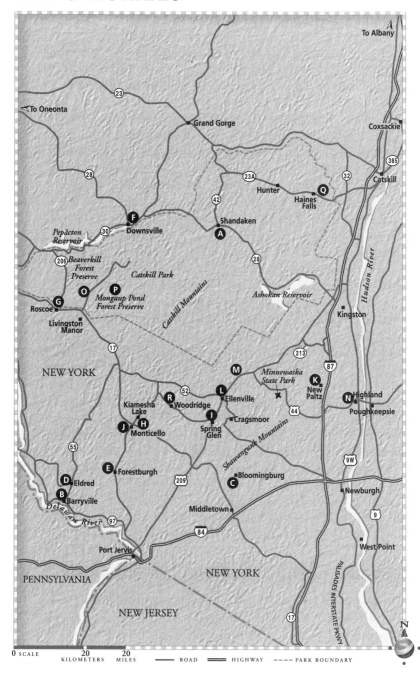

To Albany

23

To Oneonta

Grand Gorge

Coxsackie

385

28

23A

32

Catskill

42

Hunter

Haines
Falls

Q

F

Downsville

Shandaken

A

Pepacton
Reservoir

30

28

206

Beaverkill
Forest
Preserve

Catskill Park

Ashokan Reservoir

Hudson River

O

P

Mongaup Pond
Forest Preserve

Catskill Mountains

Kingston

G

Roscoe

Livingston
Manor

17

213

87

NEW YORK

M

Minnewaska
State Park

K

New
Paltz

R

52

L

Ellenville

N

Highland

Kiamesha
Lake

Woodridge

44

Poughkeepsie

J

H

I

Cragsmoor

Monticello

Spring
Glen

9W

Shawangunk Mountains

55

E

Forestburgh

D

Eldred

209

C

Bloomingburg

Newburgh

B

Barryville

9

Delaware River

97

Middletown

West Point

Port Jervis

84

NEW YORK

PENNSYLVANIA

17

PALISADES INTERSTATE PKWY

NEW JERSEY

N

0 SCALE    20    20
KILOMETERS   MILES    ——— ROAD    ═══ HIGHWAY    ‑‑‑‑ PARK BOUNDARY

## Food

**Ⓐ** Auberge des 4 Saisons

**Ⓑ** Bridge Restaurant

**Ⓒ** Eagle's Nest Hotel

**Ⓓ** Eldred Preserve Restaurant

**Ⓔ** Inn at Lake Joseph

**Ⓕ** Old Schoolhouse Restaurant

**Ⓖ** Roscoe Diner

## Lodging

**Ⓗ** Concord Resort Hotel

**Ⓘ** Gold Mountain Chalet Resort

**Ⓙ** Kutsher's Country Club

## Lodging (continued)

**Ⓚ** Mohonk Mountain House

**Ⓛ** Nevele Country Club

**Ⓜ** Pinegrove Dude Ranch

**Ⓝ** Rocking Horse Ranch

## Camping

**Ⓞ** Beaverkill Campground

**Ⓟ** Mongaup Pond
State Campsite

**Ⓠ** North and South
Lake Campground

**Ⓡ** Yogi Bear's Jellystone Park

wheelchair accessible). It has welcomed guests since 1869. There's 85 miles of hiking and skiing trails and other activities including horseback riding and golf.

The **Concord Resort Hotel**, Kiamesha Lake, (914) 794-4000 or (800) 431-3850, is one of the most enduring Catskill resorts, with 1,250 rooms, a wide range of activities, and a children's program ($95 to $130 a day per person including all meals; wheelchair accessible). The hotel annually serves more than 2.5 million strictly kosher meals in dining rooms that can seat more than 3,000. The **Nevele Country Club**, Nevele Road, Ellenville, (914) 647-6000 or (800) 647-6000, is another legendary resort with a complete range of activities and entertainment ($74 to $114 per person per night including three meals; wheelchair accessible).

**Rocking Horse Ranch**, 600 Route 44–55, Highland, (800) 647-2624, has 120 rooms and a wide array of activities including horseback riding, a private lake, archery and rifle ranges, an indoor shooting range, and downhill skiing ($92 to $125 per person per night including breakfast and dinner, $500 to $650 per week). **Kutsher's Country Club**, Anawana Lake Road, Monticello, (914) 794-6000 or (800) 431-1273, is another grand 450-room resort with a wide range of activities and children's and teen programs (wheelchair accessible). **Pinegrove Dude Ranch**, Lower Cherrytown Road, Kerhonkson, (914) 626-7345 or (800) 925-7634, is an award-winning dude ranch that welcomes children ($145 per person including meals). The **Gold Mountain Chalet Resort**, Tice Road, Spring Glen, (914) 647-4332 or (800) 395-5200, is a romantic resort and spa offering chalets with wood-burning fireplaces ($349 to $499 per couple for two nights including meals).

## CAMPING

Camping is popular in the Catskills region. The state **North and South Lake Campground**, Route 23A, Haines Falls, (518) 589-5058, is a multi-use 219-site campground and recreational area with breathtaking scenery that includes Kaaterskill Falls ($15 per night; wheelchair accessible). **Beaverkill Campground**, R.R. 1, Roscoe, (914) 439-4281, offers swimming, fishing, and 46 sites ($11 per night; wheelchair accessible). **Yogi Bear's Jellystone Park**, Woodridge, (800) 552-4724, has 252 sites and a full range of facilities ($26 per night). **Mongaup Pond State Campsite**, Livingston Manor, (914) 439-4233, has 163 campsites, a small sandy beach, and well-marked hiking trails ($13 per night).

## FISHING

It has been said that God created the Catskills for the trout fisherman. This is the birthplace of dry fly fishing. There are more than 500 miles of prime trout streams in the Catskills. **Esopus Creek**, with its excellent trout water, is a tributary of the Hudson. **Schoharie Creek** flows into the Mohawk. The **Neversink**, **Beaverkill**, **Willowemoc**, **East Branch**, and **West Branch** belong to the Delaware River drainage system. These are the main trout streams of the Catskills. In addition to the wondrous trout streams, the Catskills boast another unique fishing resource: New York City's water reservoirs. Six bodies of water make up this unusual reservoir system. They are the **Ashokan**, **Cannonsville**, **Neversink**, **Pepacton**, **Rondout**, and **Schoharie** reservoirs. Bathing, swimming, and wading are prohibited in the reservoirs, as are all boats except rowboats with a special permit. The **Beaverkill Angler School of Fly-Fishing**, in Roscoe, which calls itself "Trout Town USA," (607) 498-5194, offers classes along the banks of the legendary Willowemoc and Beaverkill Rivers.

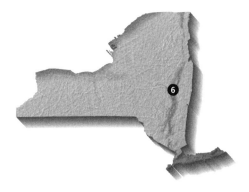

# 6

# ALBANY AND SARATOGA SPRINGS

It has long been a popular pastime to malign Albany, the state capital. H. H. Richardson, a famed architect, had this to say in 1870: "Of all the most miserable, wretched, second-class, one-horse towns, this is the most miserable." But the city, which has sent more presidents to Washington than any other city, has undergone a transformation in recent decades; Pulitzer Prize–winning Albany author William Kennedy called his hometown an "improbable city of political wizards, fearless ethnics, spectacular aristocrats, splendid nobodies and underrated scoundrels."

When the State Capitol was completed in 1898, at the then-staggering cost of $25 million, it was the most expensive building in the country. This expense proved to be relatively small compared with the Nelson A. Rockefeller Empire State Plaza. Governor Rockefeller was inspired to build the mammoth structure in 1962, after he was embarrassed by the slums he and Dutch Queen Juliana passed through while she was visiting the city.

Since the opening of the Erie Canal, the city has served as a gateway to the west and the north. Especially during August, when thoroughbred horses are racing, "north" means Saratoga Springs, a place long associated with elegance, horse racing, mineral springs, and a famous Revolutionary War battle. In the nineteenth century, Saratoga was the place to be in the summer, and people came from as far away as the Deep South to summer at the "Queen of Spas." More than 800 structures in town are listed on the National Register of Historic Places. ◼

# ALBANY AND SARATOGA REGION

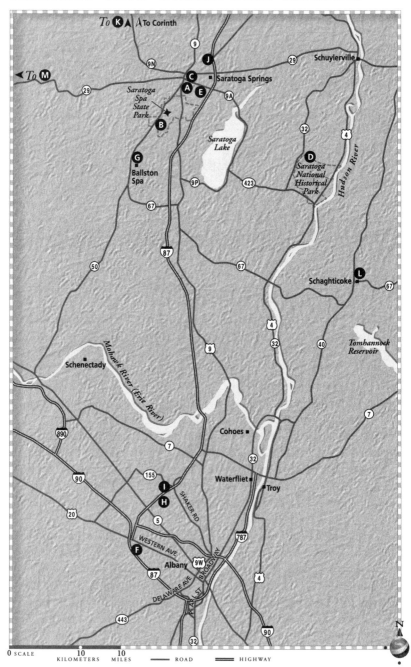

To **K** ▲ To Corinth

To **M** ◄

9

9N

**J**

**C**
**A** **E**

Saratoga Springs

9A

Schuylerville

29

29

Saratoga
Spa
State
Park

**B**

Saratoga
Lake

32

4

Hudson River

**G**

Ballston
Spa

9P

423

**D**

Saratoga
National
Historical
Park

67

87

50

67

9

67

4

32

**L**

Schaghticoke

67

40

Tomhannock
Reservoir

Mohawk River (Erie River)

Schenectady

890

7

Cohoes

32

7

90

155

**I**

**H**

SHAKER RD

Waterfliet

Troy

20

5

787

WESTERN AVE

**F**

Albany

9W

BROADWAY

PEARL ST

4

87

DELAWARE AVE

443

32

90

N

0 SCALE
10
KILOMETERS
10
MILES
ROAD
HIGHWAY

## Sights

- Ⓐ Casino and Congress Park
- Ⓑ National Museum of Dance
- Ⓒ National Museum of Racing and Hall of Fame
- Ⓓ Saratoga National Historical Park
- Ⓔ Saratoga Racetrack
- Ⓑ Saratoga Spa State Park

## Food

- Ⓕ Coco's Albany
- Ⓐ Inn at Saratoga
- Ⓐ Lillian's Restaurant
- Ⓖ Little Czechoslovakia
- Ⓐ Pennell's Restaurant

## Lodging

- Ⓐ Adelphi Hotel
- Ⓗ Albany Marriott Hotel
- Ⓘ The Desmond
- Ⓑ Gideon Putnam Hotel
- Ⓙ Sheraton Saratoga Springs Hotel

## Camping

- Ⓚ Alpine Lake Camping Resort
- Ⓛ Deer Run Campground
- Ⓜ Northampton Beach

*Note: Items with the same letter are located in the same town or area.*

## A PERFECT DAY IN ALBANY AND SARATOGA SPRINGS

If you are in Saratoga during August, start the day with a longtime tradition: have breakfast at the racetrack, where you will be served by tuxedoed waiters while champion equines work the stretch. Visit the Saratoga Battlefield, site of the the battle that turned the tide in favor of the colonists, and immerse yourself in Revolutionary War history. Reserve the afternoon for the thoroughbred races at the nation's oldest and most beautiful track. The bugler's "call to post" announces the beginning of the races. After the races many jockeys and visitors head for the soothing therapy of the Roosevelt and Washington Bath Houses in Saratoga Spa State Park. You can picnic in the park before the evening concert at the Saratoga Performing Arts Center or dine at one of the nearby restaurants or at the Gideon Putnam Hotel in the park.

## SIGHTSEEING HIGHLIGHTS

★★★ Nelson A. Rockefeller Empire State Plaza—When this was

built in 1962 at a cost of $1 billion, Governor Rockefeller predicted in his characteristic grandiose style that it would be "the most spectacularly beautiful seat of government in the world." Not everyone would agree, but the complex certainly dominates downtown Albany. The center for festivities and entertainment in the city, the plaza is a public square with reflecting pools, a skating rink in winter, flowers, fountains, and parks. The plaza is also the site of the **New York State Vietnam Memorial** and has a convention center and performing arts facility, a gallery featuring modern painting and sculpture, a state museum devoted to the cultural and natural environment, a library, a covered ¼-mile concourse, a 42-story tower with an observation gallery overlooking the Hudson River Valley, and the headquarters for nearly 50 state agencies. Wheelchair accessible. Empire State Plaza, Albany; (518) 474-2418; open daily 10 a.m. to 5 p.m. Observation Deck in Corning Tower open Monday through Friday 9 a.m. to 4 p.m., Saturday and Sunday 10 a.m. to 4 p.m. Admission free. (2 hours)

★★★ **Saratoga National Historic Park**—About 9 miles from Saratoga Springs are the park and the **Saratoga Battlefield**, according to some historians the most significant battlefield of the Revolutionary War. Every American schoolchild learns of the surrender of General John "Gentleman Johnny" Burgoyne to the colonists at Saratoga on October 17, 1777. It was a vital and sweet Colonist victory that turned the course of history.

Stop at the visitors center to see the film *Checkmate on the Hudson*, which explains the strategy and political implications of the battle. There are ten stops on the well-marked 9-mile auto tour of the battlefield. The road is one-way, so you can't change your mind and turn back, but you can skip stops. Living history encampments are regularly scheduled at **Nielson Farm**, which American generals used as their headquarters. The "boot monument" marks the spot where General Benedict Arnold was wounded in the leg. There's no name on the monument, reflecting Arnold's later traitorous switch to the British side. Routes 4 and 3, Schuylerville; (518) 664-9821; open daily 9 a.m. to 5 p.m., closed early December through early April. Admission $4 per car, $2 per person for hiking trails (free with driving tour). (3 hours)

★★★ **Saratoga Spa State Park**—For centuries people have come to Saratoga Springs to "take the waters." The Iroquois were the first to pronounce the springs therapeutic. In 1803 doctors began touting this elixir as a cure for a laundry list of ailments, and Gideon Putnam opened a boardinghouse. A spa was born, and Saratoga soon became the nation's leading resort. Visitors can still take to the baths at the state-operated Roosevelt (named after FDR, who sought relief from his polio at Saratoga) and Lincoln bathhouses, both in the 2,000-acre park.

Also in the park is the **Saratoga Performing Arts Center**, the July home of the New York City Ballet and the August home of the Philadelphia Orchestra. The center is nestled in a superb natural amphitheater. The park also contains tennis courts, two golf courses, two swimming pools, and the **Gideon Putnam Hotel**. Wheelchair accessible. Between Routes 9 and 50, Saratoga Springs; (518) 584-2000; open daily 8 a.m. to dusk. Admission free, parking $3 Memorial Day through Labor Day, parking free rest of year; charge for concerts varies; call (518) 587-3330 for concert information. (3 hours)

★★ **Casino and Congress Park**—For many years tourists came from all parts of country, especially the South, to enjoy the delights of this three-story gambling casino facing Congress Park in the center of the city. Built by John Morrissey, who also built the first racetrack, it was often called "Morrissey's Elegant Hell," and it attracted the likes of "Diamond Jim" Brady. It just may be the only gambling den that is a National Historic Landmark.

Gambling ended here in 1907, and today the casino houses the **Historical Society of Saratoga Springs**. Poker chips and dice remain, but they are now in display cases, along with other exhibits that trace the growth of the town from rural village to flamboyant resort. In Congress Park, in front of the building, is **Congress Spring** (the one that started it all), under a Greek Revival pavilion. The *Spirit of Life*, by sculptor Daniel Chester French, creator of the *Seated Lincoln* in the Lincoln Memorial, is on display here. Congress Park, Saratoga Springs; (518) 584-6920; June through August open Monday through Saturday 10 a.m. to 4 p.m., Sunday 1 p.m. to 4 p.m.; Wednesday through Sunday 1 p.m. to 4 p.m. rest of year. Admission $2 adults, $1.50 seniors and students. (1 hour)

★★ **National Museum of Racing and Hall of Fame**—Across the street from Saratoga's racetrack, this museum features a unique collection of racing artifacts, memorabilia, and lore. Paintings by the world's most renowned equine artists hang on the walls. In a simulated racetrack, videotapes of well-known trainers and jockeys explain training and racing techniques. The Hall of Fame honors horses, jockeys, and trainers. Its most colorful feature is the brilliant display of 200 of the world's most renowned racing silks, including those of Queen Elizabeth and Sir Winston Churchill. Wheelchair accessible. Union Avenue and Ludlow Street, Saratoga Springs; (518) 584-0400; during racing season (late July through Labor Day) open daily 9 a.m. to 5 p.m.; Monday through Saturday 10 a.m. to 4:30 p.m. and Sunday noon to 4:30 p.m. rest of year. Admission $3 adults, $2 seniors and students; free on off-season Sundays. (1 hour)

★★ **New York State Capitol**—The seat of the New York State government, built between 1867 and 1899 for a total cost of $25 million, was the most expensive building in the country at the time. The building is adorned with intricate and elaborate woodwork; carvings on the staircase depict famous people in American history as well as friends and relatives of the sculptors. The tour includes the **Million Dollar Staircase** and the **Legislative and Executive Chambers**. Wheelchair accessible. Empire State Plaza, Albany; (518) 474-2418; open daily. Guided tours Monday through Thursday hourly 9 a.m. to 4 p.m.; Friday 10 a.m., noon, 2 p.m., and 4 p.m.; Saturday and Sunday 10 a.m., 11 a.m., 2 p.m., 3 p.m., and 4 p.m. Admission free. (1 hour)

★★ **Saratoga Racetrack**—This is the nation's oldest and, most would say, most beautiful thoroughbred racetrack. The first races were held in town in 1863. The **Travers Stakes**, horse racing's oldest stakes race, is run yearly at Saratoga. The action starts at sunrise, when breakfast is served at the track. Guided tours of the backstretch and stables and how-to workshops on handicapping are offered during the morning. There are general admission seats for the daily races (a limited number go on sale daily at 8 a.m.), as well as seats in the clubhouse or restaurants. The grounds are dotted with booths and kiosks, and jazz combos play for passersby. The atmosphere at the track is a unique blend of country fair and garden party. A huge area is set aside for picnickers. Wheelchair accessible. Union Avenue, Saratoga Springs; (518) 584-6200; open late July through Labor Day Wednesday through Monday, post time 1 p.m. Admission $4 clubhouse, $2 general admission. (4 hours)

★★ **Schuyler Mansion State Historic Site**—Built in 1761, this is the Georgian home of Revolutionary War general Philip Schuyler. George Washington, Benjamin Franklin, Benedict Arnold, and Alexander Hamilton visited these rooms; Hamilton wed Schuyler's daughter

Elizabeth at the mansion in 1780. General Burgoyne was a prisoner here after his defeat at Saratoga. An architectural gem, the house contains an excellent collection of colonial and Federal-period furnishings, many original to the home. Following the war Schuyler served in the New York and U.S. Senate. 32 Catherine Street, Albany; (518) 434-0834; mid-April through October open Wednesday through Saturday 10 a.m. to 5 p.m., Sunday 1 p.m. to 5 p.m. Admission $3 adults, $2 New York State resident seniors, $1 children. (1½ hours)

★ **Historic Cherry Hill**—This is the Georgian-style home of Philip Van Rensselaer, once the center of a Colonial farm. It was home to five generations of the family, from 1787 through 1963. The tour depicts the changes experienced by the family and highlights their 20,000 objects. 523½ South Pearl Street, Albany; (518) 434-4791; guided tours on the hour Tuesday through Saturday 10 a.m. to 3 p.m., Sunday 1 p.m. to 3 p.m; closed January. Admission $3.50 adults, $3 seniors, $2 college students, $1 other students. (1 hour)

★ **National Museum of Dance**—Located in the Saratoga Spa State Park in a handsome building that once housed the Washington Baths, this is the only museum devoted exclusively to professional American dance. With videos, costumes, and photos, it salutes just about every great name in twentieth-century dance. Visitors can watch dance classes in session at the studios. Wheelchair accessible. South Broadway, Saratoga Springs; (518) 584-2225; open May through September Tuesday through Sunday 10 a.m. to 5 p.m. Admission $3 adults, $2 seniors and students, $1 under age 12. (1 hour)

★ **New York State Museum**—This is the oldest and largest state museum in the country. It is dedicated to researching and preserving the state's natural and cultural resources. Multimedia exhibits focus on the Adirondacks, New York City, and Native Americans in the state. There is also a hands-on discovery area for children. Wheelchair accessible. Empire State Plaza, Albany; (518) 474-5877; open daily 10 a.m. to 5 p.m. Admission free. (2 hours)

## FITNESS AND RECREATION

**Saratoga Spa State Park**, in Saratoga Springs, has walking trails as well as bikes for rent, tennis courts, golf courses, and a swimming pool.

# ALBANY

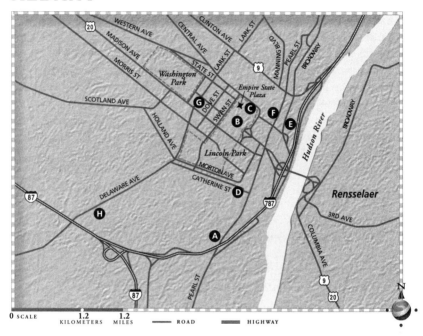

## Sights

**Ⓐ** Historic Cherry Hill

**Ⓑ** Nelson A. Rockefeller
Empire State Plaza

**Ⓒ** New York State Capitol

**Ⓓ** New York State Museum

**Ⓓ** Schuyler Mansion

## Food

**Ⓔ** Jack's Oyster House

**Ⓕ** Ogden's

**Ⓖ** Yono's

## Lodging

**Ⓗ** Ramada Inn
Downtown Albany

*Note: Items with the same letter are located in the same town or area.*

Nearby **Saratoga National Historic Park** has hiking trails as well as a 10-mile tour of the Battle of Saratoga. **John Boyd Thacher State Park**, in Voorheesville, 15 miles southwest of Albany, contains the Indian Ladder Geological trail, one of the richest fossil-bearing formations in the world, as well as cross-country skiing and hiking trails. **Five Rivers Environmental Education Center**, in Delmar, 5 miles from Albany, has outdoor educational programs as well as hiking and ski trails. **Erastus Corning Riverfront Preserve**, along the Hudson River in Albany, features hiking trails and paths for biking.

## FOOD

Albany and Saratoga Springs enjoy a surprisingly diverse selection of restaurants, helped in part by graduate chefs from the nearby Culinary Institute of America. **Jack's Oyster House**, 42 State Street, Albany, (518) 465-8854, an Albany landmark since 1913, is open 365 days a year for lunch and dinner. Also downtown is **Ogden's**, 42 Howard Street, Albany, (518) 463-6605, which is located in a 1903 building. In the summer there's dining outside overlooking the Empire State Plaza. **Yono's**, 289 Hamilton Street, Albany, (518) 436-7747, is located in historic Robinson Square; the menu combines Continental and Indonesian cuisines. **Coco's**, 1470 Western Avenue, Albany, (518) 456-0297, is a fun restaurant with four huge salad bars and a large menu selection.

In operation since 1922, **Pennell's Restaurant**, 284 Jefferson Street, Saratoga Springs, (518) 583-2423, is a long-time favorite with locals and visitors. **Lillian's Restaurant**, 408 Broadway, Saratoga Springs, (518) 587-7766, offers good food at reasonable prices. The **Inn at Saratoga**, 231 Broadway, Saratoga Springs, (518) 583-1890, is one of the town's oldest inns and features seafood, pasta, and beef. **Little Czechoslovakia**, 437 Geyser Road, Ballston Spa, (518) 885-2711, bills itself as the only Czechoslovakian restaurant between New York and Montréal and has received many awards for its food.

## LODGING

**The Desmond**, 660 Albany-Shaker Road, Albany, (518) 869-8100 or (800) 448-3500, calls itself "a one-of-a-kind hotel," and its eighteenth-century indoor courtyards and Colonial manorhouse support the claim ($134 to $147 for a double). Near the airport, the 320-room hotel comes with such modern amenities as indoor pools, saunas, and whirlpools. The **Albany Marriott Hotel**, 189 Wolf Road, Albany, (518) 458-8444 or (800) 443-8952, is also convenient to the airport ($109 to $168 for a double; wheelchair accessible). Downtown, the 386-room **Omni Albany Hotel**, State and Lodge Streets, Albany, (518) 462-6611 or (800) THE-OMNI, is close to the State Capitol ($89 to $159 for a double; wheelchair accessible). Also downtown in an historic building is the **Ramada Inn Downtown**, 300 Broadway, Albany, (518) 434-4111 or (800) 333-1177 ($60 to $80; wheelchair accessible).

In Saratoga Springs, hotel rates often double or even triple during the late July through Labor Day racing season, so some visitors stay in Albany to the south or Lake George to the north. Bed and breakfasts are popular, and some residents leave town and rent their homes during the season. The 37-room **Adelphi Hotel**, 365 Broadway, Saratoga Springs, (518) 587-4688, in the middle of downtown, is a small-scale version of the three huge hotels that once flanked it. It has been restored, and all rooms are filled with Victorian furnishings ($90 to $170 for a double, $120 to $320 during racing season). The **Gideon Putnam Hotel**, Saratoga Spa State Park, Saratoga Springs, (518) 584-3000 or (800) 732-1560, offers all the park facilities ($99 to $175 for a double, $236 to $455 during racing season; wheelchair accessible). The 240-room **Sheraton Saratoga Springs Hotel**, 534 Broadway, Saratoga Springs, (518) 584-4000 or (800) 325-3535, is a short walk from the track ($96 to $185 for a double, $259 to $650 during August; wheelchair accessible).

## CAMPING

Most area campgrounds are open from May through October. South of Saratoga National Historic Park is the 368-site **Deer Run Campground**, off Route 67, Schaghticoke, (518) 664-2804, with swimming and fishing ($18 per night). The 400-site **Alpine Lake Camping Resort**, 78 Heath Road, Corinth, (518) 654-6260, offers swimming, fishing, and a boat launch ($21 per night). **Northampton Beach** is a 224-site New York State Environmental Conservation Campground, with swimming and fishing ($13 per night).

# THE ADIRONDACKS

To say that Adirondack Park is big is something of an understatement. Established in 1892, the park covers 6.1 million acres of public and private land, or much of the northern third of New York State. The largest park outside of Alaska, it contains more than 1,000 miles of rivers, 30,000 miles of brooks and streams, and more than 2,500 lakes and ponds. Some 46 Adirondack peaks are more than 4,000 feet in elevation. Mount Marcy, a source of the Hudson River at the poetically named Lake Tear-of-the-Clouds, is the highest and most celebrated of the peaks.

People actually live in the Adirondacks, making the area far more diverse than any national park. Instead of civilization outside and wilderness inside, there's a living mixture here. The interior of the park remained silent in its splendor until after the Civil War, when a tourist boom began and changed the region forever. An entire industry grew up, spawning inns with guides who took the "city sports" hunting and fishing. Lavish hotels followed. The Adirondack region became one of the major playgrounds for the rich and famous of the Gilded Age in American history, between the end of the Civil War and the beginning of World War I. Lake Placid has hosted two Winter Olympics and still serves as an Olympic training center. Lake George, the largest in the park, has been called the "Queen of American lakes." ◼

# THE ADIRONDACKS

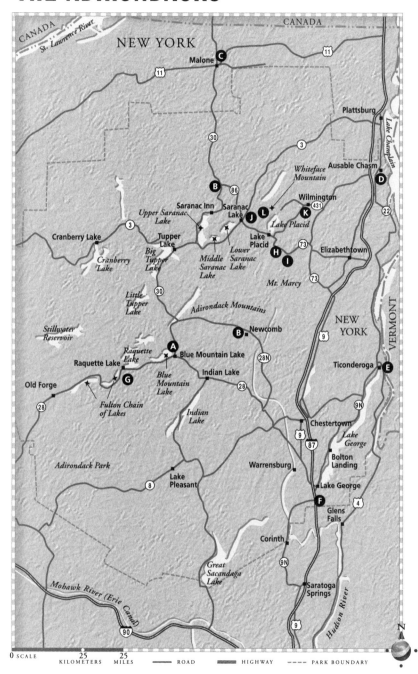

# Sights

- **Ⓐ** Adirondack Museum
- **Ⓑ** Adirondack Park Visitor Interpretive Centers
- **Ⓒ** Almanzo Wilder Homestead
- **Ⓓ** Ausable Chasm
- **Ⓔ** Fort Ticonderoga
- **Ⓕ** Fort William Henry
- **Ⓖ** Great Camp Sagamore
- **Ⓕ** Great Escape Fun Park
- **Ⓗ** John Brown Farm
- **Ⓘ** Mt. Van Hoevenberg Recreation Area
- **Ⓙ** Robert Lewis Stevenson Cottage
- **Ⓚ** Santa's Workshop
- **Ⓛ** Whiteface Mountain

*Note: Items with the same letter are located in the same town or area.*

## A PERFECT DAY IN THE ADIRONDACKS

Originally, the only way to explore the Adirondacks was by water. It is still my favorite way. Canoeing, especially, is a long-time tradition. A popular area is the St. Regis Wilderness Canoe Area, the only specially designated canoe management area in the state. But my favorite lake for canoeing or just visiting is Blue Mountain, the geographical center of the area. This tiny town is one of those jewels that manages to remain true to itself despite the thousands of visitors each year. After a morning on the lake, spend some time hiking one of the many trails and then visit the Adirondack Museum, both for its exhibits and its spectacular views. Spend the evening at a concert at the Adirondack Lakes Center for the Arts in the village of Blue Mountain Lake.

## SIGHTSEEING HIGHLIGHTS

★★★ **Adirondack Museum**—Rated as one of the finest regional museums in the country, the institution aims to chronicle the entire Adirondack experience. The 22 exhibit buildings are spread over a 30-acre compound on a peninsula nearly surrounded by **Blue Mountain Lake**. The award-winning film *The Adirondacks: The Lives and Times of an American Wilderness*, shown at regular intervals, provides a good overview of the region. In the main building, exhibits highlight the land and history of the area. Detailed dioramas are accompanied by "hearphones," headsets that provide explanations of the scenes before you.

One building contains nothing but boats—Adirondack guide boats, sail canoes, polished teak speedboats, a naphtha-fueled launch that looks like a truncated steamboat, and a Colonial-era *bateau*. Another building is given over to stagecoaches, buckboard wagons, carriages, and horse-drawn sleighs—one with a fox-fur lap robe that E. H. Harrison gave to tuberculosis pioneer Dr. Edward Trudeau. If you admire fine craftsmanship, you'll marvel at the 800 wooden miniatures made by one local man—everything from an elegant circus wagon to 407 chairs, no two the same. Wheelchair accessible. State 30, Blue Mountain Lake; (518) 352-7311; open daily 9:30 a.m. to 5:30 p.m. Memorial Day weekend through mid-October. Admission $10 adults, $9 seniors, $6 children. (3 hours)

★★★ **Whiteface Mountain**—This is the highest skiing peak in the East and the only Adirondack high peak accessible by car. Ice has shaped the mountain, and its distinctive white slash was created by avalanches. President Franklin D. Roosevelt, disabled by polio and standing with the aid of crutches, dedicated this high peak to New York's war dead.

The highway terminates just 500 feet short of the summit. A stone castle near the main parking area at the top houses historic and scientific exhibits, a cafeteria, a gift shop, and many windows for viewing the countryside. To reach the summit, most visitors take the elevator. Hardier individuals climb the ¾-mile **Whiteface Mountain Nature Trail**—be sure to wear good walking shoes. On a clear day, the view from the top is unsurpassed, encompassing the Montréal skyline, Lake Champlain, Vermont's Green Mountains, and hundreds of Adirondack peaks and lakes. World traveler and writer Lowell Thomas described it as "one of the great scenic vistas of the world." Wheelchair accessible. Whiteface Mountain Veterans' Memorial Highway, Wilmington; (518) 523-1655; June 28 through Labor Day open daily 9 a.m. to 6 p.m.; May 17 through June 27 and the day after Labor Day through October 19 open daily 9 a.m. to 4 p.m. Road open only in good weather. Admission $8 per driver, $4 each passenger. (2 hours)

★★ **Adirondack Park Visitor Interpretive Centers**—These two centers offer exhibits and tourist information in large buildings modeled after one of the park's legendary Great Camps. At **Paul Smith's**, the **Butterfly House** is a showcase for native species. The center's 5½ miles of trails are designed to allow visitors to complete one loop or all six at their own pace. The crushed-stone surface of the **Easy Access Trail**, less than a mile, is suitable for wheelchairs or strollers.

The **Newcomb Center** is adjacent to the **Santanoni Preserve**, with its Great Camp complex. Winter visitors can borrow snowshoes at no charge to explore the miles of trails. The 12,000-acre Santanoni Preserve, now deserted and empty, is owned by the state. Occasionally, the Newcomb Center sponsors guided tours of the preserve. More than 100 special events, workshops, and lectures are conducted annually at each center through the support of the Adirondack Park Institute. Wheelchair accessible. Paul Smiths, Route 30; (518) 327-3000; Newcomb, Route 28N; (518) 582-2000; both open daily 9 a.m. to 5 p.m. Admission free. (2 hours)

★★ **Ausable Chasm**—A tourist attraction since 1870, this chasm is a huge cleft with towering sandstone cliffs, formed about 500 million years ago. Visitors travel by foot, following stone steps up and down and crossing steep bridges that span the gorge. The ¾-mile walk through the chasm ends at **Table Rock**; from there you travel by boat. The highlight of the ten-minute boat journey is a bouncing ride through rapids into the **Whirlpool Basin**. When the boat ride is over, a bus takes you back to the main souvenir shop. Route 9, Ausable Chasm; (518) 834-7454; open daily 9 a.m. to 4 p.m. Memorial Day through Columbus Day. Admission $12.95 adults, $10.95 seniors, $7.95 children; walking tour $9.07 adults, $7.67 seniors, $5.57 children. (2 hours)

★★ **Fort Ticonderoga**—The French built the original fort in 1755. Because it is perched on a promontory overlooking both **Lake Champlain** and an outlet of **Lake George**, whoever controlled the fort also controlled travel between Canada and the American colonies. The fort has been nicknamed the "Key to the Continent." Between 1755 and 1777, it was attacked six times. Three times it was successfully held, and three times it fell—a record no other fort can match. You can wander through the fort independently or join a guided tour. During the summer there are dress parades, cannon firings, and fife-and-drum concerts. Route 74, Ticonderoga; (518) 585-2821; July and August open daily 9 a.m. to 6 p.m.; May, June, and September through October 20 open daily 9 a.m. to 5 p.m. Admission $8 adults, $7.20 seniors, $6 children. (2 hours)

★★ **Fort William Henry**—This fort was originally constructed by England to block an anticipated French advance from Canada into the colonies along the Lake Champlain–Hudson River Valley route. In the summer of 1757, the Marquis de Montcalm mustered a force of 10,000 French and Indians and swept south over Lake Champlain and Lake George. For six days and nights the French mercilessly pounded the log fort. Finally, the colonists and British surrendered, the fort was burned, and hundreds who surrendered were slaughtered. The tragedy is the subject of James Fenimore Cooper's *The Last of the Mohicans*.

The fort has been completely rebuilt, and artifacts recovered from the ashes of the fort and from the lake below are on display in the fort museum. Tours include a musket-firing demonstration, a grenadier bomb-toss demonstration, a cannon firing, and a musket-molding demonstration. The fort looks down the length of Lake George, and the view alone is worth the stop. An audiovisual program recounts the fort's history. Canada Street, Lake George; (518) 668-5471; July and August open daily 9 a.m. to 10 p.m.; May, June, and September through mid-October open daily 9 a.m. to 5 p.m. Admission $8 adults, $6 seniors and children. (2 hours)

★★ **Great Camp Sagamore**—When the twentieth century was young, it was a real journey to this Great Camp. Guests came by a relay of motor launch and private train, chugging along the ½-mile that made up the shortest track in the country to join the party at Alfred Vanderbilt's summer retreat. The massive main lodge was built along the lines of a Swiss music box. The 29 structures were grouped into a family and guest complex on a wooded promontory on Sagamore Lake, and a servant and service area was a ¼-mile away. A National Historic Site, the camp now is operated by the nonprofit **Sagamore Institute**. Tours are offered, but guests can also stay overnight at the camp and participate in workshops and special programs, which include Elderhostel offerings. One of the most popular programs is the **Grandparents and Grandchildren's Summer Camp**, held during three one-week periods in the summer. Route 28, Raquette Lake; (315) 792-6568; July 4th weekend through Labor Day open daily for two-hour tours, 10 a.m. and 1:30 p.m.; Labor Day through Columbus Day tours on weekends, 10 a.m. and 1:30 p.m. Admission $6 adults, $4.50 seniors, $3 children. (2 hours)

★★ **Mt. Van Hoevenberg Recreation Area**—Located on Lake Placid, this area is best known as the home of the 1932 and 1980 Winter Olympics and is the site of the only bobsled run in the country. The folks who operate the course for the public call it "the champagne of thrills." The reassuring thing about the bobsled ride is that there is a professional driver and brakeman on board, while on a luge there is no such security.

If you want to try the bobsled or luge without the cold, you can ride down the runs on wheels during the warmer months. Hitting speeds of 45 to 50 m.p.h. from the ½-mile start, riders quickly reach the bottom, with plenty of thrills along the way. There are roll-over bars, seat belts, and helmets for the passengers. Professional bobsledders drive and brake on the sleds in the summer months, too. The wheeled luge is slower than the bobsled—*only* 25 to 30 m.p.h. from the ½-mile mark where passenger rides begin. The summer luge is steered solely with the feet, not with the whole body, as with the winter luge. There are also more than 30 miles of cross-country ski trails here. Route 73, Lake Placid; (518) 523-1655; April through November open daily 9 a.m. to 4 p.m.; rest of year Tuesday through Sunday 9 a.m. to 4 p.m.; Admission $4 adults, $3 seniors, $2 children; cross-country ski area $12 adults, $10 seniors and children. Bobsled ride $30, $20 in summer. Luge ride $30. (2 hours)

★ **Almanzo Wilder Homestead**—Fans of writer Laura Ingalls Wilder will enjoy a pilgrimage to the real home of Almanzo Wilder, Farmer Boy in the Little House books. The simple home has been restored. Wheelchair accessible. Burke Road, Malone; (518) 483-1207; Memorial Day through Labor Day open Tuesday through Saturday 10 a.m. to 4 p.m., Sunday 1 p.m. to 4 p.m. Admission free. (1 hour)

★ **Great Escape Fun Park**—This is one of the state's largest amusement parks. One of the main attractions is the famous **Comet Roller Coaster**, which delighted generations at Crystal Beach, Ontario. There are more than 100 rides as well as puppet, circus, and magic shows, stage performances, high divers, and Western shootouts. Wheelchair accessible. Route 9, Lake George; (518) 792-3500; Memorial Day through Labor Day open daily 9:30 a.m. to 6 p.m. Admission $21.95 adults; $17.75 children, $16.50 seniors. (6 hours)

★ **John Brown Farm**—Many might be surprised to learn that the home and gravesite of abolitionist John Brown, immortalized in song—"John Brown's body lies a-mouldering in the grave"—are just outside Lake Placid Village. Brown is best known for leading an assault on the United States Arsenal at Harpers Ferry, West Virginia, in 1859. Trying to capture arms for use in the campaign to free Southern slaves, Brown was apprehended, convicted, and hanged for his participation in the raid. He and two sons who were killed in the raid are buried on his farm, now a State Historic Site. The house has been restored to its original appearance and is furnished in the style of a typical mid-19th-century Adirondack farmhouse. John Brown Road, Lake Placid; (518) 523-3900; late May through late October open Wednesday through Saturday 10 a.m. to 5 p.m., Sunday 1 p.m. to 5 p.m. Admission free. (1 hour)

★ **Santa's Workshop**—Young children love this place, billed as the North Pole and complete with live reindeer, Santa Claus (of course), crafts demonstrations, rides, storybook characters, live entertainment, and a gift shop with personalized magic wands for sale. Wheelchair accessible. Route 431, Wilmington; (518) 946-2212; July through Labor Day open daily 9:30 a.m. to 4:30 p.m.; open June and the day after Labor Day through Columbus Day daily 10 a.m. to 3:30 p.m.; open weekend before Thanksgiving to weekend before December 25 weekends 10 a.m. to 3 p.m. Admission $11.95 adults, $7.95 children, $6.95 seniors during summer; admission spring, fall, and December $9.95 adults, $6.95 children. (3 hours)

**Robert Lewis Stevenson Cottage**—Saranac Lake was a major tuberculosis treatment center during the late 1800s and early 1900s. Stevenson spent the winter of 1887–88 here in a futile attempt to regain his health. He began *The Master of Ballantrae* during his stay in this cottage. Stevenson Lane, Saranac Lake; (518) 891-1990; July through mid-September open Tuesday through Sunday 9:30 a.m. to noon and 1 p.m. to 4:30 p.m. Admission $1 adults, 50 cents children. (½ hour)

## FITNESS AND RECREATION

Nowhere else east of the Mississippi boasts such opportunity for a variety of sports: wilderness canoeing, hiking, rock and ice climbing, downhill and cross-country skiing, ski jumping, skating, snowshoeing, snowmobiling, fishing, hunting, golfing, mountain biking, kayaking, luging and bobsledding, horseback riding, swimming, whitewater rafting—it's all here, with expert instructors, guides, and equipment to buy or rent. More than 300 professional outdoor guides are licensed in the state and are available to teach and demonstrate their specialties. Many work in the Adirondacks. Contact the New York State Outdoor Guides Association at (518) 798-1253.

## FOOD

Most hotels and lodges welcome non-guests to their dining rooms. Lake Placid and Lake George have the largest variety of restaurants. **The Boathouse**, 89 Mirror Lake Drive, Lake Placid, (518) 523-4822, is in a lovely spot overlooking Mirror Lake. **Lake Placid Lodge**, Whiteface Inn Road, Lake Placid, offers sophisticated porch dining specializing in fish and game. **Alpine Cellar**, Route 86, Lake Placid, (518) 523-2180, is a friendly German restaurant in the heart of the village. **The Trillium**, at the Omni Sagamore Hotel, Sagamore Road, Bolton Landing, (518) 644-9400, offers elegant and expensive dining. Not far from Lake George is **Anthony's Ristorante Italiano**, Route 9, Warrensburg, (518) 623-2162, with some of the best Italian food outside of New York City, at reasonable prices. On Blue Mountain Lake, **Potter's Restaurant**, Routes 30 and 28N, (518) 352-7664, has a lofty log dining room and an old-fashioned menu. The **Park Restaurant**, 320 Park Street, Tupper Lake, (518) 359-7556, offers good family fare and is one of the few places you can enjoy fresh bullhead (the fish). **The Wawbeek**, Panther Mountain Road, Upper Saranac Lake, (518) 359-2656, offers a gorgeous view of the lake and food befitting the setting.

## LODGING

The villages of Lake Placid and Lake George have the highest concentrations and variety of lodgings. Only in the Adirondacks could the word "camp" mean both a cabin and a 68-building complex. You can live like a Rockefeller at **The Point**, the former "Great Camp" of William Avery Rockefeller, which has received rave reviews from just about everyone and maintains the atmosphere of a truly elegant house party with mountain charm and luxury; located at Upper Saranac Lake, (518) 891-5674 or (800) 255-3530; $850 to $1,025 per night per couple includes gourmet meals. **Lake Placid Resort**, Whiteface Inn Road, Lake Placid, (518) 523-2700, operated by the same family as The Point, could be called a "Point for mortals" (doubles for $150 to $400). Another Lake Placid classic is the **Mirror Lake Inn**, 5 Mirror Lake Drive, Lake Placid, (518) 523-2544, complete with an indoor pool and spa ($95 to $326 for a double).

**Hemlock Hall**, Maple Lodge Road, Blue Mountain Lake, (518) 352-7706, is a long-time favorite, with a motel unit and rustic cabins (doubles for $92 to $120). My favorite Blue Mountain Lake resort is **The Hedges**, Route 28, Blue Mountain Lake, (518) 352-7325, where you can

# THE ADIRONDACKS

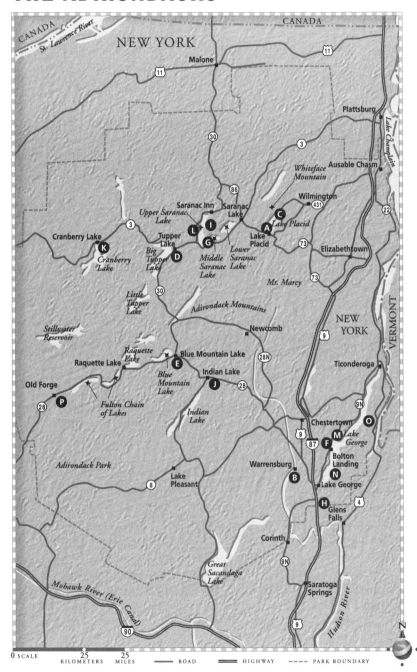

CANADA
St. Lawrence River
CANADA

NEW YORK

Malone

11

11

Plattsburg

30

3

Lake Champlain

Whiteface
Mountain

Ausable Chasm

86

Wilmington

431

22

Saranac Inn

Upper Saranac
Lake

Saranac
Lake

**L** **I**

Cranberry Lake

3

Tupper
Lake

**A**

Lake Placid

**C**

Lake
Placid

**K**

*Cranberry
Lake*

Big
Tupper
Lake

**D**

**G**

*Middle
Saranac
Lake*

Lower
Saranac
Lake

73

Elizabethtown

Mt. Marcy

73

Little
Tupper
Lake

30

*Adirondack Mountains*

NEW
YORK

VERMONT

Stillwater
Reservoir

Newcomb

9

Raquette
Lake

Blue Mountain Lake

**E**

Ticonderoga

Raquette Lake

Indian Lake

28N

Old Forge

*Blue
Mountain
Lake*

**J**

28

9N

28

**P**

*Fulton Chain
of Lakes*

*Indian
Lake*

Chestertown

**O**

9

**F** **M**

*Lake
George*

87

*Adirondack Park*

8

Lake
Pleasant

Warrensburg

Bolton
Landing

**N**

**B**

Lake George

**H**

Glens
Falls

4

Corinth

9N

*Great
Sacandaga
Lake*

Saratoga
Springs

*Hudson River*

*Mohawk River (Erie Canal)*

90

9

N

0 SCALE  25  25
KILOMETERS  MILES  —— ROAD  ══ HIGHWAY  - - - PARK BOUNDARY

## Food

- Ⓐ   Alpine Cellar
- Ⓑ   Anthony's Ristorante Italiano
- Ⓐ   The Boathouse
- Ⓒ   Lake Placid Lodge
- Ⓓ   Park Restaurant
- Ⓔ   Potter's Restaurant
- Ⓕ   The Trillium
- Ⓖ   The Wawbeek

## Lodging

- Ⓗ   Fort William Henry
     Motor Inn
- Ⓔ   The Hedges
- Ⓔ   Hemlock Hall
- Ⓗ   Hosteling International
     Lake George
- Ⓒ   Lake Placid Resort

## Lodging (continued)

- Ⓐ   Mirror Lake Inn
- Ⓕ   Omni Sagamore Hotel
- Ⓘ   The Point
- Ⓙ   Timberlock
- Ⓖ   The Wawbeek

## Camping

- Ⓒ   Adirondack Loj Campground
- Ⓚ   Cranberry Lake
- Ⓛ   Fish Creek Pond
- Ⓜ   Glen Island
- Ⓝ   Long Island
- Ⓞ   Narrow Island
- Ⓟ   Old Forge KOA
- Ⓛ   Rollins Pond

*Note: Items with the same letter are located in the same town or area.*

stay in a 100-year-old stone house or one of 14 cottages and hop on a canoe whenever you wish (doubles for $135 to $150, includes breakfast and dinner). At **Timberlock**, Sabael Road, Indian Lake, (518) 648-5494, where guests stay in log cabins, "rustic" is the operative word ($160 for a double, including meals). **The Wawbeek**, Panther Mountain Road, Upper Saranac Lake, (518) 359-2656 or (800) 953-2656, has rooms in the lodge or 11 cabins as well as boats for guests' use ($100 to $120 for a double, including breakfast). **Hosteling International Lake George** invites guests to stay in the St. James Episcopal Parish Hall, Montcalm Street, Lake George, (518) 668-2634 or (800) 444-6111 ($15 or $18 per person). The **Omni Sagamore Hotel**, Sagamore Road, Bolton Landing, (518) 644-9400 or (800) 358-3585, is on its own island on Lake George. It has attracted guests for more than 100 years and underwent a $72 million restoration and expansion in 1985 ($89 to $390 for a double). For more than 130 years there's been a hotel named "Fort William Henry" on this bluff overlooking Lake George. Currently it's the **Fort William**

**Henry Motor Inn**, 50 Canada Street, Lake George, (518) 668-3081 or (800) 234-0267 ($59 to $159 for a double).

## CAMPING

There are literally hundreds of campgrounds in this region, both public and private. In addition, camping is permitted year-round on most of the 2.5 million acres of state land. Along the Northville–Lake Placid Trail and on popular canoe routes you'll find lean-tos for camping. These three-sided log structures are a trademark of the Adirondack wilds. The Department of Environment Conservation (DEC) operates more than 40 public campgrounds, most of which are on beautiful lakes and ponds. Some are on islands, accessible only by boat. Some are also wheelchair accessible. Contact the DEC office in Warrensburg, (518) 623-3671, for information. Reservations at state campgrounds can be made by calling (800) 456-CAMP.

In Lake Placid, the Adirondack Mountain Club operates the **Adirondack Loj Campground**, Adirondack Loj Road, (518) 523-3441 ($15 per night). In the Lake George area, there are DEC campgrounds on **Glen Island**, (518) 644-9696, **Narrow Island**, (518) 499-1288, and **Long Island**, (518) 656-9426 ($15 per night). On Cranberry Lake, the DEC operates **Cranberry Lake**, Route 3, (315) 848-2315 ($11 per night). On Saranac Lake the DEC runs **Fish Creek Pond**, Route 30, (518) 891-4560, and **Rollins Pond**, (518) 891-3239 ($15 per night). In the Fulton Chain of Lakes area at Old Forge, the **Old Forge KOA**, Route 28, (315) 369-6011, offers complete facilities year-round ($20 per night).

## TOURS

A variety of boat tours and guides is offered throughout the Adirondacks. The **Lake George Steamboat Cruise Company**, Lake George, (518) 668-5777, claims to be the oldest boat-excursion company in the country and has been giving rides since 1817. **Lake Placid Marina**, Lake Placid, (518) 523-9704, has one-hour narrated boat tours of Mirror Lake. *Norridgewock III* **River Boat**, Eagle Bay, (315) 376-6200, offers a unique boat tour on the Stillwater Reservoir to remote Beaver River Lodge. The **Blue Mountain Lake Boat Livery**, Blue Mountain Lake, (518) 352-7351, takes tours of this lovely lake in a 1916 wooden launch. **St. Regis Canoe Outfitters**, Lake Clear, (518) 891-1838, offers day paddle trips and extended overnight trips as well as guide services.

# Scenic Route: Adirondack Park

This circular route travels through some of the Adirondack Park's most scenic vistas. Begin the trip in the village of **North Creek**, which gained international fame in September 1901, when Vice President Teddy Roosevelt, who had been vacationing in the mountains, was summoned to return to Buffalo after President William McKinley was assassinated. Roosevelt made his harrowing nighttime ride down the mountain in a buckboard to reach the train station in North Creek. There's a historic marker between **Minerva** and **Newcomb** that commemorates the fateful ride and Roosevelt's ascendancy to the presidency. The road has been renamed the **Roosevelt-Marcy Memorial Highway** in his honor.

    **Gore Mountain**, just outside North Creek, is the second-largest ski area in the state. Nonskiers can get a view from the top of Gore in the summer and fall, when the gondola operates for sightseers. The town is also the whitewater hub of the Adirondacks and site of the annual Whitewater Derby during the first full weekend in May.

    The drive between North Creek and **Long Lake** is one of the prettiest in the Adirondacks. The mountains and valleys are covered with beech, spruce, birch, and maples. The lake and mountain views

## ADIRONDACK PARK

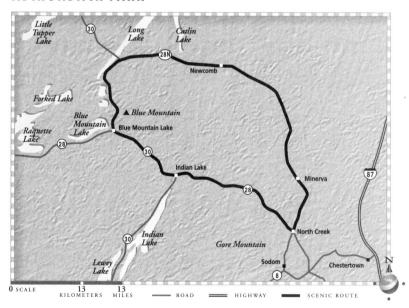

are awesome, especially so in late September, when the mountains are usually at their peak of color. Adirondack author William Chapman described the colors of the woods and mountains: "On highland and lowland, the world is red, with all the reds from marron to madder and vermilion flaring in the sun. A hillside of maples will have 50 shades."

At Long Lake, State 28N heads south along the east side of the lake following the **Adirondack Trail**. Just north of **Blue Mountain Lake**, State 28N becomes State 30 and continues into the village of **Blue Mountain Lake**, considered by many to be the most beautiful village in the Adirondacks. This is a good place to stop for a hike. There are quite literally hundreds of hiking trails in the region. One of the most popular and accessible trails is the route to the summit of the 3,759-foot **Blue Mountain**. The average hiking time for the 4-mile round trip on this trail is less than four hours. From the fire tower on the top, the views of lakes, ponds, and mountains are spectacular and hard to match in the park. From Blue Mountain Lake continue east along State 28, past **Lake Durant**, **Indian Lake**, **Lake Adirondack**, and **Lake Abanakee** to North Creek. ◼

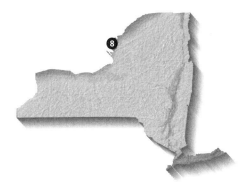

# THE THOUSAND ISLANDS

G arden Place of the Great Spirit"—Native Americans conferred this poetic name on the area now known as the Thousand Islands. An Iroquois Indian legend holds that when God summoned Eden to heaven, a thousand flowers fell and settled on the narrow channel of the St. Lawrence River between the United States and Canada; these became the Thousand Islands.

The name "Thousand Islands" is less than accurate. There are, in fact, nearly twice that number, depending on who is doing the counting and what you consider an island: "Any clump of land that could support two trees" was the definition the National Geographic Society used when it counted "1,800 or so islands" a few years back. Once a summer playground of the wealthy, the islands are an appealing vacationland for families, fishing enthusiasts, boat lovers, and anyone interested in romantic tragedies.

The coastline runs for more than 100 miles southwest from Massena to Cape Vincent, where the river meets Lake Ontario. When the St. Lawrence Seaway project was completed in 1959, it meant the formation of the longest navigable inland passage, more than 2,300 miles, in the world. The historic village of Sackets Harbor, on the shores of Lake Ontario, was the major naval port during the War of 1812; the battlefield and barracks have been restored. Napoleon's chief of police built a home for the emperor in Cape Vincent in anticipation of his escape from the island of St. Helena. Napoleon never made it to the Thousand Islands, but the village's French heritage is celebrated each summer. ◼

# THE THOUSAND ISLANDS

N

To Cornwall
To C

Massena
111
458
Potsdam
Raquette River
56
345
60
Canton
St. Lawrence River
Iroquois River
37
Ogdensburg
D
Prescott
16
812
Gouverneur
58
11
26
Watertown
Smiths Falls
29
Brockville
37
Alexandria
Bay
B  I
81
12
G  J
180
Clayton
16
15
42
Elgin
Lansdowne
A
12
Seeleys Bay
32
12E
F  3
43
Gananoque
15
12E
10
12E
H
E
Sharbot Lake
10
Perth
96
95
CANADA
NEW YORK
Sackets Harbor
Verona
Kingston
509
38
Napanee
Collins Bay
401
Odessa
Lake
Ontario
509
7
Kaladar
33
41
Picton

O SCALE   18   18
KILOMETERS   MILES

ROAD ——   HIGHWAY ══   INTERNATIONAL BOUNDARY ···

## Sights

- Ⓐ  Antique Boat Museum
- Ⓑ  Boldt Castle
- Ⓑ  Boldt Yacht House
- Ⓒ  Dwight D. Eisenhower Lock
- Ⓓ  Frederic Remington Museum
- Ⓔ  Horne's Ferry
- Ⓕ  Madison Barracks

- Ⓕ  Sackets Harbor Battlefield
- Ⓐ  Thousand Islands Museum
- Ⓖ  Thousand Islands Skydeck
- Ⓗ  Tibbett's Point Lighthouse
- Ⓘ  Uncle Sam Boat Tours
- Ⓙ  Wellesey Island State Park

*Note: Items with the same letter are located in the same town or area.*

## A PERFECT DAY IN THE THOUSAND ISLANDS

The best way to start the day is on the river, fishing. Licensed fishing charter captains offer an easy way for newcomers to be where the fish are biting, although it's also possible to catch fish right from the shore. After a morning of successful fishing, it's time for the shore dinner, a long-time tradition with charter captains. The menu always includes bacon and tomato sandwiches, fresh fish fillets, salad, and salt potatoes, topped off with French toast, real maple syrup, and freshly brewed coffee. There's time for a visit to Boldt Castle, an awesome structure on Heart Island. If it's a clear day, an ideal way to get a sense of the islands and river is to take a tour with 1000 Islands Helicopters. For dinner, pick an Alexandria Bay or Clayton restaurant overlooking the water to enjoy the river traffic while dining.

## SIGHTSEEING HIGHLIGHTS

★★★ **Boldt Castle**—At the beginning of this century, financial barons vied with each other in building sumptuous summer estates on their own private islands in the region. The grandest of all is the signature structure of the islands, Boldt Castle. Hollywood could not have dreamed up a more tragically romantic story than the tale of the castle and its creator. George C. Boldt came to the United States from Prussia in 1864 at age 13. In time he became the most famous hotel magnate in the world, owner of the Waldorf-Astoria in New York and the Bellevue-Stratford in Philadelphia. He and his beloved wife, Louise, came to the Thousand Islands on vacation and fell in love with the area.

Boldt decided to buy an island and create a full-sized Rhineland Castle to show his love for his wife. He even had the island reshaped to resemble a heart. Hearts are integrated in design elements throughout the castle. Boldt spent more than $2.5 million before tragedy struck and his wife died in January 1904. Heartsick, he ordered the 300 workers to leave, and he never returned.

The unfinished 120-room structure stands in all its haunting majesty. For 73 years, the castle and its buildings were left to the mercy of the wind, rain, ice, snow, and vandals. Since 1977 millions of dollars have gone into the restoration of Heart Island structures. Several rooms have been finished as they were intended, but most are empty. The castle is a symbol of what might have been had death not cut short a man's dreams.

There are continuous showings of a movie on Boldt's life and a snack bar next to the boat dock. The castle is accessible by private boat or tour boats from the U.S. and Canada. Wheelchair accessible. Boldt Castle, Alexandria Bay; (315) 482-2501 or (800) 8-ISLAND; mid-May through Columbus Day open daily 10 a.m. to 6 p.m. (to 7 p.m. July and August). Admission $3.75 adults, $2 children. (2 hours)

*Waterskiing near Alexandria Bay*

NYS Department of Economic Development

★★★ **Uncle Sam Boat Tours**—Since 1926 Uncle Sam has taken visitors for rides along the St. Lawrence River. There are a variety of tours as well as lunch and dinner cruises. The best way to get a feel for the river is to take a two-nation tour that includes an unlimited stop-over at Boldt Castle. A guide tells you the history of the region and points out unusual features—**Zavicon Island**, for instance, which boasts the shortest international footbridge in the world. There are 45 Canadian and New York State parks in the region, several accessible only by boat. Check out **The Price is Right Island**, which was given away in 1964 by Bill Cullen on *The Price is Right* television program. Of course, Thousand Island salad dressing originated in the islands and gained fame when George Boldt began using it in his hotels. Wheel-chair accessible. 47 James Street, Alexandria; (315) 482-2611 or (800) ALEXBAY; tours daily May through October 10 a.m. to 6 p.m. Admission for two-nation tour $12.50 adults, $6.50 children. (3 hours)

★★ **Antique Boat Museum**—The country's oldest and one of the largest collections of freshwater antique boats and engines is on display in a series of buildings. The museum is noted for its St. Lawrence Skiff and classic powerboat collection, including the world's largest runabout, the *Pardon Me*. Boats are rebuilt and refurbished here, and visitors can watch crafts at work. Every summer during the first weekend in August, the nation's oldest antique boat show brings together a magnificent collection of classic freshwater boats. 750 Mary Street, Clayton; (315) 686-4104; open daily 9 a.m. to 4 p.m. May 17 through October 14. Admission $6 adults, $5 seniors, $2 children. (2 hours)

★★ **Boldt Yacht House**—Opened in the summer of 1996 after undergoing restoration, this is George Boldt's boathouse, reachable by car from Wellesey Island or by free shuttle from Boldt Castle. Looking more like a castle than a boathouse, it was built in 1899 to hold a house-boat, two steam yachts, a sailing yacht, and a number of racing boats. Today it holds 15 antique boats, including three originally owned by Boldt; all are on loan from Clayton's **Antique Boat Museum**. Fern Island; (315) 482-9724; June through September open daily 10 a.m. to 6 p.m. Admission $2 adults, $1 children. (1 hour)

★★ **Horne's Ferry**—This is the only international car/passenger ferry crossing the St. Lawrence River; it travels back and forth between Cape Vincent, New York, and Ontario's Wolfe Island, the largest of the

Thousand Islands. After crossing the island you can connect with Wolfe Island Ferry to Kingston, Ontario. Though it's faster to cross the river by bridge, it is certainly more fun to take the ferry. Be sure to bring proof of citizenship. Lower James Street, Cape Vincent; (315) 783-0638 or (613) 385-2262; May 3 though October 27 open daily 8:15 a.m. to 7:30 p.m. Admission $6 car and driver, $1 per passenger. (30 minutes)

★★ **Madison Barracks**—This is a living museum of military architecture. The barracks played a part in every war involving the United States from the War of 1812 to World War II. It is unique as an early example of a designed military complex and for the rich diversity of its stone and brick buildings. With a sweeping parade ground and wide view of Lake Ontario, the barracks forms a National Register Historic District. Ulysses S. Grant served a four-year tour of duty here in the early 1800s. The barracks has been renovated into a country inn, apartments, a health club, and a restaurant. Walking tours are available daily. 85 Worth Road, Sackets Harbor; (315) 646-3374; open daily. Admission free. (1 hour)

★★ **Sackets Harbor Battlefield State Historic Site**—During the War of 1812, Sackets Harbor was an important military and naval base. There are guided and self-guided tours of this site overlooking Lake Ontario. There's also a restored Navy Yard and the Commandant's House. During the summer, guides dressed in military uniforms re-enact the camp life of the common soldier. Down the street on West Main Street is the former Augustus Sacket House, built in 1802. It is now the visitors center. During the War of 1812, it served as an officers' headquarters and makeshift hospital. Now renovated, it houses exhibits of the village's role in the war. 505 West Washington Street, Sackets Harbor; (315) 646-3634; open daily May 15 through October 15. Admission free. (1 hour)

★★ **Wellesley Island State Park**—This 2,636-acre park near Alexandria Bay is on the western shore of Wellesey Island, accessible by car. A highlight of the park is the **Minna Anthony Common Nature Center,** which includes a museum and wildlife sanctuary. The sanctuary encompasses a 600-acre peninsula on the southeast end of the park, with spectacular views of the St. Lawrence River. The nature center, housed in a high-ceilinged, modern building, is dedicated to conserving natural resources, promoting environmental awareness, and providing recreational programs. Interpretive naturalists conduct a variety of activities during the summer, including a voyageur canoe program, guided hikes, workshops, and a concert series. The ¼-mile **Friendship Trail** is designed for use by wheelchairs and the visually impaired. During winter the trails are maintained for cross-country skiing and snowshoeing. There's also a golf course and marina. 44927 Cross Island Road, Fineview; (315) 482-2722; open daily year-round. Admission $5 per car during the summer, free otherwise. (3 hours)

★ **Dwight D. Eisenhower Lock**—Huge cargo ships pass through this lock on their way from the Atlantic to the heartland of the United States and Canada. The process of getting a ship through the lock takes about 45 minutes, and the statistics are quite amazing: Raising or lowering a ship by more than 40 feet requires the displacement of 22 million gallons of water in the lock, and that amount can be flooded or drained in just ten minutes. There's a viewing deck and interpretive center. 180 Andrews Street, Massena; (315) 764-3213 (call to find out when a ship is scheduled to go through); May through October open daily 7 a.m. to 11 p.m. Admission free. (1 hour)

★ **Frederic Remington Museum**—Although Frederic Remington gained fame as a painter of the American West, he was born in nearby Canton. The museum houses more than 200 of his works, the largest collection in the United States. Additional collections include Dresden china, cut glass, and Victorian furnishings. 303 Washington Street, Ogdensburg; (315) 393-2425; open Monday through Saturday 10 a.m. to 5 p.m., Sunday 1 p.m. to 5 p.m. Closed Sunday and Monday January through April. Admission $3.50 adults, $2.50 students and seniors, children 12 and under free. (1 hour)

★ **Thousand Islands Skydeck**—Except for going up in a helicopter, this tower, 400 feet above the St. Lawrence River, offers the best view of the islands and the river. High-speed elevators take visitors to the three observation decks, one of which is enclosed. The tower is located between the spans of the Thousand Islands International Bridge. Hill Island, Lansdowne, Ontario; (613) 659-2335; May through October open daily 8:30 a.m. to 6:30 p.m. Admission $6.95 (Canadian) adults, $3.95 (Canadian) children. (1 hour)

★ **Tibbett's Point Lighthouse**—Standing where Lake Ontario and the St. Lawrence River meet, the lighthouse's automated beam of light reaches 14 nautical miles and has been a beacon to sailors and ships' captains since 1827. The former lighthouse keeper's house is used by American Youth Hostels. 33435 County Route 6, Cape Vincent; (315) 654-2700; grounds open daily, hostel open May 15 to October 24. Admission free (hostel charge for overnight). (½ hour)

**Thousand Islands Museum**—This museum is filled with artifacts and photos depicting life as it was in the golden years of the region, in the late nineteenth and early twentieth centuries. The **Muskie Hall of Fame**, which pays homage to the mighty muskellunge, is here, as is the **Decoy Hall of Fame**. 405 Riverside Drive, Clayton; (315) 686-5794; Memorial Day through Labor Day open daily 10 a.m. to 5 p.m. Admission free. (1 hour)

## FITNESS AND RECREATION

**Wellesley Island State Park** has miles of hiking and cross-country ski trails as well as a special trail for the disabled and a golf course. In the early 1900s, Boldt, Rockefeller, Pullman, and other tycoons enjoyed golf at the **Thousand Islands Golf Club** on Wellesey Island. Now the public can play on this 18-hole course. **Selkirk Shores State Park** has miles of hiking and cross-country ski trails. The **Clayton Recreation Park and Arena** has lighted tennis, basketball, and softball facilities, a heated pool and diving tank, and 1-mile exercise trail.

## FOOD

In Alexandria Bay, **Cavallario's Steak and Seafood House**, 26 Church Street, (315) 482-9867, is a popular restaurant, open May through November. The Riveredge Resort Hotel, 17 Holland Street, (315) 482-9917, has two restaurants open year-round: **Jacques Cartier Fine Dining** (dinner only) and **Windows on the Bay**. Bonnie Castle Manor houses the **Crystal Dining Room**, Holland Street, (315) 482-4511, overlooking the river and Boldt Castle. Open year-round, it serves all meals. In Sackets Harbor, the **1812 Steak and Seafood Company**, 212 Main Street, (315) 646-2041, is popular year-round, although hours are limited in winter. The **Barracks Inn**, Madison Barracks, Sackets Harbor, (315) 646-2376, is open May 15 through September 15 and specializes in Italian food as well as steaks and seafood. In Clayton, the **Riverside Café**, 506 Riverside Drive, (315) 686-3030, features Greek specialties and is open April through September.

# LODGING

Alexandria Bay has the largest concentration of accommodations in the area, including island homes and bed and breakfasts. The large hotels are open year-round, and prices go down in the winter. Many offer special packages in the off-season. Smaller facilities are generally open May through October. **Riveredge Resort Hotel**, 17 Holland Street, Alexandria Bay, (315) 482-9917 or (800) ENJOYUS, is a 129-room resort on the river with a great view of Boldt Castle ($74 to $258 for a double; wheelchair accessible). Next door is the 128-room **Bonnie Castle Resort**, Holland Street, Alexandria Bay, (315) 482-4511 or (800) 955-4511 ($65 to $175 a night for a double; wheelchair accessible). It also offers commanding river views. The 68-room **Capt. Thomson's Resort**, 43 James Street, Alexandria Bay, (315) 482-9961 or (800) 253-9229, is open from May through October 15 ($59 to $165; wheelchair accessible). In Sackets Harbor, the **Old Stone Row Country Inn Hotel** is in the historic Madison Barracks, (315) 646-1234 ($55 to $125 for a double; wheelchair accessible). The **Ontario Place Hotel**, 103 General Smith Drive, Sackets Harbor, (315) 646-8000, overlooks the harbor ($59 to $125; wheelchair accessible). In Clayton, the **Thousand Islands Inn**, 335 Riverside Drive, (315) 686-3030 or (800) 544-4241, is in a renovated century-old building across the street from the river; it is open from May 17 through September ($45 to $75 a night; wheelchair accessible). The **Hosteling International-Tibbetts Point Lighthouse Hostel**, 33439 County Route 6, Cape Vincent, (315) 654-3450 or (800) 909-4776, is a hostel in the lighthouse keeper's home on Lake Ontario ($15 a night or $18 for non-members), open May 15 to October 24.

# CAMPING

Camping is popular in the Thousand Islands. If you have a boat you can even camp on one of the state park islands. **Wellesley Island State Park** is, despite the name, accessible by car. One of the area's premier parks on the St. Lawrence River, it has 429 sites; call (315) 482-2722 or (800) 456-CAMP for reservations ($10 per night). In the Clayton area, **Canoe-Picnic Point State Park**, **Cedar Island State Park**, and **Mary Island State Park** are island campgrounds accessible only by boat; call (315) 654-2522 or (800) 456-CAMP for reservations ($10 per night). **Selkirk Shores State Park**, in Pulaski, is bordered by Lake Ontario,

# THE THOUSAND ISLANDS

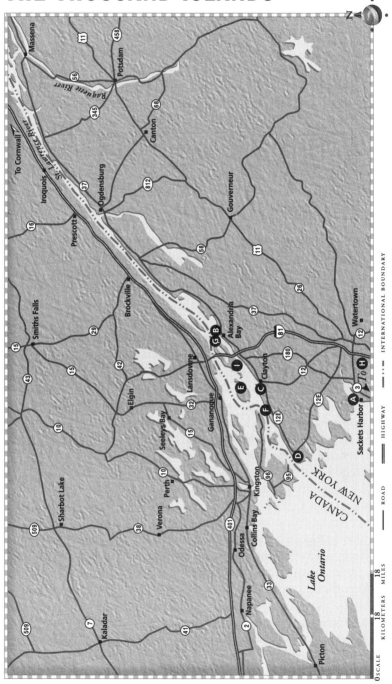

OSCALE    18 KILOMETERS    MILES   18     ROAD    HIGHWAY    INTERNATIONAL BOUNDARY

## Food

- **(A)** 1812 Steak and Seafood Company
- **(A)** Barracks Inn
- **(B)** Cavallario's Steak and Seafood House
- **(B)** Crystal Dining Room
- **(B)** Jacques Cartier Fine Dining
- **(C)** Riverside Café
- **(B)** Windows on the Bay

## Lodging

- **(B)** Bonnie Castle Resort
- **(B)** Capt. Thomson's Resort
- **(D)** Hosteling International-Tibbetts Point Lighthouse Hostel

## Lodging (continued)

- **(A)** Old Stone Row Country Inn Hotel
- **(A)** Ontario Place Hotel
- **(B)** Riveredge Resort Hotel
- **(C)** Thousand Islands Inn

## Camping

- **(E)** Canoe-Picnic Point State Park
- **(F)** Cedar Island State Park
- **(G)** Mary Island State Park
- **(H)** Selkirk Shores State Park
- **(I)** Wellesley Island State Park

*Note: Items with the same letter are located in the same town or area.*

the Salmon River, and Grindstone Creek. Visitors here enjoy the sandy beach, trails, great salmon fishing on the Salmon River, and 100 sites to choose from ($10 per night); call (315) 298-5737 or (800) 456-CAMP for reservations.

## FISHING

Legendary for its ever-elusive muskie and trophy pike and walleye, the region is considered one of the world's premier fishing destinations. The world record for muskellunge—69 pounds, 15 ounces—was set in the waters just off Clayton. Charter captains are licensed, and many belong to associations in Alexandria Bay, Clayton, and Cape Vincent. For fishing in U.S. waters, a New York State fishing license is necessary. A Canadian license is needed in Canadian waters. For information contact the **Thousand Islands International Council**, 43373 Collins Landing, Alexandria Bay, (800) 8-ISLAND. The Salmon River is also world famous for fishing, largely because of the New York State Salmon River Fish Hatchery. Thousands of anglers come to fish the river during the September-October salmon spawning season and the March-April steelhead spawning season. The village of Pulaski is one of the hot spots. For current information on Salmon River fishing conditions, call the Oswego County FISH-N-FUN line, (800) 248-4FUN or (315) 349-8322.

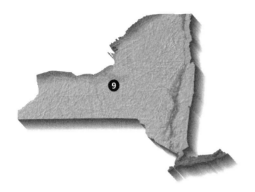

# 9

# SYRACUSE

Syracuse, known as "Salt City," is located in the geographic center of New York. The Indian chief Hiawatha chose this location as the capital of the Iroquois Confederacy in the sixteenth century. The Onondaga Indian Reservation at Nedrow is now the seat of the Indian Confederacy. Father Simon LeMoyne, a French missionary, recorded in his journal of August 16, 1654, that he had found a salt spring near the head of Onondaga Lake. Salt brought the Indians, the French, and subsequent settlers to Syracuse, and for many years Syracuse was the source of most salt in the United States. Naturally enough, there's a Salt Museum in Syracuse, which demonstrates old-time salt processing, and another museum re-creates the early days of the French and Iroquois.

Syracuse is home to Syracuse University, with more than 12,000 undergraduate and 4,500 graduate students. The university's highly regarded NCAA Division 1 football, basketball, and lacrosse teams play in the striking Carrier Dome. Since 1841 Syracuse has been home to the New York State Fair, which operates for 12 days in late August, closing on Labor Day. The fair usually attracts more than 850,000 fairgoers. The fairgrounds are used for a variety of other shows during the year. The Syracuse area usually receives a bountiful snowfall each year, and winter is celebrated in January with a Winterfest. During the Christmas season Lights on the Lake illuminates a 2-mile area along Onondaga Lake in a dazzling display. ◨

# SYRACUSE

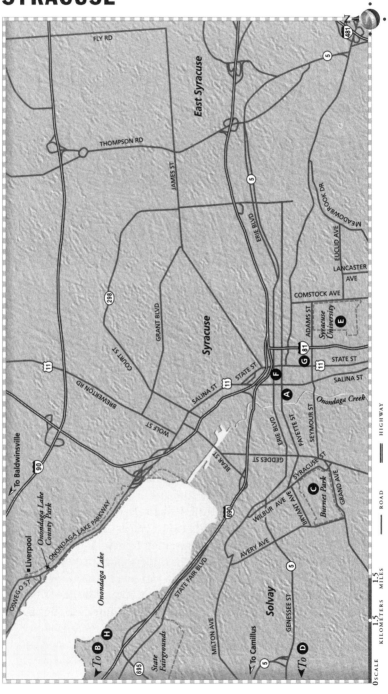

# Sights

Ⓐ Armory Square District

Ⓑ Beaver Lake Nature Center

Ⓒ Burnett Zoo

Ⓓ Camillus Erie Canal Park

Ⓔ Carrier Dome

Ⓕ Erie Canal Museum

Ⓖ Everson Museum of Art

Ⓐ Museum of Science & Technology (MOST)

Ⓓ Sainte Marie Among the Iroquois

Ⓗ Salt Museum

*Note: Items with the same letter are located in the same town or area.*

## A PERFECT DAY IN SYRACUSE

The Museum of Science & Technology, or MOST, as locals call it, is a fascinating hands-on science museum located in an old armory building. MOST is in the Armory Square historic district, the perfect place for lunch and shopping for antiques and crafts. Visitors can travel back in time at Sainte Marie Among the Iroquois, a living history compound that re-creates the lifestyles of the seventeenth-century French explorers and Iroquois natives. The museum is in Onondaga Lake Park, which features walking trails and picnic areas. If your timing is right, you might catch a concert or play on stage in the Landmark Theater. Opened in 1928, it is the last remaining Depression-era movie palace in Central New York and is lavishly adorned with ornate carvings and decorations.

## SIGHTSEEING HIGHLIGHTS

★★★ **Armory Square District**—Located in downtown Syracuse, this area was originally settled in 1804. Most of the historic buildings were built between 1860 and 1890 as factories or warehouses. The original character of the buildings has been maintained even as they have been transformed into office, residential, restaurant, and retail spaces. The district is considered an outstanding example of urban renaissance and was designated a National Historic Landmark in 1984. A popular place for dining and entertainment, it is the city's liveliest night spot. There are art galleries, craft boutiques, antique shops, free lunchtime concerts, and festivals, including Winterfest. Both the **Museum of Science & Technology** and the **Landmark Theatre** are within the district. Bounded by West Fayette Street, South Clinton Street, South Salina Street, and Onondaga Creek. (3 hours)

★★★ **Sainte Marie Among the Iroquois**—"You must have had a long journey." That's the friendly welcome you'll receive as you walk into the mission and the seventeenth century at Sainte Marie, situated high above Onondaga Lake. This museum portrays the cultures of two seventeenth-century peoples, the Iroquois and the French missionaries. Outside the museum but within the fort walls, the lives of the French occupants of the fort in 1657 are depicted. The original fort on this site was erected in 1656 by Father Simon LeMoyne. Staff wear the clothing of middle-class Frenchmen, bake bread in beaverback ovens, and respond to the chapel bells calling them to daily vespers. Blacksmithing, carpentry, and farming are also portrayed. Inside, visitors can walk through a series of interactive museum galleries that depict the culture and customs and the flora and fauna of the Native American world. Visitors can also view the interior of a typical European ship used to transport immigrants to the New World. Wheelchair accessible. Onondaga Lake Parkway, Liverpool; (315) 453-6767; May through November open Tuesday through Sunday 10 a.m. to 5 p.m.; December through April open Wednesday through Sunday 10 a.m. to 5 p.m. Admission $3.50 adult, $3 senior, $1.50 children ages 5–14. (2 hours)

★★ **Beaver Lake Nature Center**—The 200-acre wilderness lake is surrounded by forests and meadows. The visitors center, the hub of Beaver Lake's extensive interpretive programming, houses a variety of hands-on exhibits. Visitors enjoy guided nature walks, canoe tours, films, slide programs, natural history courses, and arts and crafts workshops. During the spring and fall, the nature center is a major resting place for thousands of Canada geese. There are eight trails ranging from a ¼-mile to 3 miles in length. Wheelchair accessible. East Mud Lake Road, Baldwinsville; (315) 638-2519; open daily dawn to dusk; during the winter open until 10 p.m. for cross-country skiing. Admission $1 per vehicle. (3 hours)

★★ **Burnett Zoo**—This zoo provides a habitat for more than 1,000 animals, including a popular group of elephants, members of a very successful breeding program. Visitors can trace the origins of life from 600 million years ago, learn about the unique adaptations that help animals survive, and hike the "Wild North." They can also walk through a prehistoric cave, view a rainstorm in a tropical forest, walk along a treetop boardwalk, and explore the wildlife of North America. Wheelchair accessible. 1 Conservation Place, Syracuse; (315) 435-8511; open daily 10 a.m. to 4:30 p.m. Admission $5 adult, $3 senior, $2 children ages 5–14, $12 family. (2 hours)

★★ **Erie Canal Museum**—This museum is housed in the 1850 Weighlock Building. It is the only surviving canal boat weighing station on the Erie Canal and is a National Historic Landmark. Visitors can explore the history of Syracuse as it grew from a salt marsh to a city and view the story of Syracuse narrated by E. G. Marshall. They can also board a 65-foot canal boat, the *Frank Thomson*, to experience life and work on the Erie Canal. The orientation theater provides an historical overview of the world's most successful canal. Participatory exhibits allow the visitor to operate a bilge pump and try on a diving helmet. The Erie Canal took seven years to build and was the engineering marvel of its day. Finished in 1825, it spurred the first great westward migration of American settlers, opened the only trade route west of the Appalachians, and helped make New York City the commercial capital of the country. 318 Erie Boulevard East, Syracuse; (315) 471-0593; open daily 10 a.m. to 5 p.m. Admission free. (1 hour)

★★ **Everson Museum of Art**—Built in 1968, the museum is the first in the world to be designed by internationally renowned architect I. M. Pei. Ten galleries on three levels showcase a range of work with an emphasis on American art by such artists as Winslow Homer, Andrew Wyeth, and Gustav Stickley. This museum is also the home of the **Syracuse China Center for the Study of Ceramics**, with one of the nation's most comprehensive displays of American ceramics as well as ceramics from around the world. Wheelchair accessible. 401 Harrison Street, Syracuse; (315) 474-6064; open Sunday and Tuesday through Friday noon to 5 p.m., Saturday 10 a.m. to 5 p.m. Admission by $2 donation. (2 hours)

★★ **Museum of Science & Technology (MOST)**—Officially named the Milton J. Rubenstein Museum of Science & Technology, this is a hands-on science museum with exhibits that explain scientific and technological phenomena. The museum contains displays on color, computers, gravity, light, sound, and the stars. The planetarium, a 24-foot domed star theater, offers regular shows. The IMAX theater showcases nature and science movies on a giant screen. Wheelchair accessible. Franklin Street at West Jefferson Street, Syracuse; (315) 425-9068; open Tuesday through Sunday 10 a.m. to 5 p.m. Admission $4.50 adult, $3.50 seniors and children ages 2–11. (2 hours)

★ **Carrier Dome**—The Carrier Dome, at Syracuse University, is the only major domed stadium in the country on a college campus. The 50,000-seat, multi-purpose facility can accommodate both sporting and entertainment events. The Teflon-coated roof weighs 220 tons, and 16 fans produce the necessary air pressure to inflate the roof. Once inflated, two fans keep it aloft. Wheelchair accessible. Syracuse University, Syracuse; (315) 443-4634; open Monday through Friday 8:30 a.m. to 4:30 p.m. Tours available. Admission free (except for events). (½ hour)

★ **Salt Museum**—This museum, located in Onondaga Lake Park, illustrates the Onondaga salt industry during the nineteenth century, when Syracuse earned the name "Salt City" as the country's leading salt manufacturing community. Exhibits include a full-size reconstruction of an 1856 boiling block, re-created crafts shops, and a "sights and sounds" tour of an 1800s salt workers neighborhood. Onondaga Lake Parkway, Liverpool; (315) 453-6767; May through September open daily noon to 5 p.m. Admission 50 cents, under age 14 free. (1 hour)

**Camillus Erie Canal Park**—This is a 300-acre park with 7 miles of navigable canal and towpath trails. At Camillus Landing the **Lock Tender's Shanty Museum** and the **Sims' Store Museum**, filled with artifacts and memorabilia, are authentic replicas of buildings from the Erie Canal era. DeVoe Road, Camillus; (315) 488-3409; park open daily, Sims' Store open Saturday 9 a.m. to 1 p.m. Canal boats operate May through October, Sunday 1 p.m. to 5 p.m. Admission free, canal boat rides $2 adult, $1 children. (2 hours)

## FITNESS AND RECREATION

**Onondaga Lake Park** boasts a 5-mile, vehicle-free recreational trail adjacent to the marina and boat launch. In-line skates and bicycles are available for rent. **Baltimore Woods**, in Marcellus, is a 160-acre preserve with a 4-mile trail system. **Beaver Lake Nature Center** has eight trails, guided nature walks, and cross-country skiing. **Camillus**

**Erie Canal Park** is a 300-acre park with 7 miles of towpath trails. **Highland Forest**, in Fabius, has miles of trails for horseback riding, hiking, hayrides, and sleigh tours.

## FOOD

There are a number of popular restaurants in the downtown Armory Square area. They include the award-winning **Pascale Wine Bar & Restaurant**, 204 West Fayette Street, (315) 471-3040, which offers fine food and an excellent wine selection; **Lemon Grass**, 238 West Jefferson Street, (315) 475-1111, which serves Thai food in an elegant, understated setting; and the popular **Crown Bar & Grill**, 301 West Fayette Street, (315) 474-0112. **Coleman's Authentic Irish Pub**, 100 South Lowell Avenue, (315) 476-1933, serves up Irish favorites (even green beer for St. Patrick's Day) in the Irish-dominated Tipperary Hill area, where the green light is on top of the traffic light. Menu items at Coleman's are written in both English and Gaelic. **Weber's Restaurant**, 820 Danford Street, (315) 472-0480, serves ample portions of German food at reasonable prices. **Grimaldi's**, 2950 Erie Boulevard East, (315) 445-0012, has been serving Italian specialties since 1943. **Ling Ling on the Square**, 218 West Genesee Street, (315) 422-2800, is a popular downtown Chinese restaurant. **Captain Ahab's Seafood & Steaks**, 3449 Erie Boulevard, East Syracuse, (315) 446-3272, attracts seafood and steak lovers.

## LODGING

**Hotel Syracuse/The Radisson Plaza**, 500 South Warren Street, Syracuse, (315) 422-5121 or (800) 333-3333, has 442 rooms; in the center of downtown, it is one of the Historic Hotels of America ($119 for a double; wheelchair accessible). The **Sheraton University Hotel and Conference Center**, 801 University Avenue, Syracuse, (315) 475-3000 or (800) 325-3535, is on the Syracuse University campus, with 232 rooms and an indoor pool and health club ($99 to $195 for a double; wheelchair accessible). The closest hotel to the State Fairgrounds is the **Holiday Inn–Syracuse State Fair**, 100 Farrell Road, Syracuse, (315) 457-8700 or (800) HOLIDAY ($94 for a double; wheelchair accessible). The **Embassy Suites Hotel–Syracuse**, 6646 Old Collamer Road, East Syracuse, (315) 446-3200 or (800) EMBASSY, is another good option ($109 to $138 for a double;

# SYRACUSE

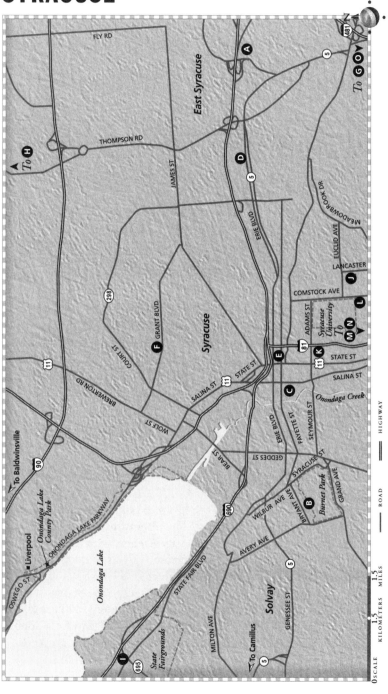

## Food

Ⓐ Captain Ahab's
   Seafood & Steaks

Ⓑ Coleman's Authentic Irish Pub

Ⓒ Crown Bar & Grill

Ⓓ Grimaldi's

Ⓒ Lemon Grass

Ⓔ Ling Ling on the Square

Ⓒ Pascale Wine Bar
   & Restaurant

Ⓕ Weber's Restaurant

## Lodging

Ⓖ Craftsman Inn

Ⓗ Embassy Suites
   Hotel–Syracuse

## Lodging (continued)

Ⓘ Holiday Inn–Syracuse
   State Fair

Ⓙ Hosteling International–
   Downing International Hostel

Ⓚ Hotel Syracuse/The
   Radisson Plaza

Ⓛ Sheraton University
   Hotel and Conference Center

## Camping

Ⓜ Empire Haven

Ⓝ Fillmore Glen State Park

Ⓞ Green Lakes State Park

*Note: Items with the same letter are located in the same town or area.*

wheelchair accessible). **Craftsman Inn**, 7300 East Genesee Street, Route 5, Fayetteville, (315) 637-8000 or (800) 797-4464, is a traditional country inn across from the Fayetteville Mall and ten minutes from the Carrier Dome ($79 to $84 for a double). **Hosteling International-Downing International Hostel**, 535 Oak Street, Syracuse, (315) 472-5788 or (800) 909-4776, is open year-round ($15 to $18 per night).

## CAMPING

**Green Lakes State Park**, 7900 Green Lakes Road, Fayetteville, (315) 637-6111 or (800) 456-CAMP for reservations, has 137 sites including cabins, as well as hiking, biking and nature trails, a beach, fishing, a golf course, and cross-country skiing and snowshoeing in the winter ($10 per night). **Fillmore Glen State Park**, RD 3, Moravia, (315) 497-0130, or (800) 456-CAMP, has 70 sites and features swimming and fishing ($10 per night). It is named in honor of Millard Fillmore, thirteenth president of the U.S., who was born about 6 miles southeast of the park. There is a replica of his birthplace in the park. For those who prefer to camp without clothes, **Empire Haven**, RD 3, Moravia, (315) 497-0135, is a nudist camp with swimming, fishing, and 50 sites ($20 per night).

## NIGHTLIFE

The **Armory Square** area, which has a number of restaurants and night spots, is popular with the younger crowd, especially on weekends. **Syracuse Stage**, 820 Genesee Street, Syracuse, (315) 443-3275, performs seven main plays during the season that runs from September through May. The **Salt City Center for the Performing Arts**, 601 South Crouse Avenue, Syracuse, (315) 474-1122, presents musicals, dramas, and comedies year-round. The **Syracuse Symphony Orchestra**, John H. Mulroy Civic Center, 411 Montgomery Street, Syracuse, (315) 424-8200 or (800) 724-0113, performs classical music, popular music concerts, family series, and other productions during its 36-week season. The **Famous Artists Series**, Hotel Syracuse, 465 South Salina Street, Syracuse, (315) 424-8210, has brought great stage artists, concerts, and cinema to Syracuse for more than 50 years. The

NYS Department of Economic Development

*The New York State Fair*

**Syracuse Opera**, the third-largest opera company in the state, performs at the John H. Mulroy Civic Center, 411 Montgomery Street, (315) 475-5915.

## SIDE TRIP: SKANEATELES

Skaneateles is both a lovely village and a lake south of Syracuse. (An Iroquois word meaning "long lake," it is pronounced "skinny-ata-less.") The village is on the northern tip of Skaneateles Lake, just 17 miles from Syracuse. The lake is the bluest of the Finger Lakes, and, according to legend, the sky spirits used to lean out of their home to admire themselves in the lake's reflection when the heavens were nearer to the earth than they are now. The lake spirits fell in love with the sky spirits and absorbed the color of the sky spirits' robes into the water, thus giving the lake its beautiful deep blue color.

After traveling around the world, William H. Seward, secretary of state under Presidents Abraham Lincoln and Andrew Johnson, proclaimed the Skaneateles Lake "the most beautiful body of water in the world." His description still rings true today, especially while you're on board the *Barbara S. Wiles*, a restored wooden tour boat that also delivers the U.S. Mail around the 16-mile-long lake. The boat tour is operated by **Mid-Lakes Navigation Co.**, 11 Jordan Street, (315) 685-8500 or (800) 545-4318, which offers various lake cruises on several tour boats from May through September.

Polo matches take place every Sunday afternoon during July and August, and the highly acclaimed **Skaneateles Festival**, a series of chamber music concerts, is held every August, (315) 685-7418. Overlooking the lake is the **Sherwood Inn**, 26 W. Genesee Street, (315) 685-3405 or (800) 3SHERWOOD, a lovely, rambling country inn that has welcomed travelers since 1807 ($75 to $145 for a double). Down the street is **The Krebs**, 53 W. Genesee Street, (315) 686-5714, which has served hungry diners since 1899. It's open from April 30 through October and features a home-cooked, plate-passing feast. Another popular eatery is **Doug's Fish Fry**, 8 Jordan Street, (315) 685-3288. The fish is flown in every day from Boston.

The village, filled with lovely old homes and quaint shops, promotes itself as stress-free with the motto, "Relax, you're in the village." Even the meter maids are helpful. They carry extra nickels to place in the meters so visitors won't suffer the stressful experience of getting a parking ticket.

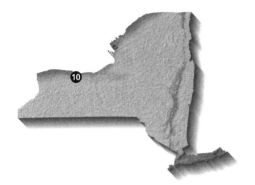

# 10

# ROCHESTER

The third-largest city in the state, Rochester owes its existence to the Genesee River and its growth and development to the Erie Canal. The city is named after Colonel Nathaniel Rochester, who built and developed flour mills by Genesee River's High Falls. After construction of the Erie Canal, Rochester became the country's first "boom town," as long lines of barges loaded with flour, lumber, and other goods moved along the canal. Originally called the "Flour City" because of its flour mills, the city later became known as "Flower City" for its many flower nurseries. Home to the world's largest collection of lilacs, the city celebrates its flower heritage every May with the Lilac Festival.

Today the city calls itself "the world's image center" because of the University of Rochester's Institute of Optics, the Rochester Institute of Technology's College of Imaging Arts and Sciences, and many imaging and optics firms, including Bausch & Lomb, Xerox, and Eastman Kodak. Surely it is George Eastman, creator of Eastman Kodak, who has brought the most fame to the city. His donations made possible the University of Rochester's Eastman School of Music and the Eastman Theatre, as well as the internationally renowned collection of photographs and cameras on display at the International Museum of Photography and Film. During his lifetime, he donated more than $100 million to various charities and schools, many of which were in his hometown. ◪

# ROCHESTER

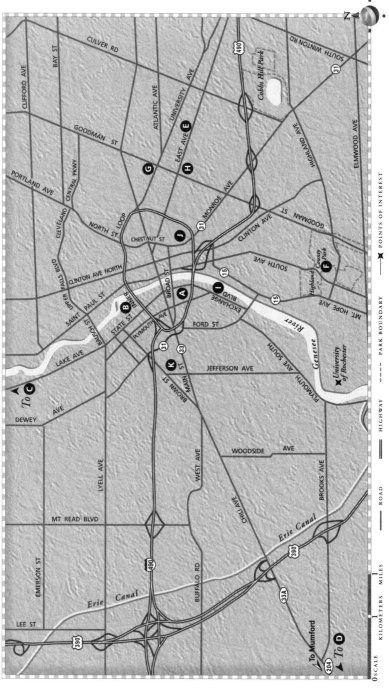

## Sights

- Ⓐ Campbell Whittlesey House Museum
- Ⓑ Center at High Falls
- Ⓒ Charlotte-Genesee Lighthouse
- Ⓓ Genesee Country Museum
- Ⓔ George Eastman House and the International Museum of Photography and Film
- Ⓕ Highland Park
- Ⓖ Memorial Art Gallery
- Ⓗ Rochester Museum and Science Center/Strasenburgh Planetarium
- Ⓘ *Sam Patch* Tour Boat
- Ⓙ Strong Museum
- Ⓚ Susan B. Anthony House

## A PERFECT DAY IN ROCHESTER

If you time your visit for May, start the day with a walk through Highland Park, home of the world's largest collection of lilacs, where the ten-day Lilac Festival is held each May. Nearby is the stately George Eastman House and the International Museum of Photography and Film, with one of the world's finest collection of photographs. The Eastman House is in the East Avenue Preservation District, an avenue filled with grand homes from the nineteenth and early twentieth centuries. For lunch go to the High Falls area, where you can enjoy the Genesee River and the falls. The downtown Strong Museum is a wondrous place full of more than 300,000 objects collected by Margaret Woodbury Strong. Children love the toys, dolls, and the children's history section. In the evening see a play at the GeVa Theatre or enjoy a symphony at the Eastman Theatre.

## SIGHTSEEING HIGHLIGHTS

★★★ **George Eastman House and the International Museum of Photography and Film**—This is two museums in one: the 50-room grand mansion of George Eastman, founder of Eastman Kodak, and the world's leading museum of photography and film. The Eastman home, a National Historic Landmark, has been renovated and is beautifully connected to the adjoining $7.8 million photography museum. Eastman never married, but he loved to entertain in his elegant and comfortable home. He had a passion for flowers, and his extensive gardens have been lovingly restored. A second-floor exhibit traces Eastman's early years at his mother's kitchen table—where he developed the photographic process that started Eastman Kodak—to his suicide in 1932.

The International Museum of Photography and Film houses one of the world's largest collections of photographs, films, photo technology, and literature, including half a million fine works of art and historical prints and the works of 8,000 international photographers from 1839 to the present. The **Dryden and Curtis Theaters** present evening and Sunday afternoon film programs. 900 East Avenue, Rochester; (716) 271-3361; open Tuesday through Saturday 10 a.m. to 4:30 p.m., Sunday 1 p.m. to 4:30 p.m. Admission $6.50 adults, $5 seniors and students. (2 hours)

★★★ **Strong Museum**—Margaret Woodbury Strong, the largest single Kodak stockholder when she died in 1969, directed that her $77 million estate be used to create this museum to hold her amazing collection of more than 300,000 objects. The museum is regarded as the nation's leading collection of cultural history and popular taste from 1820 to 1930. Special exhibits are held regularly. **History Place**, a special children's section, is a big hit with the three- to seven-year-old set. There are dolls to dress and undress, an attic filled with old clothes, games, toys, puppets, a kitchen with child-sized implements, a replica steam train, and books. A new glass atrium addition features an operating 1956 stainless steel diner and a fully restored and operating 1918 carousel. The museum now boasts the first three-dimensional museum exhibit on *Sesame Street*. Wheelchair accessible. 1 Manhattan Square, Rochester; (716) 263-2700; open Monday through Saturday 10 a.m. to 5 p.m., Sunday 1 p.m. to 5 p.m. Admission $5 adults, $4 seniors and college students, $3 children ages 3–16. (3 hours)

★★ **Center at High Falls**—At High Falls visitors can watch the Genesee River rush over a 96-foot waterfall; walk through Rochester's past, including actual 1816 factory ruins at **Triphammer Forge** and ruins of the old Granite Flour Mill; step across footbridges and look beneath the street at a replicated 240-foot section of the original raceway used to power mill wheels; walk over the Genesee River Gorge on the 858-foot-long **Pont De Rennes Bridge**; and enjoy fireworks, a laser light show, and music. A restaurant and picnic tables await diners. The 30-minute *River of Light* laser show is projected on a 500-foot section of the gorge. It relates the story of a Seneca Indian spirit, Jonesho, who tells the history of the river and Rochester to Chester, a young bear whose great, great, great, great-grandfather jumped over the falls with daredevil Sam Patch in 1829. (The bear lived but Patch did not.) Call for laser show schedule. Wheelchair accessible. 60 Brown's Race, Rochester; (716) 325-2030; open Wednesday through Saturday 10 a.m. to 5 p.m., Sunday noon to 4 p.m. Admission free. (2 hours)

★★ **Genesee Country Museum**—Spend the day in the nineteenth century, strolling through a reconstructed village of 57 buildings that were gathered from 13 counties of the Genesee Valley and represent various stages in the development of the frontier. Costumed guides and craftspeople add to the atmosphere. The museum strives to show how the average person engaged in everyday activities of the period and displays artifacts of an entire century. Authentic nineteenth-century flower, vegetable, and herb gardens are scattered throughout the grounds. Throughout the season special events designed to give an in-depth look at various aspects of nineteenth-century life are staged. The **John L. Wehle Gallery of Sporting Art** displays one of the largest collections of sporting and wildlife art. Flint Hill Road, Mumford; (716) 538-6822; mid-May through October open Tuesday through Sunday 10 a.m. to 5 p.m. Admission $10 adults, $8.50 seniors, $6 students ages 6–17. (4 hours)

★★ **Memorial Art Gallery**—George Eastman donated his collection of Old Masters to this museum that houses art spanning over 50 centuries. Notable artists of the last century on display here include Mary Cassatt, Henry Moore, Paul Cezanne, Winslow Homer, Henri Matisse, and Claude Monet. Wheelchair accessible. 500 University Avenue, Rochester; (716) 473-7720; open Tuesday noon to 9 p.m., Wednesday through Friday 10 a.m. to 4 p.m., Saturday 10 a.m. to 5 p.m., Sunday noon to 5 p.m. Admission $5 adults, $4 seniors and college students, $3 students ages 6–18. (2 hours)

★★ **Rochester Museum and Science Center and the Strasenburgh Planetarium**—This museum of natural science, history, and anthropology focuses on the cultural and natural heritage of the region. Permanent exhibits include colorful dioramas of area flora and fauna, the City of Rochester in 1838, fossil seas from 300 million years ago, and an Iroquois village. The permanent exhibit, *At the Western Door*, displays the finest examples of the museum's widely acclaimed Seneca Iroquois collection. Full-length star shows and seasonal sky mini-shows are projected on the great domed ceiling of the star theater in the Strasenburgh Planetarium. Shows Wednesday through Saturday at 8 p.m.; Saturday at 11 a.m., 2 p.m., and 3:30 p.m.; and Sunday at 2 p.m. and 3:30 p.m. Wheelchair accessible. 657 East Avenue, Rochester; (716) 271-4320; open Monday through Saturday 9 a.m. to 5 p.m., Sunday noon to 5 p.m. Admission $6 adults, $5 seniors, $3 students. (2 hours)

★ **Campbell-Whittlesey House Museum**—One of the finest examples of Greek Revival architecture in the country, this is the restored home of Benjamin Campbell, a prosperous merchant/miller. The museum represents the prosperity the Erie Canal brought to the city during the boom years of 1835 to 1850. A visitor can listen to melodies made by musical glasses, see dolls and children's toys of the period, and get a glimpse into the private life of a wealthy nineteenth-century family. 123 South Fitzhugh Street, Rochester; (716) 546-7029; open Friday through Sunday noon to 4 p.m. Admission $2 adults, 25 cents children ages 6–16. (1 hour)

★ **Highland Park**—Designed in 1888 by Frederick Law Olmsted, the park features the world's largest collection of lilacs, an outdoor amphitheater used for summer concerts, an ice-skating pond, a sledding hill, and a warming shelter. The ten-day **Lilac Festival** is held in the park every May. The park's 1,200 lilac bushes feature more than 500 varieties, from the deepest purple to the purest white. The lilac collection was started by horticulturist John Dunbar in 1892 with 20 varieties, some descending from slips carried to the New World by colonists. Today lilacs cover 22 of the park's 155 acres. The **Lamberton Conservatory** on the park grounds was designed in 1911 along the lines of a Victorian greenhouse. During the Lilac Festival there are parades, concerts, tours, and other special events. Highland Avenue, Rochester; (716) 248-6280; park open daily 10 a.m. to 11 p.m. Conservatory open May to October, Wednesday through Sunday 10 a.m. to 6 p. m.; 10 a.m. to 4 p.m. rest of year. Admission free. (2 hours)

★ *Sam Patch* **Tour Boat**—The 54-foot *Sam Patch* is operated by the Corn Hill Waterfront & Navigation Foundation on the upper Genesee River and the Erie Canal. The authentic canal boat was named after the daredevil waterfall jumper who lost his life jumping from High

Falls in Rochester in 1829. 250 Exchange Boulevard, Rochester; (716) 262-5661; May through October open Tuesday through Sunday; excursions include lunch, dinner, and Sunday brunch, evening cruises on Friday and Saturday. Admission for 1½-hour cruise $10 adults, $8 seniors, $4.50 children. Dinner cruises $35 adults, lunch cruises $16 adults. (2 hours)

★ **Susan B. Anthony House**—This National Historic Landmark was the residence of the famous advocate of women's rights. Here she met with Frederick Douglass, Elizabeth Cady Stanton, and other influential reformers. On the third floor of the restored home, which is furnished in the style of the mid-1800s, Anthony wrote *The History of Woman Suffrage*. 17 Madison Street, Rochester; (716) 235-6124; open Thursday through Saturday 1 p.m. to 4 p.m. Admission $5 adults, $3 seniors and students, $1 children under age 12 (visitors receive a Susan B. Anthony memorial coin with admission). (1 hour)

**Charlotte-Genesee Lighthouse**—This 1822 lighthouse-turned-museum is next to Ontario Beach Park, so you can combine beach-combing or swimming with a visit to the lighthouse, one of the Great Lakes' oldest. The museum traces the history of lighthouses, the port, lake transportation, and Ontario Beach Park, once considered the Coney Island of the West. 70 Lighthouse Road, Rochester; (716) 621-6179; mid-May through mid-October open Saturday and Sunday 1 p.m. to 5 p.m. Admission free. (1 hour)

## FITNESS AND RECREATION

The Rochester area enjoys a multitude of parks for hiking, walking, golf, cross-country skiing, and communing with nature. **Durand-Eastman Park** has 2 miles of frontage on Lake Ontario as well as an 18-hole golf course. **Genesee Valley Park**, on the Genesee River, has two 18-hole golf courses, tennis courts, an ice rink, canoeing, and swimming. **Mendon Ponds Park** is a 550-acre nature preserve with several self-guiding trails. The **Cumming Nature Center**, in Naples, is part of the Rochester Museum and Science Center. It is a 900-acre environmental education center with nature trails and cross-country skiing and snowshoeing in winter. Hiking and biking are popular along the **Barge Canal Trail** recreation area.

# ROCHESTER

Cobbs Hill Park

CULVER RD

BAY ST

CLIFFORD AVE

GOODMAN ST

PORTLAND AVE

CLEVELAND CENTRAL PKWY

NORTH ST LOOP

CHESTNUT ST

CLINTON AVE NORTH

UPPER FALLS BLVD

SAINT PAUL ST

STATE ST

LAKE AVE

ROCHESTER ST

BROWN ST

DEWEY AVE

LYELL AVE

EMERSON ST

MT READ BLVD

LEE ST

Erie Canal

ATLANTIC AVE

UNIVERSITY AVE

EAST AVE

GOODMAN ST

MONROE AVE

CLINTON AVE

SOUTH AVE

HIGHLAND AVE

ELMWOOD AVE

SOUTH WINTON RD

Highland County Park

MT. HOPE AVE

EXCHANGE BLVD

FORD ST

PLYMOUTH AVE

BROAD ST

INNER

JEFFERSON AVE

PLYMOUTH AVE SOUTH

University of Rochester

Genesee River

WEST AVE

WOODSIDE AVE

BROOKS AVE

CHILI AVE

BUFFALO RD

Erie Canal

To F

To G

To Mumford

To K

To Mumford

SCALE
KILOMETERS
MILES

POINTS OF INTEREST

PARK BOUNDARY

HIGHWAY

ROAD

490
31
31
31
15
15
33
490
390
390
390
33A
204

## Food

- Ⓐ  Aladdin's Natural Eatery
- Ⓑ  Big Apple Café
- Ⓒ  Brasserie Restaurant
- Ⓓ  Edwards Restaurant
- Ⓔ  Highland Park Diner
- Ⓕ  Richardson's Canal House
- Ⓖ  Spring House
- Ⓗ  Water Street Grill

## Lodging

- Ⓘ  Days Inn Downtown
- Ⓙ  428 Mt. Vernon
- Ⓚ  Genesee Country Inn
- Ⓛ  Holiday Inn-Genesee Plaza
- Ⓜ  Hyatt Regency Rochester Riverside
- Ⓝ  Radisson Hotel Rochester Plaza
- Ⓞ  Strathallan

## FOOD

The Rochester area has a wide array of dining establishments, many of them housed in historic buildings. Downtown in the historic Academy Building is **Edwards Restaurant**, 13 S. Fitzhugh, Rochester, (716) 423-0140, considered one of the city's best. Across from the Eastman Theatre is the **Brasserie Restaurant**, 387 E. Main Street, Rochester, (716) 232-3350, which offers fine food and outdoor dining in good weather. The **Water Street Grill**, 175 N. Water Street, Rochester, (716) 546-4980, on restored Water Street, serves American regional cuisine. For Greek and Mediterranean specialities, the place to be is **Aladdin's Natural Eatery**, 141–145 State Street, Rochester, (716) 546-5000. The **Big Apple Café**, 682 Park Avenue, Rochester, (716) 271-1039, in the heart of the Historic Park Area, is a popular European-style cafe. The **Spring House**, 3001 Monroe Avenue, Rochester, (716) 586-2300, a National Landmark, is a former 1822 Erie Canal inn that offers moderately priced meals in an elegant setting. **Richardson's Canal House**, 1474 Marsh Road, Pittsford, (176) 248-5000, is a restored 1818 Erie Canal tavern serving French country and American regional cooking. The **Highland Park Diner**, 960 South Clinton Avenue, (716) 461-5040, invites diners to enjoy the nostalgia of the city's last classic diner.

## LODGING

In the downtown area, the **Hyatt Regency Rochester Riverside**, 125 E. Main Street, Rochester, (716) 546-1234, is the city's newest hotel, with 337 rooms and skyway connections to the convention center and shopping mall ($135 to $189 for a double; wheelchair accessible). The top floors of the neighboring **Holiday Inn-Genesee Plaza**, 120 E. Main Street, Rochester, (716) 546-6400, have good views of the river and the falls ($103 to $109; wheelchair accessible). Also overlooking the river downtown is the **Radisson Hotel Rochester Plaza**, 70 State Street, Rochester, (716) 546-3450 ($124 to $134). **Days Inn Downtown**, 384 East Avenue, Rochester, (716) 325-5010 or (800) 329-7466, is just outside downtown ($69 to $74). The elegant 150-suite **Strathallan**, 550 East Avenue, Rochester, (716) 461-5010, is in the heart of the city's museum district ($105 to $155; wheelchair accessible). **428 Mt. Vernon**, 428 Mt. Vernon, Rochester, (716) 271-0792 or (800) 836-3159, is a country inn in the city adjacent to Highland Park ($110). Down the road from the Genesee Country Museum is the **Genesee Country Inn**, 948 George Street, Mumford, (716) 538-2500 or (800) NYSTAYS, a lovely bed and breakfast inn in an 1833 former stone mill ($85 to $130).

## NIGHTLIFE

In Rochester, **EZ Rider Shuttle** makes it easy to go out on the town; the shuttle offers free transportation between hotels, restaurants, night spots, and entertainment venues. The **Rochester Philharmonic Orchestra** plays in the magnificent **Eastman School of Music**'s **Eastman Theatre**, 26 Gibbs Street, Rochester, (716) 454-2620, from October through May (wheelchair accessible). Frequent performances by talented students attending the University of Rochester's world-renowned Eastman School of Music are open to the public. **GeVa Theatre**, 75 Woodbury Boulevard, Rochester, (716) 232-GEVA, is the city's only professional resident theater (wheelchair accessible). The **Downstairs Cabaret Theatre**, 151 St. Paul Street, Rochester, (716) 325-4370, is a professional theater that produces popular comedies and musicals (wheelchair accessible). **Little Theatre**, 240 East Avenue, Rochester, (716) 258-0444, is one of the country's oldest and largest art movie houses. The theater, which opened in 1929, is on the National Register of Historic Places.

## SIDE TRIP: LETCHWORTH STATE PARK

**Letchworth State Park**, about an hour south of Rochester, has been dubbed the "Grand Canyon of the East." Though considerably smaller than Arizona's canyon, it is still a spectacular gorge. It is here that the Genesee River runs fast and deep between towering rock walls, forming a

17-mile gorge with three waterfalls. The park is named after nineteenth-century Buffalo industrialist William Pryor Letchworth, who rescued and preserved the area. An early and ardent conservationist, he restored the once-scarred landscape into a place of beauty. Nearly every species of North American tree grows here, thanks to Letchworth.

The park's creator was also determined to preserve the nation's rich Indian lore. In 1871 he relocated the last remaining Genesee Valley Seneca Council House near his home, Glen Iris. In 1906 Letchworth deeded his land and home to the state. He died four years later at his beloved home. The history of the lands and of Letchworth is told in the **William Pryor Letchworth Museum** in the park. The park now comprises 14,350 acres of magnificent scenery that encompass dramatic cliffs along the Genesee, three waterfalls (one 107 feet high), lush forests, a perfect country inn and restaurant, cabins and campsites, a swimming pool, a fishing pond, and guided nature programs. The **Glen Iris Inn**, (716) 493-2622, overlooks the Middle Falls and offers fine dining, comfortable rooms, and a wonderful porch with rocking chairs. It is open April through November. For an extraordinary view of the park and countryside, take a hot air balloon ride with **Balloons Over Letchworth**, (716) 237-2660. For park information call (716) 493-2611, or (800) 456-CAMP for campsite reservations.

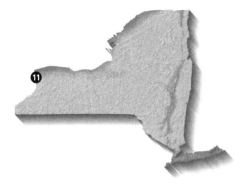

# 11
# NIAGARA FALLS

The first recorded tourist to witness the wonder of mighty Niagara Falls was the Reverend Louis Hennepin, who reported seeing the "incredible Cataract or Waterfall, which has no equal." Ever since that cold December day in 1678, Niagara Falls has been one of North America's greatest tourist attractions. More than 12 million visitors come each year to look upon the relentless waters. They drink in the vista from every conceivable angle: they line the promenade opposite the Falls, gape from the deck of a boat below, peer out from the caves behind, gaze from towers, and ogle from helicopters above.

Writers have long struggled to capture the immensity of the Falls. Charles Dickens gushed, "I seemed to be lifted from the earth and to be looking into Heaven." Mark Twain wrote simply, "Niagara Falls is one of the finest structures in the known world." The Falls is indeed an awesome spectacle: a sprawling 182-foot-high cataract of thundering water surrounded by towering clouds of mist and spray. There are taller cataracts elsewhere, but the sheer size—more than a ½-mile wide—and tremendous volume of Niagara are unsurpassed. The Falls drain four Great Lakes—Superior, Michigan, Huron, and Erie—into a fifth, Ontario, at a rate of 700,000 gallons per second in the summer.

The Falls border the United States and Canada. The American and Bridal Veil Falls are in the United States, and the Horseshoe Falls is on the Canadian side. Bridges make border crossings easy, but be sure to bring proof of citizenship. ◪

# NIAGARA FALLS

NIAGARA FALLS

WALMORE RD

NIAGARA RD

BERGHOLTZ RD

62

WILLIAMS RD

Falcon Manor

LOCKPORT RD

CAYUGA DR

PINE AVE

NIAGARA FALLS BLVD

TUSCARORA RD

MILITARY RD

62

190

Pletchers Corners

NEW YORK STATE THRUWAY

PORTER RD

PACKARD RD

190

River

River Road

RIVER ROAD EAST

Sandy Beach

190

LOCKPORT RD

Hyde Park

HYDE PARK BLVD

ONTARIO AVE

PINE AVE

WALNUT AVE

FERRY AVE

62

NIAGARA ST

FALL ST

BUFFALO AVE

PORTAGE RD

ROBERT MOSES PKWY

Niagara Falls, New York

NEW YORK
CANADA

Niagara

NIAGARA PKWY

Chippawa

NIAGARA PKWY

PORTAGE RD

To E

COLLEGE AVE

LEWISTON RD

MAIN ST

10TH ST

QUAY AVE

MAIN ST

3RD ST

A

G

H

F

D

C

B

ROBERT MOSES PKWY

Whirlpool State Park

NIAGARA RIVER BLVD

VICTORIA AVE

Prospect Park

American Falls

Goat Island

Horseshoe Falls

Niagara Falls, Ontario

BRIDGE ST

STANLEY AVE

FERRY ST

Queen Victoria Park

PORTAGE RD

STANLEY AVE

STANLEY AVE

PORTAGE

FERRY

0 SCALE

1.5 MILES

1.5 KILOMETERS

0

ROAD

HIGHWAY

# Sights

- Ⓐ Aquarium of Niagara Falls
- Ⓑ Cave of the Winds
- Ⓒ Goat Island
- Ⓓ *Maid of the Mist*
- Ⓓ New York State Park Observation Tower
- Ⓔ Niagara Power Project Visitor's Center
- Ⓕ Niagara Reservation State Park
- Ⓖ Schoellkopf Geological Museum
- Ⓗ Wintergarden

*Note: Items with the same letter are located in the same town or area.*

## A PERFECT DAY AT NIAGARA FALLS

As many times as you visit the Falls, you'll never tire of a ride on the *Maid of the Mist*, always an exciting experience. A walk through the Niagara Reservation State Park allows close-up views of the brink of the Falls. Flower lovers will enjoy the meticulously maintained formal gardens along the Niagara Parkway on the Canadian side. While on the Canadian side, stop at the Butterfly Conservatory and marvel at the hundreds of amazing butterflies. At night, under the glow of multicolor floodlights, the Falls are even more magical.

## SIGHTSEEING HIGHLIGHTS

★★★ **Goat Island**—This island, part of the state park, offers the closest possible views of the American Falls and the upper rapids. Niagara Viewmobile sightseeing trains can be boarded at several locations on both Goat Island and Prospect Point. Terrapin Point on Goat Island provides a great viewing area for the Horseshoe Falls. Goat Island, Niagara Falls; (716) 285-3891; open daily. Admission free. (1 hour)

★★★ *Maid of the Mist*—President Theodore Roosevelt called a ride on the *Maid of the Mist* boat "the only way fully to realize the Grandeur of the Great Falls of Niagara." Boat rides have been offered since 1846, and there are four *Maid of the Mist* boats that can be boarded on either side of the Falls for a 30-minute ride past the Bridal and American Falls and into the thunderous deluge of the Horseshoe Falls. The powerful engines fight the raging currents, and for a moment it seems as if the world is coming to a watery end. Of course, it's all perfectly safe. Disposable blue raincoats are provided, and you can count on getting wet. Wheelchair accessible. 151 Buffalo Avenue, Niagara Falls; (716) 284-8897; open daily mid-May (depending on the break-up of the ice in the river) through October 24; during the spring and fall open Monday through Friday 10 a.m. to 5 p.m., Saturday and Sunday 10 a.m. to 6 p.m.; third week in June through Labor Day open 9:30 a.m. to 8 p.m. Admission $7.75 adults plus 50 cents for the elevator, $4.25 children ages 6–12, ages 5 and under free. (1 hour)

★★★ **Niagara Reservation State Park**—Opened in 1885, this is the country's first state park and offers close-up views of the Falls as well as the **Great Lakes Garden**. Thousands of flowers, trees, shrubs, and ornamentals make up this colorful garden, which includes a scaled replica of the Great Lakes Region—a living map that makes geography fun for kids. The visitors center houses a restaurant, displays, and hourly showings of *Niagara Wonders*, a fanciful, fun, 20-minute virtual reality

Marshall Brown

*On board* Maid of the Mist, *Niagara Falls*

film projected on a giant 40-by-60-foot curved screen. Prospect Park, Niagara Falls; (716) 278-1770; open daily. Admission free. Parking $4; film $2 adults, $1 children ages 6–12. (2 hours)

★★ **Cave of the Winds**—A guide takes your group, attired in yellow rain slickers, through a tunnel in the rock behind the falls. A web of catwalks and staircases leads to numerous points with astounding views. Rainbows abound here. The last stop, **Hurricane Deck**, is just 25 feet from the Bridal Veil Falls. Spray and mist are ever-present. Goat Island, State Park, Niagara Falls; (716) 278-1730; mid-May through mid-October open daily 9 a.m. to 7 p.m. Admission $5.50 adults, $5 children ages 6–12. (1 hour)

★★ **New York State Park Observation Tower**—An elevator takes visitors to the base of the falls for the *Maid of the Mist* boat ride. There's also an elevator to the top and an open deck that offers a panoramic view of all three falls. Prospect Park, Niagara Falls; (716) 285-3891; July and August open daily 9 a.m. to 11 p.m.; open 9 a.m. to 4:30 p.m. during fall, winter, and spring. Admission 50 cents. (30 minutes)

★ **Aquarium of Niagara Falls**—This attraction, befitting the watery theme of Niagara Falls, showcases marine mammals and sea lions as well as fish and other aquatic creatures who make their homes in the Great Lakes region. Wheelchair accessible. 701 Whirlpool Street, Niagara Falls; (716) 285-3575; open daily 9 a.m. to 5 p.m. Admission $6.25 adults, $4.25 children ages 6–12. (2 hours)

★ **Niagara Power Project Visitor's Center**—This is one of the largest hydroelectric power projects in the world. Displays, computer games, paintings, and more explain the history of electricity. The observation deck offers a great view of the Niagara Gorge below the Falls. Niagara River is world-renowned for salmon, trout, and steelhead fishing; the fishing platform and fish-cleaning station are helpful to successful anglers. Wheelchair accessible. 5777 Lewiston Road, Lewiston; (716) 285-3211; open daily 10 a.m. to 5 p.m. Admission free. (1 hour, unless the fish are biting)

★ **Schoellkopf Geological Museum**—Though often overlooked by visitors to the Falls, this museum tells the 435-million-year geologic history of the Niagara Gorge and the 12,000 years of the Falls' recession. The museum hosts park interpretive walks and programs that enhance your visit. Wheelchair accessible. Robert Moses Parkway, Niagara Falls; (716) 278-1780; Memorial Day through Labor Day open daily 9:30 a.m. to 7 p.m.; Labor Day through October open daily 10 a.m. to 5 p.m.; open Thursday through Sunday 10 a.m. to 5 p.m. rest of year. Closed holidays. Admission 50 cents. (1 hour)

★ **Wintergarden**—This seven-story, indoor tropical garden is just a short walk from the Falls and the state park. It's a popular spot for weddings and, during the winter, an especially welcome escape from the cold. There are ponds, waterfalls, and hundreds of trees and plants. During the **Festival of Lights** (late November through early January), the gardens are decorated with thousands of lights. Wheelchair accessible. Old Falls Street, Niagara Falls; (716) 285-8007; open daily 9 a.m. to 9 p.m. Admission free. (30 minutes)

## FITNESS AND RECREATION

The **Robert Moses Parkway** and the **State Park** offer some of the most spectacular venues for joggers anywhere. On the Canadian side the Niagara Parkway extends from Fort Erie just across the river from Buffalo 35 miles north to Niagara-on-the-Lake. There are jogging and bike paths and bike rentals in Niagara-on-the-Lake.

## FOOD

**John's Flaming Hearth Restaurant**, 1965 Military Road, Niagara Falls, (716) 297-1414, across from the Factory Outlet Mall, is a long-time favorite of residents and visitors alike. Its fine steaks are most popular. For one of the best views of the Falls while dining, try the revolving dining room at the **Skylon Tower**, on the Canadian side, 5200 Robinson Street, Niagara Falls, Ontario, (905) 356-2651. The **Pinnacle Restaurant** offers more great views from the Canadian side in the Minolta Tower Centre, 6732 Oakes Drive, Niagara Falls, Ontario, (905) 356-1501 or (800) 461-2492. On the U.S. side the closest restaurant to the Falls is the **Top of the Falls Restaurant**, Goat Island in the State Park, (716) 278-0337 or (716) 278-0340, open from mid-April through Labor Day. The **Red Coach Inn**, 2 Buffalo Avenue, Niagara Falls, (716) 282-1459, is a popular dining spot overlooking the Upper Rapids. **Clarkson House**, 810 Center Street, Lewiston, (716) 754-4544, in an 1818 landmark building, is especially popular during the Artpark summer theater season.

## LODGING

The price of accommodations varies with the season and the proximity to the Falls. Summer is the high season, and, typically, the closer to the Falls, the more expensive the hotel. Children usually stay free in the room with their parents. If you are driving, you can stay farther afield and still enjoy the Falls. Buffalo is only a 20-minute drive away.

The closest hotel to the Falls is the **Comfort Inn–The Pointe**, 1 Prospect Pointe, (716) 284-6835 or (800) 28HOTEL ($63 to $119 for a double; wheelchair accessible). The **Radisson Hotel Niagara Falls**, Third and Old Falls Street, the largest city hotel, is just a block from the Falls and across from the Convention Center, (716) 285-3361 or (800) 333-3333 ($80 to $140 per night; wheelchair accessible). Other close-by hotels include the **Quality Inn Rainbow Bridge**, 443 Main Street, (716) 284-8801 ($59 to $149); **Holiday Inn**, 231 Third Street, (716) 282-2211 ($69 to $150; wheelchair accessible); **Best Western Inn on the River**, 7001 Buffalo Avenue, (716) 283-7612 or (800) 245-7612 ($72 to $118; wheelchair accessible); and **Ramada Inn at the Falls**, 240 Rainbow Boulevard, (716) 282-1212 ($52 to $125; wheelchair accessible). The **Red Coach Inn**, 2 Buffalo Avenue, overlooking the Upper Rapids, (716) 282-1459 or (800) 282-1459, has suites with fireplaces ($99 to $129).

Less expensive motels on Niagara Falls Boulevard in Niagara Falls include the **Budget Inn/Americana**, 9401 Niagara Falls Boulevard, (716) 297-2660 ($34 to $95; wheelchair accessible); and **Best Western Summit Motor Inn**, 9500 Niagara Falls Boulevard, (716) 297-5050 ($58 to $98; wheelchair accessible). The **International Bed & Breakfast Club Reservation Service**, 7009 Plaza Drive, handles bed and breakfast reservations; call (800) 723-4262. **Hosteling International Niagara Falls**, 1101 Ferry Avenue, Niagara Falls, (716) 282-3700, offers dormitories and rooms for families with a communal kitchen lounge ($13 for members, $16 for non-members).

## CAMPING

There are many good campgrounds in the Niagara Falls area. **Four Mile Creek State Campgrounds**, Route 18, Youngstown ($10 to

# NIAGARA FALLS

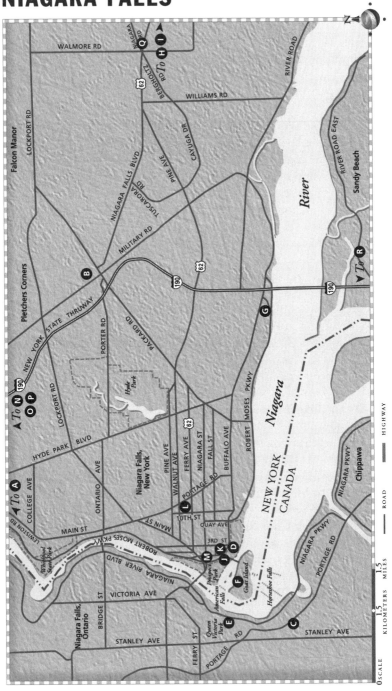

## Food

- Ⓐ Clarkson House
- Ⓑ John's Flaming
  Hearth Restaurant
- Ⓒ Pinnacle Restaurant
- Ⓓ Red Coach Inn
- Ⓔ Skylon Tower
- Ⓕ Top of the Falls Restaurant

## Lodging

- Ⓖ Best Western Inn on the River
- Ⓗ Best Western Summit
  Motor Inn
- Ⓘ Budget Inn/Americana
- Ⓙ Comfort Inn–The Pointe
- Ⓚ Holiday Inn
- Ⓛ Hosteling International
  Niagara Falls

## Lodging (Continued)

- Ⓜ Quality Inn Rainbow Bridge
- Ⓜ Radisson Hotel Niagara Falls
- Ⓚ Ramada Inn at the Falls
- Ⓓ Red Coach Inn

## Camping

- Ⓝ Four Mile Creek
  State Campgrounds
- Ⓞ Golden Hill
  State Park Campgrounds
- Ⓟ Harbor Inn & Campground
- Ⓠ Niagara Falls Campground
- Ⓡ Niagara Falls KOA
- Ⓐ Niagara Falls North KOA

*Note: Items with the same letter are located in the same town or area.*

$12 per night), and **Golden Hill State Park Campgrounds**, 9691 Lower Lake Road, Barker ($9 to $11 per night) are both state parks; reserve your campsite by calling (800) 456-CAMP. Closer to the falls is the **Niagara Falls Campground**, 2405 Niagara Falls Boulevard, Niagara Falls, (716) 731-3434 ($16 per night). On Lake Ontario in the picturesque community of Olcott is the **Harbor Inn & Campground**, 5764 W. Lake Road, (716) 778-5190 ($8 to $15 per night). On Grand Island, south of the Falls, is the **Niagara Falls KOA**, 2570 Grand Island Boulevard, (716) 773-7583 ($18 per night). The **Niagara Falls North KOA**, 1250 Pletcher Road, (716) 754-8013, is in Lewiston ($18 per night).

## NIGHTLIFE

The dazzling **Casino Niagara**, just across the Rainbow Bridge in Canada, is operated by the Canadian government. The casino,

Canada's largest, opened in December 1996 to large crowds and is open 'round-the-clock, seven days a week. **Hard Rock Café** fans have been flocking to the bar-restaurant since its opening in the summer of 1996. The lights stay on at the Falls until midnight during the summer months, making them even more romantic and magical.

## SHOPPING

Factory outlet shopping is popular in Niagara Falls. The **Niagara Factory Outlet Mall**, 1900 Military Road, is one of the country's largest, with more than 150 stores. The **Rainbow Centre Factory Outlet Mall** is just a short walk from the State Park and Falls. Nearby is **Artisans Alley**, with shops representing more than 600 American craftspeople.

## HELPFUL HINTS

July and August are the peak season at Niagara Falls. If you can plan your trip for May or September, you will still be able to enjoy all the attractions and warm weather but with fewer crowds. Beginning the Saturday before Thanksgiving and continuing through early Janurary, the **International Festival of Lights** bills itself as "Niagara's Gift to the World." The festival includes thousands of lights, big name entertainment, animated displays, fireworks, and a dazzling New Year's Eve celebration on both sides of the border. Be sure to bring a photo I.D. and proof of citizenship if you plan to cross the border into Canada.

# Scenic Route: Seaway Trail

From Niagara Falls travel north along the Robert Moses Parkway. The route follows the river and the Seaway Trail, which hugs Lakes Erie and Ontario and the Niagara and St. Lawrence Rivers. In 1996 the Seaway Trail was named one of the top 20 scenic highways in the country by the U.S. Department of Transportation. Stop at **Devil's Hole State Park** or **Whirlpool State Park** to enjoy a picnic, hiking and nature trails, and fishing.

The first village you'll come to is **Lewiston**, where Niagara Falls had its origins 12,000 years ago. In 1974 **Artpark,** the only state park in the United States devoted to the visual and performing arts, was opened on 200 acres overlooking the river. In the summer, musical and theatrical performances are held in the Artpark Theater, with lawn seating and spectacular views of the Niagara River Gorge, especially at sunset. The park is wheelchair accessible. Fishing enthusiasts flock to the fishing dock, which provides access to the world-famous Niagara River fishing.

For many years the **Frontier House**, built in 1824, welcomed weary travelers. It now serves Big Macs as the country's only McDonald's in a registered National Landmark.

## SEAWAY TRAIL

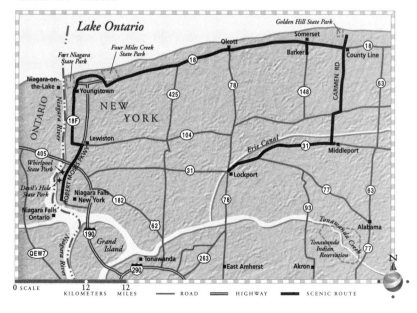

Continue north on Route 18F to **Youngstown**, home to **Fort Niagara State Park** and **Old Fort Niagara**. Located at the mouth of the Niagara River and overlooking Lake Ontario, the fort has a commanding view of the river and lake; on a clear day you can see across Lake Ontario 40 miles to Toronto and its futuristic skyline. Occupied at various times by the French, British, and Americans, the fort's original stone buildings have been preserved in their pre-Revolutionary state. Built in 1726, **French Castle** is the oldest building in the Great Lakes area, and it schedules military reenactments, battles, grand reviews, tent camps, fife-and-drum concerts, and archaeological digs. The fort's proudest possession is a flag captured by the British at Fort Niagara on December 19, 1813. The flag, one of oldest in the country, was returned by Great Britain in 1994.

From Youngstown, continue on Route 18, along the shore of Lake Ontario. Stop in **Olcott Beach**, a pleasant lakeside village with many fishing charters. From there, go to Barker, home to the **Thirty Mile Point Lighthouse** at **Golden Hill State Park**. This 1875 lighthouse, built of hand-carved stone, provides a great view of Lake Ontario. Campsites are available. The lighthouse was honored in 1995 with its own U.S. postal stamp.

From Barker, take Carmen Road, designated the **Niagara Historic Trail**, south to **Middleport**, an historic village on the Erie Canal. There are more cobblestone buildings in this area than anywhere else in the world. This unique form of regional architecture owes its existence to the Erie Canal: After the canal was completed, the English stonemasons who had built the canal needed work and convinced local residents to face their homes with water-rounded stones.

The last stop is **Lockport**, named for the canal locks in town. The best way to experience the locks is to hop on board a canal boat operated by **Lockport Locks & Canal Tours**, which travels through Locks 34 and 35—rising nearly 50 feet to overcome the difference in elevation of the Niagara Escarpment. The boat passes by Lockport's original locks and under the widest bridge in the country. As guests motor along, old canal songs play on the boat's sound system:

*I've got an old mule and her name is Sal*
*Fifteen miles on the Erie Canal.*
*She's a good ol' worker and a good ol' pal*
*Fifteen miles on the Erie Canal.*

At the base of Lock 34 is the **Erie Canal Museum**, which depicts the history of the canal from 1821. ◼

# 12

# BUFFALO

Although it is the second largest city in the state, Buffalo still manages to convey the feeling of an overgrown small town. It is well-situated as a port city at the head of the Niagara River, where Lake Erie empties into the river. The city's fortunes changed forever in 1825, when the Erie Canal opened, linking the city and Lake Erie with the Atlantic Ocean.

Buffalo has the dubious distinction of being "Blizzard City," but much of the snow falls south of the city in the ski country (Syracuse actually beats Buffalo in the snow Olympics). Strong ethnic neighborhoods and identities define Buffalo. This is also a city of taverns and churches, though the taverns are now sedate compared to their character in the nineteenth century, when the 2-block-long Canal Street on the waterfront buzzed with 93 saloons and 15 dance halls. The city has received worldwide recognition for its rich architectural treasures; Allentown, just north of downtown, is one of the nation's largest historic preservation districts. The area also has a strong cultural heritage, with a revitalized theater district.

Buffalo is well-known for its enthusiastic or, some would say, fanatic sports fans. Though one of the smallest markets in the nation, the region regularly leads the National Football League in football attendance, and baseball fans regularly set attendance records in the lovely downtown baseball field. Hockey fans enjoy one of the nation's most dazzling venues, at the new Marine Midland Arena. ◣

# BUFFALO REGION

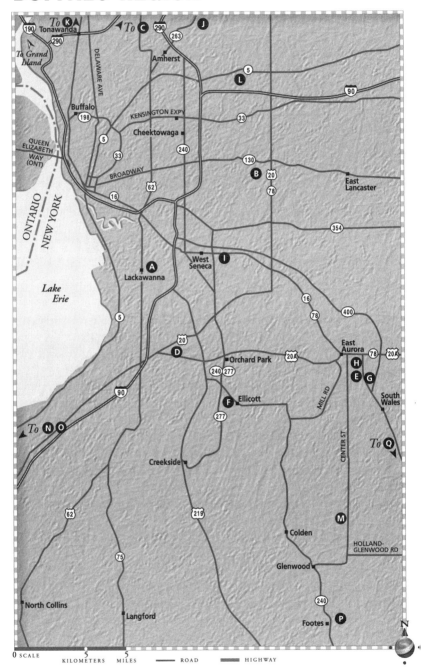

## Sights

Ⓐ Buffalo and Erie County
   Botanical Gardens
Ⓑ Dr. Victor Reinstein Woods
   Nature Preserve
Ⓒ Herschell Carousel Factory
   Museum
Ⓓ Rich Stadium
Ⓔ Toy Town Museum

## Food

Ⓕ Eckl's Beef on
   Weck Restaurant
Ⓖ Old Orchard Inn
Ⓗ Roycroft Inn
Ⓘ Schwabl's Restaurant

## Lodging

Ⓙ Buffalo/Niagara Marriott
Ⓚ Holiday Inn
   Grand Island Resort
Ⓛ Radisson Hotel and Suites
Ⓗ Roycroft Inn

## Camping

Ⓜ Colden Lakes Resort
Ⓝ Evangola State Park
Ⓞ Point Breeze
   Campground and Marina
Ⓟ Sprague Brook Park
Ⓠ Three Valley Campground

## A PERFECT DAY IN BUFFALO

Spend the morning at the Albright-Knox Art Gallery, known world-wide for its superb collection of modern art. If it is a pleasant day, eat lunch at an outside table in the Sculpture Court. The food is great, and the ambiance can't be beat. Enjoy a drive down Delaware Avenue, home to elegant nineteenth- and early-twentieth-century mansions. It's a short distance to the Erie Basin Marina, one of the city's loveliest spots, with a dramatic view of the skyline and gorgeous gardens. Then take a ride aboard *Miss Buffalo*, which cruises the Niagara River and the Black Rock Canal. Spend the evening in the city's Theater District.

## SIGHTSEEING HIGHLIGHTS

★★★ **Albright-Knox Art Gallery**—Though the art in this museum spans the centuries, the modern art collection is considered one of the nation's finest, with magnificent works by the masters of that period. This was the first United States museum to buy works by Picasso and Matisse. Overlooking Hoyt Lake, the museum also has a lovely restaurant and a gift shop. Wheelchair accessible. 1285 Elmwood Avenue, Buffalo; (716) 882-8700; open Tuesday through Saturday 11 a.m. to

5 p.m., Sunday noon to 5 p.m. Admission $4 adults, $3 senior citizens and students, children 12 and under free. (2 hours)

★★★ **Erie Basin Marina**—One of the crown jewels on Buffalo's waterfront, the marina is a popular spot for boaters, water lovers, joggers, and anyone who just enjoys relaxing and watching boats and the Buffalo skyline. The delightful grounds include test gardens for new flowers and lovely rose gardens. There are restaurants here, and it's a great spot for a picnic. 329 Erie Street, Buffalo; (716) 842-4141; open May through October. Admission free. (2 hours)

★★ **Buffalo and Erie County Historical Society**—Housed in the only building left from the Pan-American Exposition of 1901, the museum offers a look into the history of the area. **Bflo Made!** features more than 700 products and inventions created in Buffalo, including Cheerios, the pacemaker, and kazoos. 25 Nottingham Court, Buffalo; (716) 873-9644; open Tuesday through Saturday 10 a.m. to 5 p.m., Sunday noon to 5 p.m. Admission $3.50 adults, $2 seniors, $1.50 children ages 7–15, $7.50 family. (2 hours)

★★ **Buffalo and Erie County Naval and Military Park**—Next to the Erie Basin Marina, this is the largest inland naval park in the country. Climb aboard the U.S.S. *Sullivans*, named in honor of the five Sullivan brothers who lost their lives together in World War II. Tour the decks of the U.S.S. *Little Rock*, a guided missile cruiser, and the U.S.S. *Croaker*, a battle-decorated World War II submarine, where it definitely paid to be small. There's also a military museum. 1 Naval Park Cove, Buffalo; (716) 847-1773; April through October open daily 10 a.m. to 5 p.m., November open weekends only. Admission $6 adults, $3.50 seniors and children ages 6–16. (2 hours)

★★ *Miss Buffalo* and *Niagara Clipper* **Cruise Boats**—The perfect way to learn about of the role of Lake Erie and the Niagara River in the development of this port city is to take a cruise on *Miss Buffalo* or *Niagara Clipper*. The boats pass through the historic Black Rock Lock and Canal, by the 1833 lighthouse, Old Fort Erie, and the Peace Bridge, one of the world's busiest international bridges. Wheelchair accessible. 79 Marine Drive, Buffalo; (716) 856-6696; July and August cruises Tuesday through Sunday at 3 p.m., Friday and Saturday also at 8 p.m., weekends also at 12:30 p.m.; June and

September cruises only weekends at 3 p.m. Admission for afternoon cruises is $9 adults, $6.50 children under 12; evening cruises $15. (3 hours)

**★★ North AmeriCare Park**—Home to Triple "A" Buffalo Bison Baseball, the ballpark has received national recognition for its design, and it regularly breaks season attendance records. Many games are happenings, with pre- and post-game parties, fireworks, and concerts. It's an affordable, fun way for families to attend a baseball game. Wheelchair accessible. 275 Washington Street, Buffalo; (716) 846-2000; seasonal, April through September. Admission $4.25 to $8.25. (4 hours)

**★★ Rich Stadium**—A must-see for football fans, Rich Stadium is where the greatest comeback in the history of the National Football League was staged, by the Buffalo Bills under the leadership of backup quarterback Frank Reich. The Bills were down 35–3 to the Houston Oilers. Many fans left the stadium in despair and disgust. The Bills came back to win 41-38 in an overtime victory. Of course, it was also here that running back O.J. Simpson ran into the history books and earned a place in the Football Hall of Fame.

Parking lots start filling early because tailgating has become as much a part of the festivities as the game itself. Some tailgaters bring elaborate menus, while others are content with standard picnic fare in a cooler. There's music, footballs for impromptu touch football games, and area radio stations broadcasting live from the lots. Wheelchair accessible. 1 Bills Drive, Orchard Park; (716) 649-0015; Sunday, September through December. Admission $26 or $34. (4 hours)

**★ Buffalo and Erie County Botanical Gardens**—Flower lovers flock to these gardens year-round, but they are especially wonderful during the winter when everything is white outside. The glass conservatory is listed on the State and National Register of Historic Places. 2655 S. Park Avenue at McKinley Parkway, Buffalo; (716) 696-3555; open Monday through Friday 9 a.m. to 4 p.m., Saturday and Sunday 9 a.m. to 5 p.m. Admission free. (1 hour)

**★ Buffalo Zoological Gardens**—Though limited in size compared to some of the country's more expansive zoos, this is the nation's third-oldest zoo and home to more than 1,000 animals. Many are displayed in settings that simulate their natural environments. The zoo contains a children's zoo, gift shop, and picnic area. 300 Parkside Avenue, Buffalo; (716) 837-3900; spring and summer open daily 10 a.m. to 5 p.m.; fall and winter open daily 10 a.m. to 4:30 p.m. Admission $6 adults, $3 seniors and children ages 4–16. (3 hours)

★ **Dr. Victor Reinstein Woods Nature Preserve**—It is thanks to Dr. Reinstein, a land developer, that this 290-acre preserve exists at all. Located in one of the area's most developed suburbs, there are 65 acres of primeval forest within the preserve that existed before the first European settlement of the area in the 1820s. Visitors are allowed only on guided walks, where they will likely spot deer, great blue herons, and other birds. 77 Honorine Drive, Depew; (716) 683-5959; May through August guided walks on Wednesday and Saturday (except the first Saturday of the month) at 9 a.m. and 1 p.m.; rest of year walks at 9 a.m. only. Admission free. (1½ hours)

★ **Herschell Carousel Factory Museum**—Allan Herschell was the best-known carousel maker in the United States. This museum showcasing his work is filled with hand-carved wooden carousel figures. Children delight in riding the 1916 hand-carved wooden carousel. 180 Thompson Street, North Tonawanda; (716) 693-1885; July and August open daily 11 a.m. to 5 p.m.; open Wednesday through Sunday 1 p.m. to 5 p.m. rest of year. Closed January and February. Admission $3 adults, $1.50 children ages 2–12. (2 hours)

★ **Theodore Roosevelt Inaugural National Historic Site**—If you are a Teddy Roosevelt fan, you'll enjoy a visit to this home in the heart of the elegant and historic Delaware Avenue neighborhood. Theodore Roosevelt was inaugurated here as the 26th president on September 14, 1901, following the assassination of President William McKinley. The Teddy Bear Picnic is held here in August, and the Victorian Christmas celebration is in December. 641 Delaware Avenue, Buffalo; (716) 884-0095; open Monday through Friday 9 a.m. to 5 p.m., Saturday and Sunday noon to 5 p.m. Admission $3 adults, $2 seniors, $1 children ages 6–14, $6.50 family. (1 hour)

★ **Toy Town Museum**—Children and adults who love toys will be amazed at this Fisher-Price toy collection in the hometown of the toy giant. The museum features many rare and one-of-a-kind toys. Toys are on display—not available for play. 636 Girard Avenue, East Aurora;

(716) 687-5151; open Monday through Saturday 10 a.m. to 4 p.m.
Admission free. (1 hour)

## FITNESS AND RECREATION

During the warmer weather the **Erie Basin Marina** is a favorite place
for joggers. The Frederick Law Olmsted–designed **Delaware Park** is
another popular jogging area. The **Riverwalk**, which follows the river
from downtown Buffalo north, is also another good jogging route.
**Chestnut Ridge Park**, in Orchard Park, offers wonderful trails and a
great view of Buffalo and Lake Erie.

## FOOD

Buffalo is well-known for local and ethnic specialties, including Buffalo
chicken wings and beef on weck sandwiches (thinly sliced beef on a fresh
kimmelweck roll with a dash of horseradish). The **Anchor Bar**, 1047
Main Street, Buffalo, (716) 886-8920, is the birthplace of the wings.
**Eckl's Beef on Weck Restaurant**, 4936 Ellicott Road, Orchard Park,
(716) 662-2262, and **Schwabl's Restaurant**, 789 Center Road, West
Seneca, (716) 674-9821, are well-known for the beef dish. For the best in
steak, try **E. B. Green's Steakhouse**, 2 Fountain Plaza, Buffalo, (716)
855-4870. **Chef's Restaurant**, 291 Seneca Street, Buffalo, (716) 856-
9187, is a long-time favorite for Italian food, within a few blocks of both
the baseball park and the hockey arena.

Visit the **Roycroft Inn**, 40 S. Grove Street, East Aurora, (716) 652-
5552, to see the wondrous $8-million restoration and enjoy a fine meal.
Nearby is the **Old Orchard Inn**, 2095 Blakeley Road, East Aurora, (716)
652-4664, offering beautiful home-in-the-country ambiance. For a
romantic French meal, try **Rue Franklin Restaurant**, 341 Franklin
Street, Buffalo, (716) 852-4416. The **Towne Restaurant**, 186 Allen
Street, Buffalo, (716) 884-5128, in the heart of historic Allentown, offers
plentiful Greek food at reasonable prices.

## LODGING

Buffalo area hotels are mostly centered downtown in the area around
the airport, and in the rapidly growing suburb of Amherst, home to the
State University of New York at Buffalo. Many offer special weekend
and other package plans, so be sure to ask for the best rates.

# BUFFALO

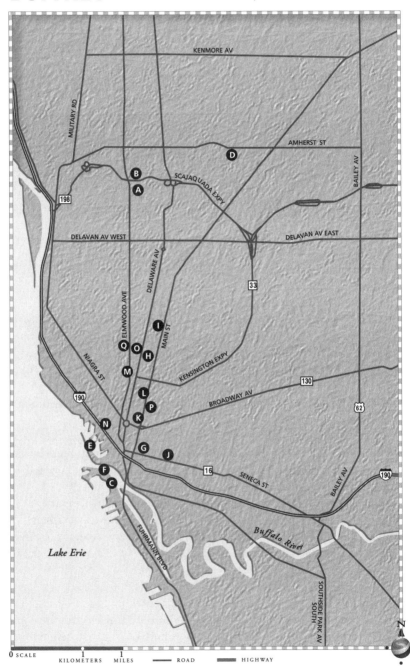

## Sights

**(A)** Albright-Knox Art Gallery

**(B)** Buffalo and Erie County Historical Society

**(C)** Buffalo and Erie County Naval and Military Park

**(D)** Buffalo Zoological Gardens

**(E)** Erie Basin Marina

**(F)** *Miss Buffalo* and *Niagra Clipper* Cruise Boats

**(G)** North AmeriCare Park

**(H)** Theodore Roosevelt Inaugural National Historic Site

## Food

**(I)** Anchor Bar

**(J)** Chef's Restaurant

**(K)** E. B. Green's Steakhouse

**(L)** Rue Franklin Restaurant

**(M)** Towne Restaurant

## Lodging

**(N)** Buffalo Hilton

**(O)** Holiday Inn Downtown

**(P)** Hostel Downtown Buffalo

**(Q)** Hotel Lenox

**(K)** Hyatt Regency Buffalo

**(P)** Radisson Suites Downtown

*Note: Items with the same letter are located in the same town or area.*

Downtown, the major hotels include the **Buffalo Hilton**, 120 Church Street, Buffalo, (716) 845-5100 or (800) 445-8667, with many rooms with good views of the lake and river ($99 to $139 for a double; wheelchair accessible). Nearby is the **Hyatt Regency Buffalo**, 2 Fountain Plaza, Buffalo, (716) 856-1234 or (800) 233-1234, which began life as the E. B. Green–designed Genesee Building and retains much of the early architectural charm ($89 to $164 for a double; wheelchair accessible). Down the street is the **Radisson Suites Downtown**, 601 Main Street, Buffalo, (716) 854-5500. The suites are popular with business travelers and families ($79 to $125 for a double; wheelchair accessible). **Holiday Inn Downtown**, 620 Delaware Avenue, (716) 886-2121, offers rooms with breakfast included ($89 for a double; wheelchair accessible). Around the corner is the **Hotel Lenox**, 140 North Street, Buffalo, (716) 884-1700, popular with visitors on extended stays. Many rooms have kitchenettes (doubles begin at $69). Also downtown is the new **Hostel Downtown Buffalo**, 667 Main Street, (716) 852-5222, where rooms are $15 per night for Hosteling International members and $18 for non-members. Guests share a communal kitchen, laundry room, and lounges in the historic renovated building (wheelchair accessible).

The **Roycroft Inn**, 40 S. Grove Street, East Aurora, (716) 652-5552, reopened in 1995 after an award-winning $8-million restoration true to its founder, Elbert Hubbard ($120 to $210 for a suite; wheelchair accessible). At the airport, **Radisson Hotel and Suites**, 4243 Genesee Street, Cheektowaga, (716) 634-2300 or (800) 333-3333, offers doubles for $69 to $102 (wheelchair accessible). The **Holiday Inn Grand Island Resort**, 100 Whitehaven Road, Grand Island, (716) 773-1111, has a golf course, pools, and a grand location on the Niagara River ($59 to $129 for a double; wheelchair accessible). In Amherst, the **Buffalo/Niagara Marriott**, 1340 Millersport Highway, Amherst, (716) 689-6900 or (800) 228-9290, is a long-time favorite ($69 to $129 for a double; wheelchair accessible).

## CAMPING

**Colden Lakes Resort**, 9504 Heath Road, Colden, (716) 941-5530, is open May through October ($15 to $20 per night). **Evangola State Park**, on the shores of Lake Erie, Shaw Road, Irving, (716) 549-1760 or (800) 456-CAMP, is open May 15 through October 15 ($10 to $12 per night). **Three Valley Campground**, Route 16, Holland, (716) 537-2372, is open May 1 through October 15 ($15 per night). **Sprague Brook Park**, 9674 Foote Road, Glenwood, (716) 592-2804, is open year-round ($9 to $12 per night). **Point Breeze Campground and Marina**, also on Lake Erie, 9456 Lake Shore Road, Angola, (716) 549-3768, is open April 15 through October 15 ($20 to $23 per night).

## NIGHTLIFE

Buffalo's downtown theater district is thriving. **Shea's Performing Arts Center**, 646 Main Street, (716) 847-0850, was built in 1926 and is one of the finest movie palaces of its period. It presents the best of Broadway touring shows, concerts, operas, dance, and children shows. **Studio Arena Theatre**, 710 Main Street, (716) 856-5650 or (800) 77-STAGE, is the only professional regional theater company and has served as the showcase for many of America's stage stars. **Pfeifer Theatre**, 681 Main Street, (716) 847-6461, stages performances in the intimate theater. **Marquee at the Tralf**, 100 Theatre Place, (716) 852-0522, is a first-class nightclub in the heart of the district. Nearby is the acoustically perfect **Kleinhans Music Hall**, home to the renowned Buffalo Philharmonic Orchestra, 71 Symphony Circle, (716) 885-5000.

# 13

# CHAUTAUQUA COUNTY

C hautauqua County takes its name from its largest lake, called "Jad-dah-gwah" by the Native Americans. The county follows the shores of Lake Erie south of Buffalo to the border of Pennsylvania.

The area's focal point for many visitors is the Chautauqua Institution. Established in 1874 as a training center for Sunday school teachers, the Institution rapidly grew into a summer-long cultural camp. The center for arts, education, religion, and recreation boasts a full complement of schools and day camps, a lecture series, and top-name performances in its 5,000-seat amphitheater. President Clinton chose Chautauqua as a weekend to retreat study for his presidential debates with Senator Robert Dole. President Teddy Roosevelt, who visited five times and enjoyed muskie fishing, called it "the most American place in America." In keeping with the nineteenth-century atmosphere, a paddlewheeler, the *Chautauqua Belle*, offers cruises around the lake.

At nearby Cassadaga Lake is the Lily Dale Assembly, the country's largest spiritualist center, which began in 1879. Other regional high-lights include the Amish community in the Conewango Valley; the Chautauqua Wine Trail; Westfield, the self-proclaimed Grape Juice Capital of the world and home to Welch's Foods; and historic Fre-donia, the one-time Seed Capital of the United States. During July and August, Fredonia State College is a popular spot for football fans because it hosts the Buffalo Bills' summer camp. Jamestown, home-town of actress and comedienne Lucille Ball, houses the Lucille Ball–Desi Arnaz Center and the Lucille Ball Festival of New Comedy. ◤

# CHAUTAUQUA COUNTY

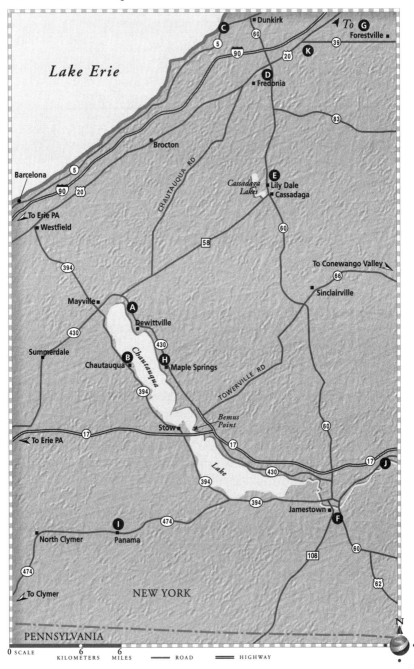

Dunkirk

To **G**
Forestville

**C**

**K**

Lake Erie

**D**
Fredonia

Brocton

Cassadaga
Lakes
**E** Lily Dale
Cassadaga

Barcelona

To Erie PA
Westfield

CHAUTAUQUA RD

Mayville
**A**
Dewittville

Summerdale

**B** Chautauqua
Chautauqua
**H** Maple Springs

To Conewango Valley

Sinclairville

TOWERVILLE RD

To Erie PA
Stow

Bemus
Point

Lake

**J**

North Clymer
**I**
Panama

Jamestown
**F**

To Clymer

NEW YORK

PENNSYLVANIA

N

0 SCALE    6       6
   KILOMETERS   MILES         ROAD           HIGHWAY

# Sights

- Ⓐ *Chautauqua Belle*
- Ⓑ Chautauqua Institution
- Ⓒ Dunkirk Lighthouse and Veteran's Park Museum
- Ⓓ Fredonia Opera House
- Ⓔ Lily Dale Assembly
- Ⓕ Lucille Ball–Desi Arnaz Museum
- Ⓖ Merritt Estate Winery
- Ⓗ Midway Park
- Ⓘ Panama Rocks
- Ⓙ Roger Tory Peterson Institute
- Ⓚ Woodbury Vineyards

## A PERFECT DAY IN CHAUTAUQUA

Get an early start to try to catch the wily muskie or lake trout on Chautauqua Lake. There are many choices for classes and activities if you are staying at the Chautauqua Institution, but the morning lectures at the amphitheater are usually thought-provoking. The *Chautauqua Belle* offers an ideal way to see the lake. Afterwards, there's time for a swim before dinner. The dining room at the Athenaeum Hotel is a long-time favorite. Ordering two desserts is standard, perfect for someone with a sweet tooth. The rocking chairs on the hotel porch provide an ideal way relax and watch the lake before an evening concert in the amphitheater.

## SIGHTSEEING HIGHLIGHTS

★★★ **Chautauqua Institution**—Many people spend the entire nine-week summer season on the grounds of this unique center for the arts, religion, sports, and education. But visitors are also welcome for a day, evening, weekend, or week. Admission is by gate ticket, and, in keeping with the Institution's religious heritage, Sundays are free. The 750-acre Victorian village is a National Historic Landmark and has been welcoming visitors interested in a learning vacation on the shore of Chautauqua Lake since 1874.

The season is filled with classes, concerts, opera, plays, and big name entertainers. The 5,000-seat amphitheater overflows on Sundays for the morning religious services, during the day for lectures, and in the evening for concerts. The Institution is also home to the oldest book club in America, and the grounds offer golf, tennis, sailing, hiking, swimming, and fishing. Some hotels and the bookstore are open during the off-season, and it's a popular spot for cross-country skiing. Route 394, Chautauqua; (716) 357-6200 or (800) 836-ARTS; summer season from late June through August. No charge for entrance during off-season. (1 day)

★★ *Chautauqua Belle*—The *Chautauqua Belle* is one of only three genuine steam-powered boats east of the Mississippi River. In the 1880s and 1890s, the steamboats, called the "Great White Fleet," could each carry as many as 3,000 passengers up and down 16-mile-long Chautauqua Lake. The *Chautauqua Belle*, a much smaller version of the nineteenth- century behemoths, comfortably accommodates 120 passengers. It's painted a festive blue and white with an enormous red paddlewheel powered by steam, sending the wheel around 18 times per minute. 15 Water Street, Mayville; (716) 753-2403 or (800) 753-2506; June through September the *Belle* departs daily from Mayville at 11 a.m., 1:15 p.m., and 3 p.m. Admission $12 adults, $6 children ages 6–12. (2 hours)

★★ **Midway Park**—If you like amusement parks, you'll love Midway Park, a throwback to another era. It opened in the summer of 1898. Admission is free, unlike just about every other park in the country. Visitors enjoy miniature golf, a roller rink, bumper boats, an arcade, a beach, and docking facilities (you can come by boat). Route 430, Maple Springs; (716) 386-3165; late May through late June open weekends; late June through Labor Day open Tuesday through Sunday. Closed Monday, except holidays. Admission free; charges on a per-ride basis. (5 hours)

★ **Dunkirk Historic Lighthouse and Veteran's Park Museum**—This lighthouse on the shores of Lake Erie offers a great view of the lake and surrounding countryside. The museum has 11 rooms of displays on maritime history and military service. 1 Lighthouse Point Drive, Dunkirk; (716) 366-5050; July and August open daily 10 a.m. to 4 p.m.; April through June and September through November open every day except Wednesday and Sunday, 10 a.m. to 3 p.m. Admission $4.50. (1½ hours)

★ **Fredonia Opera House**—This beautifully restored nineteenth-century theater adds to the ambiance of this historic village. 9–11 Church Street; (716) 679-1891; open Monday through Friday 10 a.m. to 5 p.m. Theater offers live performances and films during the evening. Admission $2 for tours. (1 hour)

★ **Lily Dale Assembly**—This is the world's largest Spiritualist community, where you can have your fortune told or your palms read or attend daily clairvoyance demonstrations, lectures, or healing workshops. Located on the shores of Cassadaga Lake, the Assembly features a bookstore, museum, library, and overnight accommodations. 5 Melrose Park, Lily Dale; (716) 595-8721; open daily late June through early September. Admission $5. (3 hours)

★ **Lucille Ball–Desi Arnaz Museum**—Named in honor of the Jamestown native, this center has received strong support from Lucille Ball's family. The museum is filled with interactive displays and Lucy memorabilia donated by her family. Each Memorial Day weekend the community sponsors the Festival of New Comedy, with films and new comedy acts. 212 Pine Street, Jamestown; (716) 484-7070; open Monday through Friday noon to 5 p.m., Saturday 11 a.m. to 5 p.m., Sunday 1 p.m. to 5 p.m. Admission $5 adults, $3.50 seniors and students. The comedy festival is held at the **Reg Lenna Civic Center**, 116 E. Third Street, Jamestown; (716) 484-7070. Admission varies for festival programs. (2 hours)

★ **Merritt Estate Winery**—This winery hosts a variety of special events and festivals throughout the year, including strawberry and fall festivals. Free tours and tastings. 2264 King Road, Forestville; (716) 965-4800; open Monday through Saturday 10 a.m. to 5 p.m., Sunday 1 p.m. to 5 p.m. (1 hour)

★ **Panama Rocks**—It's always cool in this private park filled with towering rocks, crevice passageways, and deep cavernous dens. Walk along the hiking path through lush forests. Native Americans used these rocks and caves for shelter long before the arrival of French explorers in the mid-1600s. Local legend has it that there is a gold shipment buried somewhere here, hidden and then lost by the robbers of a nearby bank. Special programs include a Folk Fair and Fall Foliagefest. 11 Rock Hill Road, Panama; (716) 782-2845; May through October 20 open daily 10 a.m. to 5 p.m. Admission $3 adults, $2 children ages 6–12. (3 hours)

★ **Roger Tory Peterson Institute**—Named in honor of the late Roger Tory Peterson, who grew up in this area and published his first *Field Guild to the Birds* in 1934, the institute sponsors nature training workshops and programs. The fieldstone exterior and rough-sawn siding on the building, as well as the use of wood interiors, complement the meadows and woods that surround it. The area retains the rural character that Dr. Peterson knew as a boy, with woods and fields to roam in search of birds, butterflies, and moths. Regular exhibits include wildlife photography and paintings. Roger Tory Peterson served as the honorary chairman of the board until his death in 1996. 311 Curtiss Street, Jamestown; (716) 665-2473; open Tuesday through Saturday 10 a.m. to 4 p.m., Sunday and most holidays 1 p.m. to 5 p.m. Admission varies with exhibits but usually $3 adults, $2 seniors, $1 students and children. (2 hours)

**Woodbury Vineyards**—This winery produces award-winning wines and offers free samples and tours. South Roberts Road, Dunkirk; (716) 679-WINE; open daily 10 a.m. to 5 p.m., Sunday noon to 5 p.m. (1 hour)

## FITNESS AND RECREATION

Early morning walks at the **Chautauqua Institution** are delightful, and the mostly car-free 750-acre village makes an ideal spot for jogging or cross-country skiing in the winter. The 73-acre **Thayer Road Overview Park** escarpment is more than 1,000 feet above Lake Erie. Hiking trails include a viewing station accessible to those with disabilities. On a clear day you can see the Buffalo skyline and Canadian shoreline. The **French Creek Preserve** is a nature preserve with easily accessible, self-guided trails. The **Westside Overland Trail**, a part of the **National Trail System**, begins just outside Mayville and extends 25.5 miles south into Panama.

## FOOD

The **Athenaeum Hotel**, South Lake Drive, Chautauqua, (716) 357-4444 or (800) 821-1881, on the grounds of the Chautauqua Institution, welcomes the public to its old-fashioned, elegant dining room overlooking the lake. No alcohol is served, but two desserts are standard. In Bemus Point, both the **Italian Fisherman**, 61 Lakeside Drive, (716) 386-7000, and **Ye Hare'n Hound Inn**, 64 Lakeside Drive, (716) 386-2181, overlook the lake and are popular dining spots. Close to the lake in Stow is **Good Morning Farm**, Route 17, (716) 763-1773, which serves fresh food in a 150-year-old restored farmhouse. **Webb's**, West Lake Road, Mayville, (716) 753-3960, overlooks the lake and offers several dining rooms, including an outdoor deck. **Lazzaroni's Lakeside Expresso Bar & Restaurant**, 282 Dale Drive, Cassadaga, (716) 595-2557, offers fine dining on Cassadaga Lakes. Nearby is the **White Horse Inn**, Route 60, Cassadaga, (716) 595-3523, with good food in a friendly setting. A welcome idea: optional smaller portions at reduced prices for all ages. The **White Inn**, 52 E. Main Street, Fredonia, (716) 672-2103, has a reputation for fine dining and a delectable chocolate cake. Close to Amish Country and across from Cockaigne Ski Area is the **Grainery Restaurant**, 1494 County Route 66, Cherry Creek, (716) 287-3500, with fresh food from the area served in a century-old converted barn.

# LODGING

The grounds of the Chautauqua Institution have a wide variety of accommodations, including hotels, inns, guest houses, rooms, condos, apartments, private homes, and denominational houses operated by various Protestant denominations. Call (800) 836-ARTS or (716) 357-6200 for information and a directory. **Chautauqua Lake Vacation Rentals**, (716) 789-2600 or (800) 344-2198, lists more than 125 homes, condos, cottages, and townhouses for rent. Many are on the Institution grounds. Everyone staying on the Institution grounds needs a gate ticket (except children under 12 and adults 90 and over).

The venerable **Athenaeum Hotel**, South Lake Drive, Chautauqua, (716) 357-4444 or (800) 821-1881, is the grande dame of Chautauqua hotels, wired for electricity by Thomas Alva Edison himself, son-in-law of one of the founders. It welcomes guests on the American Plan only—breakfast, lunch, and dinner, with two desserts at lunch and dinner, of course ($215 to $314 for a double, includes meals). The **William Baker Hotel**, 14 S. Lake Drive, Chautauqua, (716) 357-2805 or (800) 522-2805, is also on the Institution grounds and has a loyal following ($84 to $120 for a double). **Plumbush**, P.O. Box 864, Chautauqua, (716) 789-3093, is a charming bed and breakfast just a mile from the Institution gates and adjacent to the golf course ($75 to $100). **We Wan Chu Cottages**, Route 394, Chautauqua, (716) 789-3383, is a mile from the Institution and on the lake. All cottages have kitchens. Weekly rates only during summer ($480 to $750) and minimum two nights otherwise ($125 to $270).

In Bemus Point, on Chautauqua Lake, the **Hotel Lenhart**, 20–22 Lakeside Drive, Bemus Point, (716) 386-2715, has a long history and wonderful rocking chairs on the porch painted in primary colors ($44

# CHAUTAUQUA COUNTY

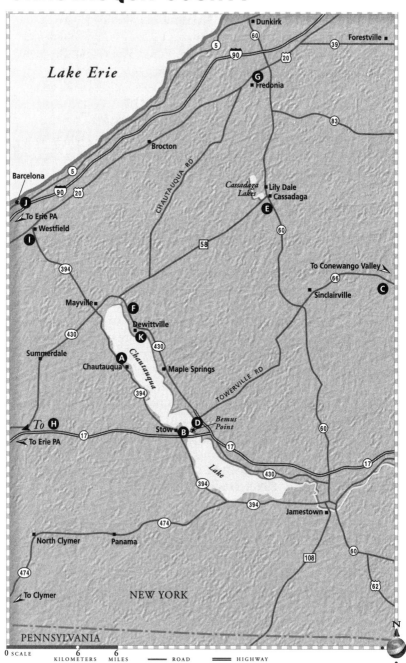

Lake Erie

Dunkirk
Forestville
Fredonia G
Brocton
Barcelona
To Erie PA
Westfield
Cassadaga Lakes
Lily Dale
Cassadaga E
To Conewango Valley
Sinclairville
C
Mayville
Dewittville
F
K
Summerdale
Chautauqua A
Maple Springs
TOWERVILLE RD
Bemus Point
To H
Stow B D
To Erie PA
Lake
Jamestown
North Clymer
Panama
NEW YORK
To Clymer
PENNSYLVANIA

CHAUTAUQUA RD

0 SCALE 6 6
KILOMETERS MILES ROAD HIGHWAY

N

## Food

Ⓐ Athenaeum Hotel

Ⓑ Good Morning Farm

Ⓒ Grainery Restaurant

Ⓓ Italian Fisherman

Ⓔ Lazzaroni's Lakeside Expresso
Bar & Restaurant

Ⓕ Webb's

Ⓔ White Horse Inn

Ⓖ White Inn

Ⓓ Ye Hare'n Hound Inn

## Lodging

Ⓐ Athenaeum Hotel

Ⓓ Hotel Lenhart

Ⓗ Peek 'n Peak Resort and
Conference Center

## Lodging (Continued)

Ⓐ Plumbush

Ⓕ Webb's Year-Round Resort

Ⓐ We Wan Chu Cottages

Ⓖ White Inn

Ⓐ William Baker Hotel

Ⓘ William Seward Inn

## Camping

Ⓙ Blue Water Beach
Campground

Ⓑ Camp Chautauqua

Ⓚ Chautauqua Heights
Campground

Ⓙ Westfield-Lake Erie KOA

*Note: Items with the same letter are located in the same town or area.*

to $127 for a double). At the other end of the lake is **Webb's Year-Round Resort**, 115 W. Lake Road, Mayville, (716) 753-2161. Rates vary with the season ($59 to $229). The **White Inn**, 52 East Main Street, Fredonia, (716) 672-2103, has been beautifully restored ($59 to $159 a night). The **William Seward Inn**, 6645 South Portage, Westfield, (716) 326-4151 or (800) 338-4151, was the one-time home of Seward, the secretary of state under President Lincoln who was credited with buying Alaska ($85 to $175). **Peek 'n Peak Resort & Conference Center**, 1405 Olde Road, Clymer, (716) 355-4141, offers a hotel and condos, a ski resort, golf course, and conference facilities ($85 to $235 at hotel, $75 to $335 a night at condo).

## CAMPING

Camping is popular in the Chautauqua area. Most campgrounds are open mid-April through October. **Camp Chautauqua** is on Chautauqua Lake, in Stow, (716) 789-3435 ($20 to $30 per night).

**Blue Water Beach Campground**, 7364 E. Lake Road, Westfield, (716) 326-3540, is also on the lake ($18 per night). Nearby is the **Westfield-Lake Erie KOA**, 8001 Route 5, Westfield, (716) 326-3573 ($19 to $23 a night). **Chautauqua Heights Campground**, 5652 Thumb Road, Dewittville, (716) 386-3804, isn't on the lake but does have a pool ($12 to $22.50 per night).

## NIGHTLIFE

There are concerts, operas, ballet, plays, and other programs every evening during the nine-week season at the **Chautauqua Institution**; call (716) 357-6200 or (800) 836-ARTS for reservations or program information. In keeping with its Methodist origins, no alcohol is sold on the grounds, although people may partake in their rooms or homes. The absence of alcohol adds to the genteel atmosphere of the Institution.

# 14

## CATTARAUGUS COUNTY

The name "Cattaraugus" traces its roots to the Native Americans who still live in the area. The county is home to the only city in the nation on Native American lands, and the Seneca Indian Nation, a branch of the Iroquois, has a proud history, chronicled at the Seneca-Iroquois National Museum.

Allegany State Park, New York's largest state park, annually attracts hundreds of thousands of visitors, who come to camp, hike the trails, swim in the two lakes, fish in the streams, ponds, and lakes, snowmobile, cross-country ski, hunt, ride horses, and just take in nature's bountiful beauty. Adjoining the park is the Allegheny Reservoir, which spans the New York–Pennsylvania border. Holiday Valley, in the historic and picturesque village of Ellicottville, is a thriving year-round resort. But it really comes alive during the winter, when skiers flock to the state's largest ski center.

Artists have long been drawn to the peace and serenity of the area. Griffis Sculpture Park is a private park that welcomes visitors to picnic and hike amidst more than 200 colossal sculptures. Surprisingly, one of the country's major herds of buffalo grazes on a ranch just outside Ellicottville. The state's largest community of old-order Amish people live here, forsaking all modern conveniences. Many sell their unique furniture, quilts, and baked goods from their homes. ◪

# CATTARAUGUS COUNTY

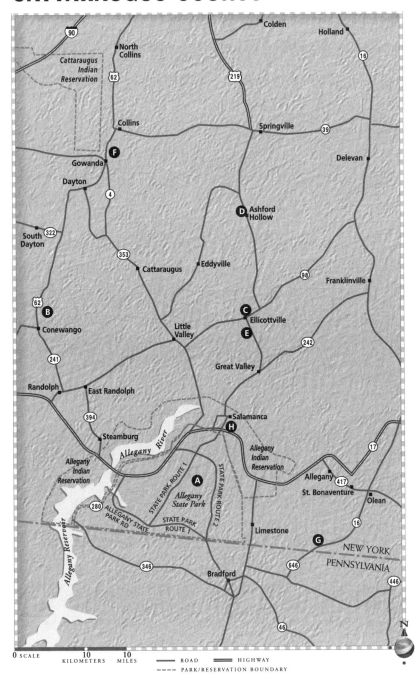

## Sights

Ⓐ  Allegany State Park

Ⓑ  Amish Community

Ⓒ  B&B Buffalo Ranch

Ⓓ  Griffis Sculpture Park

Ⓔ  Holiday Valley

Ⓒ  Nannen Arboreteum

Ⓕ  New York and Lake Erie
     Railroad

Ⓖ  Rock City Park

Ⓗ  Salamanca Rail Museum

Ⓗ  Seneca-Iroquois
     National Museum

*Note: Items with the same letter are located in the same town or area.*

## A PERFECT DAY IN CATTARAUGUS COUNTY

Though this area is blessed with a bountiful snowfall and winter is a favorite season for many, it's hard to match a fine fall day, when the hillsides are ablaze with color. There's no better place for a brisk morning hike than Allegany State Park. Park rangers lead guided nature walks. Stop at the Red House administrative building for a trail map and pick a route. Afterwards, take a drive through Amish Country, in the western section of the county. Largely undiscovered by tourists, the Amish area has road signs illustrated with a buggy, warning motorists that they now share the roads with horse-drawn vehicles. In the evening head to Ellicottville, an historic village that has been called "the Aspen of the East," filled with restaurants, inns, shops, and boutiques. It's the perfect spot for dinner and after-dinner drinks in one of the many nightspots, always busy on weekends.

## SIGHTSEEING HIGHLIGHTS

★★★ **Allegany State Park**—The largest state park has more than 65,000 acres along the Pennsylvania border. The park is surrounded on three sides by the Allegheny Indian Reservation. It's a beautiful and wild land with mountains, streams, and lakes. The Erie and Seneca Indian Nations once lived here; *Allegany* is an Indian word meaning "beautiful waters." Despite Allegany's popularity, it's possible to find solitude here. Wildlife you might spot include deer, wild turkey, pheasant, raccoon, and even bear. Red House and Quaker are the two main recreational areas.

The park has two 100-acre lakes with sand beaches and lifeguards,

80 miles of hiking trails, and cross-country skiing and snowmobile trails. Nearly 400 cabins (130 of them are winterized) are available, as well as three restaurants; a camp store; and bicycles, rowboats, and paddleboats for rent. A variety of seasonal programs attracts visitors to the park. During January the highlight is the Trappers Special Sled dog races, and in February the Winter Funfest welcomes snowmobilers and anyone interested in taking a ride. Snowmobile trails connect with Pennsylvania trails. Be sure your snowmobile is registered in both states if you are crossing the border. Off Route 17, Salamanca; (716) 354-2535 or (800) 456-CAMP for camping reservations; open year-round. Admission $4 per car during summer (late June through Labor Day), otherwise free. (5 hours)

★★★ **Holiday Valley**—This is the state's largest ski resort, with 52 slopes and 12 lifts, including the **Mardi Gras Express High Speed Quad**. The resort has grown tremendously since it opened in 1957. An average 210 inches of snowfall, supplemented by a snowmaking system, cover the slopes and trails, insuring skiers a long ski season. During the winter of 1995–96, the resort opened on November 16 and stayed open until April 14, a record 151 days of skiing. The resort encompasses a snowboard park, cross-country ski trails, a complete ski school for adults and children, and a licensed childcare center. Condos and townhouses built on the slopes allow guests the freedom to ski in and ski out their front door. When the season is over, visitors enjoy an 18-hole golf course, a three-pool complex, hiking, and mountain bike trails. Holiday Valley Resort, Ellicottville; (716) 699-2345; open daily 8:30 a.m. to 10:30 p.m. Admission $21 to $35 for lift ticket depending on day of week and time of day. Special prices for juniors and seniors; weekend and three-, four-, and five-day lift ticket packages available, as well as season passes and various packages with lodging included. (1 day)

★★ **Amish Community**—This is the largest community of old-order Amish people in the state. They began coming to the area from Ohio in 1949, seeking farmland. Primarily farmers and carpenters, they live much as their ancestors did, without modern conveniences such as cars, tractors, electricity, telephones, television, or radio. The Amish live in the western region of the county between Randolph and South Dayton. You will know you are in the Amish community when you see simple wooden homes without electric wires and road signs illustrated with horse-drawn buggies. The Amish sell their leather work, quilts, furniture, and baked goods from their homes. All are of the finest hand-made quality. Remember, no photographs, and no business conducted on Sundays. (3 hours)

★★ **Griffis Sculpture Park**—This is a unique private park, a 400-acre nature preserve with 10 miles of hiking trails. It is also filled with 200 colossal abstract and representational sculptures, so you can commune with nature and enjoy art at the same time. Tours are available by appointment, but visitors are also free to walk, hike, and picnic amidst the sculptures. Concerts and special programs are held in the summer and fall. Ahrens Road, Ashford Hollow; (716) 257-9344; May through October open daily 9 a.m. to 9 p.m.; closed November through April. Admission free. (2 hours)

★★ **New York and Lake Erie Railroad**—This excursion train offers a step back in time. One route provides a two-hour ride through the countryside with a stop at the **South Dayton** depot, where scenes from the movies *The Natural*, starring Robert Redford, and *Planes, Trains and Automobiles*, starring Steve Martin and John Candy, were filmed. In South Dayton, there's time to shop in quilt and antique stores or enjoy an ice cream soda. 50 Commercial Street, Gowanda; (716) 532-5716; 20-mile round trip mid-June through last weekend in October, Saturday and Sunday at 1 p.m., also Wednesday at noon during July and August; special excursions rest of year including Santa Claus Express in December, and Dinner Train and Murder Mystery Dinner Train. Admission $9 adults, $8 seniors, $4 children ages 3–11, family fares (two adults and up to four children) $25. (2½ hours)

★★ **Seneca-Iroquois National Museum**—The Senecas were known as the Keepers of the Western Door of the Iroquois Confederacy. They still live in the area, and this museum located on Seneca lands is devoted to the history of their culture. The Senecas are one of the original five native nations of the Haudenosaunee, or "People of the Longhouse." At one time their territory spread from northern Canada to South Carolina and from the Hudson River to the Mississippi. Broad Street Extension, Salamanca; (716) 945-1738; April through September open daily 9 a.m. to 5 p.m.; October through March open Monday through Friday 9 a.m. to 5 p.m. Closed January. Admission $4 adults, $2 children. (2 hours)

★ **Rock City Park**—Once an Indian fortress and signal station, this park is filled with gigantic rock formations, one in the shape of a teepee. Some of the rocks tower 80 feet high. Once the bottom of a prehistoric ocean, this area contains the largest deposit of cemented quartz conglomerate irregular rock formation. Rock fans can buy rocks in the rock shop. There's also a museum and black-light room to see more rocks. 505 Rock City Road, Olean; (716) 372-7790; May, June, September, and October open daily 9 a.m. to 6 p.m.; July and August open daily 9 a.m. to 8 p.m. Admission $4. (2 hours)

★ **Salamanca Rail Museum**—This Buffalo, Rochester, and Pittsburgh Depot was built in 1912 and has been beautifully restored to house this museum of railroad history. Railroad buffs will especially enjoy the train memorabilia, including an actual rail car to explore. 170 Main Street, Salamanca; (716) 945-3133; May through September open Monday through Saturday 10 a.m. to 5 p.m., Sunday noon to 5 p.m.; April and October through December closed Monday. Closed January through March. Admission by donation. (1 hour)

**B&B Buffalo Ranch**—It is quite surprising to see a large herd of buffalo grazing on a ranch within view of Ellicottville's ski resorts. Visitors can stop and watch the 300-head herd, the largest east of the Mississippi River, from the road. The store is filled with buffalo-related items, including buffalo meat. Horn Hill Road, Ellicottville; (716) 699-8813; **Buffalo Boutique and Gift Shop** open May through December, Monday through Saturday 10 a.m. to 5 p.m., Sunday 11 a.m. to 5 p.m.; open January through April 30, Thursday through Saturday 10 a.m. to 5 p.m., Sunday 11 a.m. to 5 p.m. Buffalo burgers served on weekends, May to October. Admission free. (1 hour)

**Nannen Arboretum**—This peaceful and lovely spot in the heart of Ellicottville has perennial gardens, more than 260 species of trees, the **Lowe Herb Garden**, the **Ryoanji Temple Stone Garden**—an abstract garden of stone and sand created to encourage contemplation—and the **Amano-Hashidate Bridge**, or "Japanese Bridge to Heaven." The **Chapman Nature Sanctuary** contains formal plantings of Kentucky coffee trees, park benches, and a stone altar in case you want to get married here or hold other special celebrations. 28 Parkside Drive, Ellicottville; (716) 699-2377; open daily. Admission free. (1 hour)

## FITNESS AND RECREATION

**Allegany State Park** is one of the most popular spots for recreation of all kinds, including hiking, cross-country skiing, and snowmobiling in the winter. There are six golf courses in the area. **Holiday Valley** boasts 52 slopes and 12 lifts for skiing enthusiasts. During the summer and fall, the resort welcomes hikers and mountain bike fans.

## FOOD

Though largely a rural area, a wide range of restaurants offer everything from casual to sophisticated dining. Because of the influx of visitors who come for the ski season and the number of second homes and condos in the area, Ellicottville has more restaurants than might be expected in a small town. (The village has a population of just 500 year-round residents.) **Ellicottville Brewing Co.**, 28A Monroe Street, Ellicottville, (716) 699-ALES, is a popular microbrewery and grill house. The **Barn Restaurant and Lounge**, 7 Monroe Street, Ellicottville, (716) 699-4600, is another long-time favorite, housed in a converted 100-year-old barn. **Fenton's**, 8–10 Washington Street, Ellicottville, (716) 699-2373, is in the Ellicottville Inn and is a favorite with skiers. The **Silver Fox Restaurant**, 8 Milks Alley, Ellicottville, (716) 699-4672, offers fine food and a warm welcome. **Dina's**, 15 Washington Street, Ellicottville, (716) 699-5330, is a popular village eatery. The **Old Library Restaurant**, 120 S. Union Street, Olean, (716) 373-6662, is on the Register of National Historic Sites, is an award-winner and favorite with locals and visitors. **R & M Restaurant**, 265 Main Street, Randolph, (716) 358-5141, is in the heart of Amish Country and serves family-style meals at reasonable prices.

## LODGING

Many overnight accommodations are available in the Ellicottville area because of the ski resort. Most Ellicottville lodgings have higher rates on weekends and during the winter. **Ye Olde Towne & Country Realty**, 30 Washington Street, Ellicottville, (716) 699-2456 or (800) 680-0863, handles rentals for chalets, condos, townhouses, and private homes. The **Inn at Holiday Valley**, Route 219, Ellicottville, (716) 699-2345, is an award-winning inn with an indoor/ outdoor pool and easy access to the slopes ($85 to $278 for a double). The **Ellicottville Inn**, 4–10 Washington Street, Ellicottville, (716) 699-2373, is in the heart of the village in a

# CATTARAUGUS COUNTY

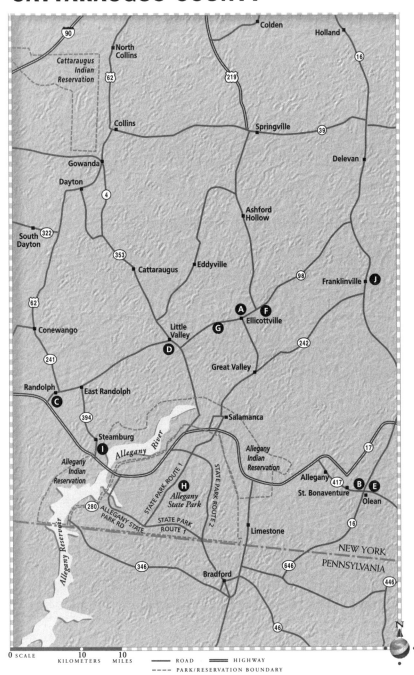

Colden
Holland
90
North Collins
Cattaraugus Indian Reservation
62
219
16
Collins
Springville
39
Delevan
Gowanda
Dayton
4
Ashford Hollow
South Dayton
322
353
Eddyville
Cattaraugus
98
Franklinville
J
62
A
F
Conewango
Little Valley
G
Ellicottville
241
D
242
Great Valley
Randolph
East Randolph
C
394
Salamanca
Steamburg
I
Allegany River
17
Allegany Indian Reservation
Allegany Indian Reservation
Allegany
417
B
E
St. Bonaventure
Olean
STATE PARK ROUTE 1
STATE PARK ROUTE 2
H
280
Allegany State Park
16
Allegany Reservoir
ALLEGANY STATE PARK RD
STATE PARK ROUTE 1
Limestone
NEW YORK
PENNSYLVANIA
346
646
446
Bradford
46
N

0 SCALE
10
KILOMETERS
10
MILES
ROAD HIGHWAY
PARK/RESERVATION BOUNDARY

## Food

- Ⓐ The Barn Restaurant and Lounge
- Ⓐ Dina's
- Ⓐ Ellicottville Brewing Co.
- Ⓐ Fenton's
- Ⓑ Old Library Restaurant
- Ⓒ R & M Restaurant
- Ⓐ Silver Fox Restaurant

## Lodging

- Ⓓ Bush Bed & Breakfast
- Ⓔ Castle Inn

## Lodging (Continued)

- Ⓐ Ellicottville Inn
- Ⓕ Ilex Inn
- Ⓖ Inn at Holiday Valley
- Ⓐ Jefferson Inn

## Camping

- Ⓗ Allegany State Park
- Ⓘ Highbanks Campground
- Ⓒ J.J.'s Pope Haven
- Ⓙ Triple R Campground

*Note: Items with the same letter are located in the same town or area.*

restored, century-old building ($65 to $120 for a double). Also in the middle of the village is the **Jefferson Inn**, 3 Jefferson Street, Ellicottville, (716) 699-5869, a lovely Victorian bed and breakfast ($90 to $135 for a double). The **Ilex Inn**, Route 219, Ellicottville, (716) 699-2002 or (800) 496-6307, is another elegant bed and breakfast ($95 to $185 per double). Outside Ellicottville, **Bush Bed & Breakfast**, Route 353, Little Valley, (716) 938-6106, is a nearly century-old home updated for today's guests ($44 to $99 for a double). The **Castle Inn**, 3220 W. State Street, Olean, (716) 372-1050 or (800) 422-7853, is just across from St. Bonaventure University and is a complete resort with a golf course, pool, and ski packages ($48 to $93 for a double).

## CAMPING

Naturally, **Allegany State Park** contains the most popular and biggest campground, with nearly 400 sites (including 130 winterized cabins) and a full year-round park program ($10 to $12 per night). It is located off Route 17, Salamanca; call (716) 354-2535 or (800) 456-CAMP for reservations. **J.J.'s Pope Haven**, Pope Road, Route 241, Randolph, (716) 358-4900, is in the heart of Amish Country ($15 per night). **Highbanks Campground**, operated by the Seneca Nation of Indians, is on the Allegany Reservoir, Route 394, Steamburg, (716) 354-4855 or (888) 341-8890 ($10 per night). **Triple R Campground**, 3491 Bryant Hill Road, Franklinville, (716) 676-3856, is a full-service RV facility with a tent area ($15 per night).

# 15

# CORNING AND ELMIRA

Glass, Mark Twain, and soaring help to define the Corning and Elmira area, which anchors the Finger Lakes Region near the Pennsylvania border. Corning is the hometown of Corning Glass Works. Bulbs for Thomas Edison's incandescent lamps were one of the company's early products; today, Steuben Glass creations are often given as gifts by American presidents to foreign heads of state. The Corning Glass Center opened in 1951 to mark the 100th birthday of Corning Glass Works and is now one of the top tourist attractions in the state. Housing the world's largest collection of glass objects, the Corning Museum of Glass has objects ranging from weapons chipped from volcanic glass by prehistoric people to exquisite hand-blown pieces by contemporary artists.

Nearby Elmira is known as "Mark Twain Country." Samuel Clemens, a.k.a. Mark Twain, called the area "a garden of Eden." He married an Elmira native, Olivia Langdon, and the family spent 20 summers at Olivia's sister and brother-in-law's home atop East Hill. In his beloved Octagon Study, he brought to life Huck, Tom Sawyer, the Connecticut Yankee, and many other characters. Since 1930, when a national soaring contest was held on a mountaintop south of the city, Elmira has also been called the Soaring Capital of America. The National Soaring Museum tells the story of soaring; just outside, sailplanes and pilots stand by to take visitors into the air on a motorless flight. The Near Westside Historic District in Elmira, listed on the National Register of Historic Places, contains the largest number of Victorian-style buildings in the state. ◼

# CORNING AND ELMIRA REGION

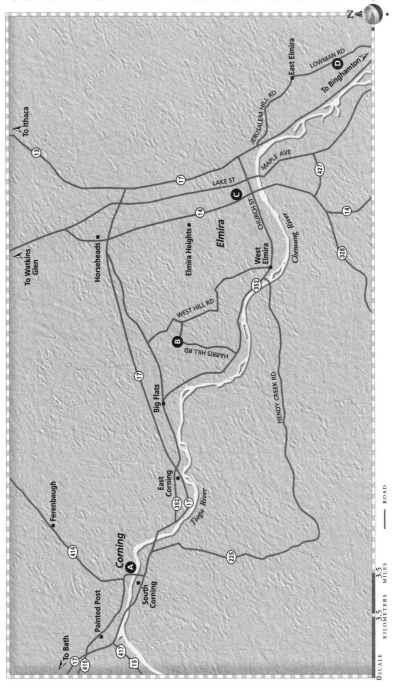

# Sights

- Ⓐ **Benjamin Patterson Inn**
- Ⓐ **Corning Glass Center**
- Ⓑ **Harris Hill Soaring Corp.**
- Ⓒ **Mark Twain Study**
- Ⓐ **Market Street**

- Ⓑ **National Soaring Museum**
- Ⓓ **Newtown Battlefield Reservation**
- Ⓐ **Rockwell Museum**

*Note: Items with the same letter are located in the same town or area.*

## A PERFECT DAY IN CORNING AND ELMIRA

The Corning Glass Center is always a fascinating place. Watch talented craftspeople in the magical act of glass blowing in the Steuben Glass Factory. After a morning at the center, hop on the free double-decker bus that operates in the summer and ride to Market Street (it's a short walk if the buses aren't running). Stop at the Ice Cream Works, in the middle of the historic Market Street District, for lunch and ice cream. Take time to stroll through the district and admire the nineteenth- century architecture. Mark Twain called the area "a foretaste of heaven." It's easy to accept his assessment from a sailplane more than 3,000 feet in the air. Soaring is exhilarating and fun, pure and simple. Top off the day with dinner at Pierce's 1894 Restaurant in Elmira, complete with a glass of fine Finger Lakes wine.

## SIGHTSEEING HIGHLIGHTS

★★★ **Corning Glass Center**—Housed in a spectacular Gunnar Birkerts building, this complex is made, appropriately enough, mostly of glass. The Glass Center is currently undergoing a multimillion-dollar renovation, to be completed by 2001 in commemoration of the company's 150th anniversary and the 50th anniversary of the opening of the Glass Center and the **Corning Museum of Glass**. The museum displays the world's greatest collection of glass—more than 26,000 objects in all—dating from 1400 B.C. through the twentieth century. Visitors may gently touch the bottom of a bottle found in a 2,000-year-old Roman tomb. Methods of making and decorating glass are described and shown in short movies.

The next stop is the **Hall of Science and Industry**, where you can experience the amazing world of glass through many hands-on exhibits and demonstrations. A dramatic display features one of the largest pieces of glass ever made by a human being: the first casting of the 200-inch mirror disk for the Mount Palomar telescope. A favorite feature in this area is the lampworker demonstration, where a crafts-person melts rods of glass and forms them into tiny glass animals, for sale in the center gift shops.

The final stop is the **Steuben Factory**, the only place in the world where Steuben glass artisans create crystal masterpieces from molten glass. Visitors are invited to sit in the tiered gallery to watch the process. Visitors can also enjoy close-up views of the artisans using rotating copper wheels to engrave intricate designs in the crystal. The Steuben showroom has $150 paperweights and art objects selling for $4,000 or more. The center's gift shops sell all manner of glass objects, including Corningware and Pyrex cookware. Wheelchair accessible. Route 17, Corning; (607) 974-2000; open daily 9 a.m. to 5 p.m. Closed Thanks-giving, December 24 and 25, and January 1. Admission $7 adults, $6 seniors, $5 children ages 6–17, $16 family maximum. (4 hours)

★★★ **Harris Hill Soaring Corp.**—This soaring club in Harris Hill Park sits next to the National Soaring Museum. Many people enjoy coming to the park just to watch the sailplanes take off and land—scenes reminiscent of the old barnstorming days. If you are willing to accept that these fragile-looking planes can transport you into the sky and then safely back to earth, the club is ready to indulge your fantasy. It offers rides daily (weather permitting) during the summer and on weekends the rest of the year, or by special arrangement. Some 3,500 feet above the earth, it is incredibly quiet and peaceful. In today's noisy world it's harder and harder to find quiet, but here there are no engines, just the soft rush of the wind outside. The Wright Brothers once were asked why they kept flying sailplanes after they invented powered flight. Their answer: "Everyone knows sailplanes are more fun." Most everyone who has experienced a sailplane ride would agree. 63 Soaring Hill Drive, Elmira; (607) 739-7899 (office) or (607) 734-0641 (field). Open daily 10 a.m. to 6 p.m. during the summer; open weekends rest of year. Admission $45 for a ride in a sailplane trainer, $60 for a ride in a high-performance sailplane. No charge if you just want to watch, of course. (1 hour)

★★ **Mark Twain Study**—Mark Twain spent 20 summers in Elmira. It was at his wife's sister and brother-in-law's farm that he wrote some of his classics, including *The Adventures of Huckleberry Finn*. Twain loved his study at the farm: "It is the loveliest study you ever saw. It is octagonal, with a peaked roof, each face filled with a spacious window . . . It is a cozy nest and just room in it for a sofa, table and three or four chairs . . . imagine the luxury of it." The study has been moved from Quarry Farm to the campus of **Elmira College**, where there is also an exhibit of photographs and memorabilia relating to Twain's connection to Elmira. The exhibit displays a typewriter similar to the one Twain used—he was one of the first authors to submit a typewritten manuscript to his publisher. Elmira College Campus, Elmira; (607) 735-1941; late June through August open daily 10 a.m. to 5 p.m. or by appointment. Admission free. (1 hour)

★★ **Market Street**—Brick sidewalks lead pedestrians down Market Street, Corning's commercial center, which has thrived for a century and a half. Now a National Historic District, the area's buildings have been beautifully restored. During the summer authenic British red double-decker buses stop along Market Street and at the Glass Center. Rides are

*Mark Twain Study, Elmira*

NYS Department of Economic Development

free. This street is ideal for window shoppers and browsers, with more than 100 antique shops, bookstores, clothing shops, glass studios, outlets, and restaurants. Benches and outdoor tables and chairs offer places to relax and dine in warmer weather. Wheelchair accessible. Market Street, Corning; (607) 936-4686. (2 hours)

★★ **National Soaring Museum**—Anyone with an interest in flying will enjoy this museum. It boasts the world's largest collection of sailplanes, along with the only full-scale replica of the Wright Glider No. 5. This was the one in which Orville Wright started the world soaring movement in 1911 with his then-record-breaking flight of nine minutes, 45 seconds. The flight simulator is open to anyone who wants to climb in and imagine what it's like to fly off into the wild blue yonder. The museum includes a restoration area and exhibits sprinkled with quotes from the town's most famous summer resident, Mark Twain. Wheelchair accessible. 51 Soaring Hill Drive, Elmira; (607) 734-3128; open daily 10 a.m. to 5 p.m. Closed Thanksgiving, December 25, and January 1. Admission $3. (1 hour)

★★ **Rockwell Museum**—This museum is filled with the eclectic collection of art and objects amassed by the Robert F. Rockwell Jr. family, whose fortune came from a small chain of department stores in the Corning area. It is located in the heart of town in a huge Romanesque building that once housed the city hall and jail. Rockwell was a friend of Frederick Carder, founder of Steuben Glass, who spent 80 of his 100 years designing and making glass in town. More than 2,000 pieces of Carder glass are on display. The museum also houses an outstanding collection of Western art—the largest such collection east of the Mississippi—including paintings and sculptures by Frederic Remington and Charles M. Russell, the most famous cowboy artists of all. The wonderful collection of antique toys appeals to the child in all of us. Wheelchair accessible. 111 Cedar Street, Corning; (607) 937-5386; open daily 10 a.m. to 5 p.m., Sunday noon to 5 p.m.; closed Thanksgiving, December 24 and 25, and January 1. Admission $4 adults, $3.60 seniors, $2 children ages 6–17. (2 hours)

★ **Benjamin Patterson Inn**—This inn re-creates what life was like for the area's early settlers. The original inn was constructed in 1796 and has been carefully restored. The grounds also display the 1784 **DeMonstoy Log Cabin**, a 1878 one-room schoolhouse, a blacksmith shop, and a barn. 59 W. Pulteney Street, Corning; (607) 937-5281; open Monday through Saturday 10 a.m. to 4 p.m.; closed major holidays. Admission $3 adults, $1 children ages 6–18. (2 hours)

**Newtown Battlefield Reservation**—This is the site of General Sullivan's famous Revolutionary War battle. Sullivan, under the command of George Washington, destroyed 41 settlements in the area. The reservation marks a decisive victory for Sullivan over a large force of Indians and Tories. Not far from the actual battlefield is **Sullivan's Monument**, which commemorates this confrontation on August 29, 1779. Today the reservation is part of a 330-acre park with facilities for camping, hiking, and picnicking. Route 17, Elmira; (607) 732-6067; open daily. Admission free. (2 hours)

## FITNESS AND RECREATION

**Harris Hill Park**, 599 Harris Hill Road, Big Flats, (607) 737-2907, offers a chance to watch planes landing and taking off, and to gaze at hang gliders and the lovely Chemung River Valley below. There are trails for walking or hiking, a pool, an amusement park, and picnic facilities. During the winter there are cross-country ski trails, slopes for toboggans and sleds, and a frozen pond for skating. The **Tanglewood Nature Center**, West Hill Road, Elmira, (607) 732-6060, has marked trails through flora and fauna. Visitors can hang glide, cross-country ski, hike, picnic, and enjoy panoramic views at **Mossy Bank Park**, off County Route 10, Bath, (607) 776-3811.

## FOOD

**Pierce's 1894 Restaurant**, 228 Oakwood Avenue, Elmira Heights, (607) 734-2022, is an award-winning, family-owned restaurant in a rambling brick building with Victorian parlors; the wine list features New York State wines. **Hill Top Inn**, 171 Jerusalem Hill, Elmira, (607) 732-6728, offers outstanding views from atop the hill and indoor and outdoor dining. **Moretti's Restaurant**, 800 Hatch Street, Elmira, (607) 734-1535, has welcomed diners since 1917. **Sorge's Restaurant**, 66–68 Market Street, Corning, (607) 937-5422, is a popular Italian-food establishment. **Taste of China**, 84 E. Market Street, Corning, (607) 962-6176, features an extensive Cantonese/Szechuan menu. **Ice Cream Works**, West Market Street and Centerway Square, Corning,

# CORNING AND ELMIRA REGION

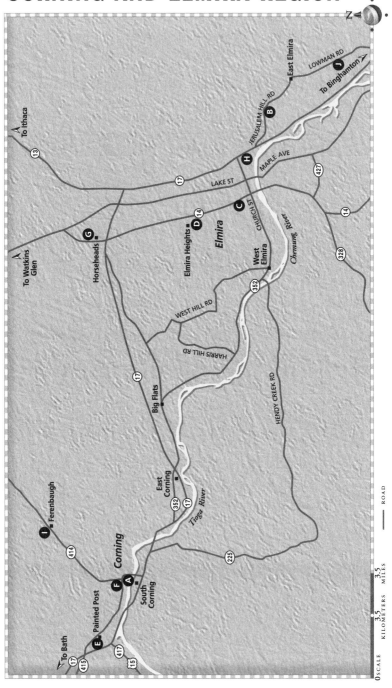

## Food

- Ⓐ Boomers
- Ⓑ Hill Top Inn
- Ⓐ Ice Cream Works
- Ⓐ London Underground Café
- Ⓒ Moretti's Restaurant
- Ⓓ Pierce's 1894 Restaurant
- Ⓐ Sorge's Restaurant
- Ⓐ Taste of China

## Lodging

- Ⓔ Best Western Lodge
  on the Green

## Lodging (Continued)

- Ⓕ Days Inn of Corning
- Ⓖ EconoLodge
- Ⓗ Holiday Inn Riverview
- Ⓐ Radisson Hotel Corning
- Ⓕ Rosewood Inn

## Camping

- Ⓘ Ferenbaugh Campsite
- Ⓙ Newtown Battlefield
  Reservation

*Note: Items with the same letter are located in the same town or area.*

(607) 962-8481, offers light meals and a big selection of ice cream creations in a restored 1880s ice cream parlor. The **London Underground Café**, 69 E. Market Street, Corning, has fine dining in a three-level setting. **Boomers**, 35 E. Market Street, Corning, (607) 962-6800, is a good choice for families and offers 99-cent kids meals.

## LODGING

The **Radisson Hotel Corning**, Denison Parkway East, Corning, (607) 962-5000 or (800) 333-3333, anchors the Market Street Historic District ($79 to $127 for a double). Also well-located is the **Days Inn of Corning**, 52 Ferris Street, Corning, (607) 936-9370 or (800) DAYS-INN ($47 to $67 for a double). A few miles outside Corning is the **Best Western Lodge on the Green**, Routes 15 and 417, Painted Post, (607) 962-2456 ($74 to $99 for a double). The **Rosewood Inn**, 134 E. First Street, Corning, (607) 962-3253, is a charming bed and breakfast inn just two blocks from Market Street ($85 to $125 for a double). Each of the antique-filled rooms is named after a famous Corning area resident. The **EconoLodge**, 871 County Route 64, Elmira, (607) 739-2000, is just 5 miles from Harris Hill ($53 for a double). **Holiday Inn Riverview**, 760 East

Water Street, Elmira, (607) 734-4211, is right on the Chemung River and in the heart of downtown Elmira ($68 for a double).

## CAMPING

In Corning, the **Ferenbaugh Campsite**, 4121 State Route 414, (607) 962-6193, has 140 campsites as well as swimming and fishing ($16 per night); it is open from April 15 to October 15. The **Newtown Battlefield Reservation**, 599 Harris Hill Road, Elmira, (607) 737-2907, is a small campground in an historic setting, with 19 sites ($8 per night); it is open from May 12 to October 9.

## SHOPPING

A large store at the **Corning Glass Center** stocks all manner of Corning glass, jewelry, kitchenware, and other items. Bargains can be had here on seconds and discontinued items. The **Steuben Glass Store** in the Glass Center carries lovely glass art works but no bargains or seconds (if a Steuben piece is not perfect, it is destroyed). Along **Market Street** there are more stores with glass objects and studios where artists create glass works of art in front of shoppers. There are also several factory outlets along the historic street. Call (607) 936-4686 for information on Market Street shopping.

# 16

# THE FINGER LAKES

Cayuga, Canandaigua, Keuka, Hemlock, Honeoye, Otisco, Owasco, Canadice, Conesus, Skaneateles, and Seneca—these names sound like a roll call for the Indians of the Iroquois Confederacy, who dominated this area in the middle of the state for more than two centuries. But they are also the names of the Finger Lakes. Iroquois legend has it that the Finger Lakes region was formed when the Great Spirit placed his hand in blessing on this favored land. Geologists have a more prosaic explanation: the lakes were created when Ice Age glaciers retreated about a million years ago. The intense pressure of those ice masses created the long narrow lakes lying side by side, the deep gorges with rushing falls, and the wide, fertile valleys that extend south for miles. These features are found nowhere else in the world.

The Finger Lakes region is the land of dreamers—dreamers who founded a religion, began the women's rights movement, pioneered the motion picture industry, and founded prestigious schools and universities. Viniculture is another of the region's many offerings. Not only did the retreating glaciers create the lakes, they also created ideal conditions for grape growing by depositing a shallow layer of topsoil on sloping shale beds above the lakes. The deep lakes also provide protection from the climate by moderating temperatures along their shores. ◣

# THE FINGER LAKES

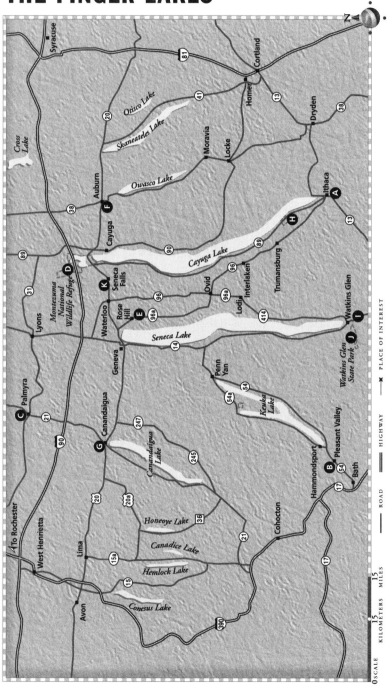

## Sights

- **Ⓐ** Cornell University Plantations
- **Ⓑ** Glenn H. Curtiss Museum of Local History
- **Ⓐ** Herbert F. Johnson Museum of Art
- **Ⓒ** Hill Cumorah Visitor Center
- **Ⓓ** Montezuma National Wildlife Refuge
- **Ⓔ** Rose Hill Mansion

- **Ⓐ** Sciencenter
- **Ⓕ** Seward House
- **Ⓖ** Sonnenberg Gardens
- **Ⓗ** Taughannock Falls State Park
- **Ⓘ** Watkins Glen Racetrack
- **Ⓙ** Watkins Glen State Park
- **Ⓚ** Women's Rights National Historical Park

*Note: Items with the same letter are located in the same town or area.*

## A PERFECT DAY AT THE FINGER LAKES

Begin the day with a hike along the Gorge Trail in Taughannock Falls State Park. At 215 feet, this is the highest vertical waterfall in the East. The flat, easy walk heads through a rugged canyon and quiet woods, along a peaceful stream to the falls. Take a tour of one of the nearby wineries. A long-time favorite is Wagner Vineyards, home to the Ginny Lee Café, overlooking the vineyards and deep blue Seneca Lake. During the warmer months it's the perfect spot to enjoy lunch and a glass of wine. Ithaca, home to Cornell University, is a beautiful and cosmopolitan small city with a wide array of dining choices. Finish your day at Watkins Glen State Park for the production of *Timespell*, a sound and light show set against the spectacular natural stage of the gorge.

## SIGHTSEEING HIGHLIGHTS

★★★ **Watkins Glen State Park**—This is the most famous of the parks in the region. The best way to experience the beauty of the glen is to hike the gorge trail. This trail and others are accessible from the main, south, and upper entrances. Most visitors walk uphill from the main entrance and return. Others take a shuttlebus to the upper entrance and walk the 1½ miles back down to the main entrance. The trail has more than 800 stone steps. It is not a difficult walk, but the footing can get slippery, so be sure to wear suitable footwear. The park encompasses 19 waterfalls, bearing such names as Rainbow, Diamond, and Pluto, plus a series of grottos, caves, and cataracts. You'll pass over and under bridges, and through handcut tunnels—the "narrows," with a microclimate almost like that of a rainforest.

Some 302 campsites are available here, divided into villages named for the Native Americans who lived in the area. At dusk the haunting voice of the narrator explains the creation of Watkins Glen as vivid laser lights dance off waterfalls and cliffs, and sounds convey erupting volcanoes, crackling ice, and the rhythmic beating of the Senecas' drums. It is a stirring performance set against a spectacular stage—the gorge of the park.

Amenities at the park include a main swimming pool, a children's pool, a recreation building, a picnic area, a playground, playing fields, and other hiking trails. The main entrance is on State 14 in the village of Watkins Glen, at the southern tip of Seneca Lake. Franklin Street, Watkins Glen; (607) 535-4511; open daily year-round, but the camping area and Gorge Trail are open only from mid-May to Columbus Day. Admission $5 per car during summer, otherwise free. *Timespell* $5.25 adults, $4.75 for seniors and children ages 6–11. (3 hours)

★★ **Hill Cumorah Visitor Center**—This is the site of the founding of the Mormon Church and is believed to be where Joseph Smith received a history of ancient American people on gold plates, which became the *Book of Mormon*. The **Hill Cumorah Pageant**, held here during the second week of July, is America's largest outdoor drama, attracting more than 100,000 annually. The pageant, which is free, features a costumed cast of 600, high technology, and magnificent music. It has been presented by the Church of Jesus Christ of Latter-day Saints since 1935. Joseph Smith's home, built in 1820, has been restored and is open for touring. Route 21, Palmyra; (315) 597-5851; open daily 9 a.m. to 5 p.m. Admission free. (1 hour for tour)

★★ **Montezuma National Wildlife Refuge**—This refuge, at the north end of Cayuga Lake, was established in 1938 as a breeding ground for migratory birds and other wildlife as a unit of the Atlantic Flyway. Motorists crossing the state via the New York Thruway pass through it, but it's hard to see much at highway speed. The refuge is worth a stop, especially for bird lovers. A total of 315 species of birds have been identified here. While birds are in abundance year-round, it's best to time your visit for the fall or spring migration seasons to see hundreds of Canada geese, ducks, and snow geese. Stop first at the visitors center, where rangers are on duty to answer questions and provide up-to-date information on the latest sightings. The observation deck and tower provide excellent opportunities to see wildlife. During our recent visit the highlight was the sight (through a telescope) of a bald eagle sitting on her nest. Wheelchair accessible. 3395 Routes 5 and 20 East, Seneca Falls; (315) 568-5987; open daily during daylight hours. Visitors center staffed on weekends, most Tuesdays, and holidays. Admission free. (2 hours)

★★ **Sciencenter**—This hands-on museum adjoins an outdoor science park and is popular with families. Over 50 exhibits include a water raceway, computer voyage through the galaxy, you-build-it bridge, and a flume exhibit where visitors can control the speed and direction of the flowing water. Wheelchair accessible. 601 First Street, Ithaca; (607) 272-0600; open Tuesday through Saturday 10 a.m. to 5 p.m., Sunday noon to 5 p.m. Admission $3.75 adults, $2.75 children ages 4–12. (2 hours)

★★ **Sonnenberg Gardens**—A great bronze Buddha sits in the lotus position in the Japanese Garden, an oasis of serenity under sheltering trees and one of the ten formal gardens here. Sonnenberg, meaning "sunny hill" in German, is a beautiful, 50-acre, turn-of the-century garden estate the Smithsonian Institution called "one of the most magnificent late-Victorian gardens ever created in America." This was the summer home of Frederick Ferry Thompson and his wife, Mary Clark Thompson. The home, completed in 1887, is on the National Register of Historic Places and has been beautifully restored. Tours of the gardens are offered daily, or you may stroll on your own. 151 Charlotte Street, Canandaigua; (716) 924-5420; May through October open daily 9:30 a.m. to 5:30 p.m.; open December for Festival of Lights. Admission $7.50 adults grounds and mansion ($6.50 for grounds only), $6.50 seniors grounds and mansion ($5.50 grounds only), and $3 children ages 6–16 ($2.50 grounds only). (2 hours)

★★ **Taughannock Falls State Park**—Taughannock Falls, 215 feet high, is the highest vertical waterfall in the eastern United States. There are two falls lookout points: one from below at the end of the **Gorge Trail**, the other from above at the Falls Overlook on **Taughannock Park Road**. You can reach the base by walking along a gentle ¾-mile trail. Pick up a Gorge Trail brochure in the park office and follow the numbered markers, which correspond to those described in the brochure.

The park includes more than a mile of Cayuga Lake shore, 783 acres, 76 campsites, 16 cabins, a swimming beach, a boat launch, playgrounds, and playing fields; it hosts camper recreation programs and a summer music festival. 2221 Taughannock Park Road, Trumansburg; (607) 387-6739, or (800) 456-CAMP for reservations; open daily. Camping is available from the last weekend in March to mid-October. Admission $5 per car during the summer season, otherwise free. (2 hours)

★★ **Women's Rights National Historical Park**—The park includes a visitors center, the **National Women's Hall of Fame**, and the **Elizabeth Cady Stanton home**. Elizabeth Cady Stanton was one of the organizers of the first Women's Rights Convention, held in Seneca Falls on July 19 and 20, 1848, and was the author of the *Declaration of Sentiments* read at the convention. She became the major author, policymaker, and speechmaker for the Women's Rights Movement. The house, at 32 Washington Street, has been restored to its 1848 appearance. The permanent exhibits of the Hall of Fame focus on the lives of women inducted through public nomination. Changing exhibits provide an interpretation of women's roles in society. Wheelchair accessible. 136 Fall Street, Seneca Falls; (315) 568-2991; open daily 9 a.m. to 5 p.m. Admission free. (2 hours)

★ **Cornell University Plantations**—From early spring until late fall, blooms can always be found at the 1,500-acre Cornell Plantations, a unit of Cornell University that includes the arboretum, botanical gardens, and natural acres of the university. The plantations were the dream of Liberty Hyde Bailey, often called "the dean of American plant scientists." One of the unique specialty gardens is the **Walter C. Muenscher Poisonous Plants Garden**, dedicated to the late Professor Muenscher, an eminent Cornell botanist and author of a classic text on poisonous plants. The **Robinson York State Herb Garden** has been designed to serve as a living reference library for herb study and research. There are more than 800 herbs to be seen, studied, and just enjoyed for their color, texture, or fragrance. The **International Crop Garden** displays the nine major crops that feed the world. The **Heritage Crop Garden** showcases old-time crops. 1 Plantation Road, off Route 366, Ithaca; (607) 255-3020; open daily 9 a.m. to dusk. Admission free. (1 hour)

★ **Glenn H. Curtiss Museum of Local History**—This museum displays the accomplishments of native son Curtiss, a pioneer in aviation, motorcycling, cycling, engineering, and other fields. The famous *June Bug* and *Curtiss Jenny* planes are on display. There's also an eclectic collection of antique toys, farm equipment, photographs, quilts, fire engines, and many other items that help to tell story of life in the area during the late nineteenth and early twentieth centuries. Wheelchair accessible. Route 54, Hammondsport; (607) 569-2160; Admission $4 adult, $3.50 seniors, $2.50 children ages 7–18. (1 hour)

★ **Herbert F. Johnson Museum of Art**—The building was designed by world-renowned architect I. M. Pei. Its collection is particularly strong in American, Asian, and contemporary art and graphics. The **George and Mary Rockwell Galleries**, on the fifth floor, offer panoramic views of Cornell, Ithaca, and Cayuga Lake. Wheelchair accessible. Cornell University Campus, Ithaca; (607) 255-6464; open Tuesday through Sunday 10 a.m. to 5 p.m. Admission free. (1 hour)

★ **Rose Hill Mansion**—Located just outside the lovely city of Geneva overlooking Seneca Lake, this mansion is a National Historic Landmark and considered one of the country's finest examples of Greek Revival architecture. Guided tours lead through 24 rooms decorated with wood and plaster moldings and furnished in the Empire style. The Jenny Lind bedroom contains the original bed in which the "Swedish Nightingale" slept when it was in a Connecticut home. During the nineteenth century, Robert Swan lived in the house and turned the property into one of the most productive farms in the state. The restored gardens are lovely when in bloom. Route 96A, Geneva; (315) 789-3848; May through October open Monday through Saturday 10 a.m. to 4 p.m., Sunday 1 p.m. to 5 p.m. Admission $3 adults, $2 seniors and children ages 10–18. (1 hour)

★ **Seward House**—This was the home of William Henry Seward, New York governor, U.S. senator, and secretary of state under Presidents Lincoln and Johnson. He was a leading figure in the founding of the Republican Party and in the Alaska purchase. At the time of its purchase, Alaska was referred to as "Seward's Ice-Box" and "Seward's Folly," but at two cents an acre, it has to be regarded as one of the best bargains ever. The home was built in 1816 by Judge Elijah Miller, Seward's father-in-law, and the only residents have been four generations of the Seward family. The Federal-style mansion is a registered National Historic Landmark. Each room in the 30-room house is furnished only with original family pieces and gifts and memorabilia collected by Seward in his travels. Guests in the dining rooms have included U.S. presidents John Adams, Martin Van Buren, Andrew Johnson, and William McKinley. 33 South Street, Auburn; (315) 252-1283; April to December open Tuesday through Saturday 1 p.m. to 5 p.m. Admission $3 adults, $2 children ages 7–18. (1½ hours)

★ **Watkins Glen Racetrack**—The first auto race in Watkins Glen took place on October 2, 1948. It was run on a 6.6-mile course of backroads and highways east of Watkins Glen and through village streets. For safety reasons the races were moved to a 2.3-mile track outside of the village. Over the years the course has hosted Formula One, Can-Am, CART Indy, Formula 5,000, and TransAm races. Wheelchair accessible. There are usually five to eight events at the track each summer. On race weekends practice and qualifying runs are made on Thursday and Friday, and races are run on Saturdays and Sundays. Camping is permitted on the grounds. Route 16, Watkins Glen; (607) 535-2481. Admission $7 to $40; packages available. (4 hours)

## FITNESS AND RECREATION

A host of trails throughout the region are used for walking, hiking, and cross-country skiing in the winter. The **Finger Lakes Trail** consists of 785 miles of hiking trails and connects Canada's Bruce Trail with the Appalachian Trail. **Finger Lakes National Forest**, between Seneca and Cayuga Lakes, 4 miles from Watkins Glen, is the state's only national forest and boasts more than 25 miles of connecting trails, including the 12-mile **Interlaken National Recreation Trail** and 2 miles of the **Finger Lakes Trail**. **Cumming Nature Center**, in Naples, has 6 miles of walking trails. The state parks in the Ithaca area—**Buttermilk Falls**, **Taughannock Falls**, **Robert H. Treman**, and nearby **Watkins Glen**—all have well-marked hiking trails. The 6,100 acre **High Tor Wildlife Management Area**, in Naples, has miles of hiking trails. **Bristol Mountain**, in Canandaigua, is a popular ski resort.

## FOOD

Because of Cornell University and Ithaca College, Ithaca offers the widest range of dining opportunities in the region. Popular spots include the **Station Restaurant**, West Buffalo Street, Ithaca, (607) 272-2609, located in the restored Lehigh Railroad Station or one of the three railroad cars. The famous **Moosewood Restaurant**, DeWitt Mall Downtown, (607) 273-9610, is a vegetarian restaurant that publishes its own cookbooks. Since 1932 **Joe's Restaurant**, 602 W. Buffalo Street, Ithaca, (607) 273-2693, has been a popular Italian eatery. **Oldport Harbour Restaurant**, 702 W. Buffalo Street, Ithaca, (607) 272-4868, offers waterfront dining and fine dining. **Turback's**, Route 13 South, Ithaca, (607) 272-6484, located in a converted nineteenth-century mansion, is considered the grande dame of Ithaca and specializes in New York regional cooking and New York wines. **Thendara Inn & Restaurant**, 4356 E. Lake Road, Canandaigua, (716) 394-4868, offers fine dining and a wonderful view of Canandaigua Lake. The **Belhurst Castle**, Route 14 South, Geneva, (315) 781-0201, overlooks Seneca Lake and provides fine food in a magnificent setting.

## LODGING

Some of the state's most unique accommodations are in this region. In many cases rates go up during the summer months. Geneva has two very special inns: Geneva-on-the-Lake and the Belhurst Castle, within a mile of each other on the shores of Seneca Lake. **Geneva-on-the-Lake**, 1001 Lochland Road, Route 14 South, Geneva, (315) 789-7190 or (800) 3-GENEVA, is a 1911 Italianate villa modeled after Villa Lancellotti, a sixteenth-century villa near Rome. It has been a Capuchin monastery, an apartment complex, and, since 1981, a small elegant resort with 30 luxurious suites ($158 to $338 for a double or suite with kitchen). **Belhurst Castle**, Lochland Road, Route 14 South, Geneva, (315) 781-0201, with 12 guest rooms, was constructed from 1885 to 1889 in Richardson Romanesque style. There's a suite on the third floor in the former ballroom with a turret overlooking the lake and another with an 1810 four-poster bed that requires a stool to get in ($85 to $225).

The **Inn on the Lake**, 770 S. Main Street, Canandaigua, (716) 394-7800 or (800) 228-2801, is a popular Canandaigua resort with 147 rooms ($59 to $185 for a double; wheelchair accessible). On Keuka Lake, the **Viking Resort**, 680 E. Lake Road, Penn Yan, (315) 536-7061, boasts 1,000 feet of lakeshore and a wide range of accommodations, including efficiency apartments and cabins ideal for families ($38 to $122 for a

# THE FINGER LAKES

Syracuse
81
Cortland
Orisco Lake
20
41
Homer
13
Dryden
38
Cross Lake
Skaneateles Lake
Moravia
Locke
Auburn
Owasco Lake
Ithaca
B
38
Cayuga
13
D
89
90
Cayuga Lake
89
I
Trumansburg
Montezuma National Wildlife Refuge
Seneca Falls
G
Ovid
96
Interlaken
Watkins Glen
31
Lyons
96
96a
Lodi
414
Rose Hill
96a
Waterloo
A
Seneca Lake
E
Watkins Glen State Park
J
Palmyra
Geneva
14
Penn Yan
F
21
Canandaigua
247
54
To Rochester
90
C
54a
H
Keuka Lake
Pleasant Valley
West Henrietta
20
208
Canandaigua Lake
245
Hammondsport
54
Bath
17
Lima
151
Honeoye Lake
36
Cohocton
21
Avon
15
Canadice Lake
Hemlock Lake
17
Conesus Lake
390

SCALE
15 KILOMETERS
15 MILES

ROAD — HIGHWAY ══ ✱ PLACE OF INTEREST

# Food

- Ⓐ Belhurst Castle
- Ⓑ Joe's Restaurant
- Ⓑ Moosewood Restaurant
- Ⓑ Oldport Harbour Restaurant
- Ⓑ Station Restaurant
- Ⓒ Thendara Inn & Restaurant
- Ⓓ Turback's

# Lodging

- Ⓐ Belhurst Castle
- Ⓑ Best Western University Inn–Ithaca
- Ⓐ Geneva-on-the-Lake

## Lodging (Continued)

- Ⓒ Inn on the Lake
- Ⓔ Rainbow Cove Motel
- Ⓑ Statler Hotel
- Ⓕ Viking Resort

# Camping

- Ⓑ Buttermilk Falls State Park
- Ⓖ Cayuga Lake State Park
- Ⓗ Keuka Lake State Park
- Ⓘ Taughannock Falls State Park
- Ⓙ Watkins Glen State Park

*Note: Items with the same letter are located in the same town or area.*

double). The Viking is open May 15 to October 15 and also operates Viking Spirit Cruises. **Rainbow Cove Motel**, Route 14, Himrod, (607) 243-7535, is on Seneca Lake, 14 miles north of Watkins Glen, ($55 to $65 for a double). The 150-room **Statler Hotel**, Cornell University Campus, Ithaca, (607) 257-2500 or (800) 541-2501, is a Cornell landmark and serves as a training ground for students in the School of Hotel Administration ($125 to $300 for a double; wheelchair accessible). **Best Western University Inn–Ithaca**, East Hill Plaza, Ithaca, (607) 272-6100 or (800) 528-1234, is adjacent to the Cornell University campus and has some rooms with fireplaces ($80 to $110 for a double; wheelchair accessible).

## CAMPING

Camping is popular in the Finger Lakes Region, and it has a number of top-rated state and private campgrounds. For reservations at state campgrounds, call (800) 456-CAMP. **Taughannock Falls State Park**, Route 89, Trumansburg, near Ithaca, (607) 387-6739, is on Cayuga Lake and has a small beach, boat launch site, and trails to the falls and beyond ($10 per night). **Keuka Lake State Park**, Route 54A,

Bluffpoint, (315) 536-3666, has a prime location on the shores of Keuka Lake ($10 per night). **Buttermilk Falls State Park**, Route 13, Ithaca, (607) 273-5761, was the site for the filming of the *Perils of Pauline* back in the 1920s ($10 per night). The waterfalls end in a wonderful swimming hole. **Cayuga Lake State Park**, 2678 Lower Lake Road, Seneca Falls, (315) 568-5163, is on Cayuga Lake and has 286 sites ($10 per night). **Watkins Glen State Park**, Route 14, Watkins Glen, (607) 535-4511, has 305 sites, swimming, fishing, and a popular trail through the glen ($10 per night).

# Scenic Route: The Finger Lakes Wine Region

Wineries galore grace the slopes of **Keuka Lake** and **Seneca Lake**. **Hammondsport**, on Keuka Lake, is the birthplace of grape culture in the Finger Lakes wine region. In 1829 Reverend William Bostwick transplanted Isabella and Catawba grapevines from the Hudson Valley to his garden at St. James Episcopal Church. The grapes flourished, and news of Bostwick's success spread rapidly among nearby farmers.

The 22-mile-long Keuka Lake, one of the loveliest in the region, is the only lake shaped like a Y. Nineteenth-century settlers called it "Crooked Lake" and "the Lady of the Lakes." Even the wines taste better when you are within sight of the lake. For the best view of the lake and the vineyards along the hillsides, take a ride on the **Keuka Maid**, which hosts lunch and dinner cruises from May to October.

From the village take State 76 north. Just a mile outside town are the famed **Bully Hill Winery** and the **Greyton H. Taylor Wine Museum**. Walter S. Taylor named the museum in honor of his father, one of the sons of the founder of the Taylor Wine Co. Walter S. Taylor is known throughout the wine world for his court battles with the Coca-Cola Co. (which owned Taylor Wine Co. at the time) over

## THE FINGER LAKES WINE REGION

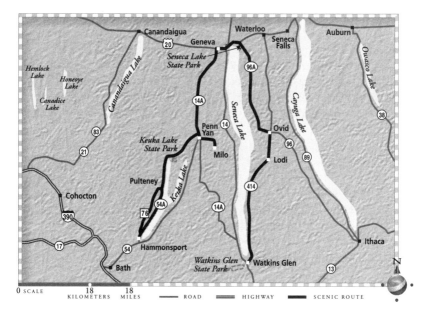

the use of his name on Bully Hill Wines. Although Walter S. lost the court battles, he won public opinion. Free tours and tastings are offered at the winery.

For other wineries follow the **Keuka Winery Route**, marked by red and white signs. Although State 54A hugs the lake, the higher State 76 offers some of the most scenic vantage points in the region, and most of the wineries can be reached from this route.

State 54A continues into **Penn Yan**, the world's largest producer of buckwheat products. Tours of Birkett Mills are given during the **Annual Buckwheat Harvest Festival**, held the last weekend in September. In 1987 the largest pancake ever made—28 feet, 1 inch across—was made at the festival. If you are traveling on a Saturday between May and December, take a detour south from Penn Yan on State 14A to the **Windmill Farm & Craft Market**. More than 150 vendors offer farm-fresh foods, plants, crafts, antiques, quilts, cheeses, baked good, Mennonite specialties, and more. Going north on State 14A from Penn Yan, there are road signs illustrated with a horse and buggy, indicating a Mennonite community in the area. You may spot a horse and buggy clip-clopping down the road.

Continue on to **Geneva**, named after the town on the shores of Lake Geneva in Switzerland. Geneva is on the northern tip of Seneca Lake, the self-proclaimed "Lake Trout Capital of the World." There is an air of elegance and solid permanence about Geneva, which was one of the earliest settlements in this part of the state. During the nineteenth century, the town prospered, becoming a place where many residents "enjoyed, rather than made, their fortune." The legacy of early Geneva lies in the variety and quality of its buildings. The city's **South Main Street** has been proclaimed "the most beautiful street in America."

Continue south on Route 96A along the east side of Seneca Lake and follow the signs for the **Seneca Lake Wine Trail**. The first stop and the perfect choice for lunch or dinner overlooking the lake and vineyards is **Wagner Vineyards**, in Lodi, home of the **Ginny Lee Café**. The next stop is **Poplar Ridge Vineyards**, and a few miles farther down is **Hazlitt 1852 Vineyards**. Continue south on State 414 to **Watkins Glen**, best known for the gorge and the state park of the same name, on the southern end of the 38-mile-long Seneca Lake. ◼

# CENTRAL LEATHERSTOCKING

The Leatherstocking area takes its name from James Fenimore Cooper's *Leatherstocking Tales*. It was the author's father, William, who bought up rights to a colonial land grant surrounding Lake Otsego and founded Cooperstown in 1786 in the wilds of Upstate New York (about 70 miles from Albany and 200 miles from New York City). While most people know Cooperstown as the birthplace of America's favorite pastime, it would still be a classic without baseball. The village, population 2,300, looks as if it were created by Disney. Cooperstown sometimes describes itself as the "Village of Museums," but the well-preserved, prosperous, old-time village is itself a museum. The streets, lined with Victorian houses, have changed little since Abner Doubleday pitched the first ball. Baseball greats converge every summer for the Annual Induction Ceremonies and Hall of Fame Game at Doubleday Field.

Cooper dubbed Lake Otsego "Glimmerglass." You can tour the lake in a classic turn-of-the-century wooden boat, the *Chief Uncas*. The Otesaga Resort Hotel is a grand old summer hotel, built in 1909, which maintains an atmosphere of a genteel, simpler era. One of the country's most highly acclaimed opera houses is also here, overlooking the shimmering lake.

Beyond the village lie a multitude of unexpected surprises: miles of country roads filled with antique shops; underground caverns; an Indian museum hosting storytellers; the state's only casino; and even a yellow brick sidewalk in "Oztown USA," better known as Chittenango, which honors *Wizard of Oz* author Frank Baum. ◨

# CENTRAL LEATHERSTOCKING

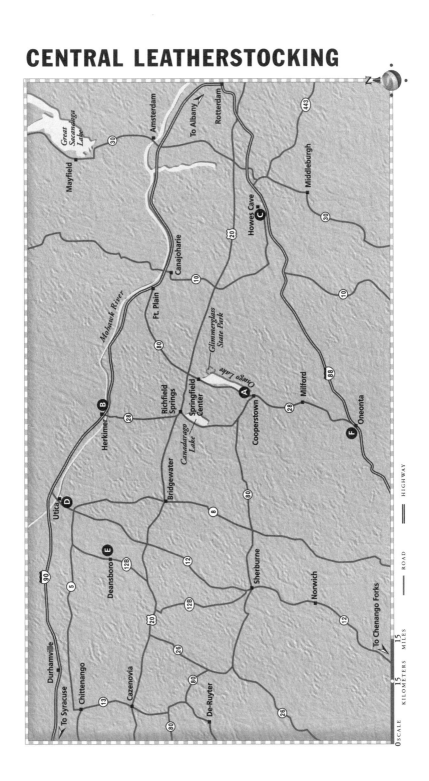

## Sights

- Ⓐ Classic Boat Tours
- Ⓐ Corvette-Americana Hall of Fame
- Ⓐ Doubleday Field
- Ⓐ Farmers' Museum
- Ⓐ Fenimore House Museum
- Ⓑ Herkimer Diamond Mines
- Ⓒ Howe Caverns
- Ⓒ Iroquois Indian Museum
- Ⓓ Munson-Williams-Proctor Institute
- Ⓔ Musical Museum
- Ⓐ National Baseball Hall of Fame
- Ⓕ National Soccer Hall of Fame

*Note: Items with the same letter are located in the same town or area.*

## A PERFECT DAY IN CENTRAL LEATHERSTOCKING

In Cooperstown, one is never far from lovely, 9-mile-long Otsego Lake. One of the best introductions to the lake is on board the *Chief Uncas*. After the cruise, stroll through the picturesque village before visiting the Fenimore House Museum, built on the site of the Cooper family farm overlooking the lake. The museum houses a wondrous collection of American Indian art as well as Cooper memorabilia. Across the road is the Farmer's Museum, which re-creates a nineteenth-century village. Almost everyone who visits Cooperstown pays homage to America's favorite pastime by visiting the National Baseball Hall of Fame. Even non–baseball fans find the museum fascinating. Cap off your day with an evening performance at the Glimmerglass Opera.

## SIGHTSEEING HIGHLIGHTS

★★★ **Classic Boat Tours**—A boat tour offers the best way to experience Lake Otsego and learn a little history at the same time. The *Chief Uncas* is a 60-foot Honduran mahogany boat, built for the Anheuser-Busch family in 1912. The hour-long cruise begins at the foot of the lake, near the headwaters of the Susquehanna River. Next to the river is Council Rock, where Indians held tribal meetings. The boat passes the village's two historic golf courses as well as Fenimore House. From the vantage of this spring-fed glacial lake, it's easy to appreciate the wisdom of William Cooper, who established a community of landowners in the wilds of New

York, and of Edward Clark, who bought up the lakefront to protect it from developers. Foot of Fair Street, Cooperstown; (607) 547-5295; Memorial Day weekend through Columbus Day weekend daily one-hour tours available; July and August six tours offered per day; two tours per day rest of season. Admission $8.50 adults, $5 children. (1 hour)

★★★ **National Baseball Hall of Fame**—The red brick facility on Cooperstown's Main Street traces its beginnings to the discovery of a misshapen, homemade ball stuffed with cloth, believed to be the baseball used by Abner Doubleday in the first game. It was purchased by Stephen C. Clark, the grandson of one of the village's first families, and put on exhibit along with other baseball objects. The exhibit was so popular that the National Baseball Hall of Fame was created, officially opening in 1939, to commemorate the game's 100th anniversary.

The Hall of Fame is really the Hall of Nostalgia, where grown men and women can return to the magical times of their youth. Even non–baseball fans will find themselves drawn into this wondrous museum with over 6,000 items on display. A 200-seat grandstand theater is the setting for a fast-paced multimedia presentation that captures the spirit of the game. During the baseball season, the Game-of-the-Week plays continuously on video screens. Tributes to Babe Ruth include his Yankee Stadium locker; the ball, bat, and uniform from his 60th home run; and photos galore. There's Ty Cobb's glove, the bat Ted Williams used when he slammed his 521st home run in his very last time at the plate, and Shoeless Joe Jackson's shoes. Wheelchair accessible. Main Street, Cooperstown; (607) 547-7200; May through September open daily 9 a.m. to 9 p.m.; October through April open daily 9 a.m. to 5 p.m. Admission $9.50 adults, $4 children ages 7–12. Cooperstown Discovery Passes available for reduced admission to three village museums. (3 hours)

★★ **Doubleday Field**—This baseball field is a must-see for baseball fans. You can sit in the stands to absorb the atmosphere and watch a practice if there is one going on. It is just down the street from the Baseball Hall of Fame. The annual **Hall of Fame Game** is played here every summer as part of the Hall of Fame induction ceremonies. The semi-professional **Oneonta Macs** play here on weekends from May through Labor Day. Main Street, Cooperstown; (607) 563-8970. Admission (for the games) $2 adults, $1 youth. (3 hours per game)

★★ **Farmers' Museum**—This living history museum of New York's frontier period, 1790 to 1860, includes a collection of a dozen historic buildings assembled from a 100-mile radius of Cooperstown. Sheep graze on the common and horse-drawn wagons travel through the village. Stop at the print shop to learn the latest news or visit the general store, where you can play a game of checkers and learn the latest gossip. Craftspeople give visitors a glimpse of nineteenth-century technologies at work. This is also home of the Cardiff Giant, America's most famous hoax. The Leatherstocking Baseball Club plays here on the Village Crossroads from May to October. It is a scene reminiscent of Abner Doubleday's era. Wheelchair accessible. Lake Road, Route 80, Cooperstown; (607) 547-1400; June through Labor Day open daily 9 a.m. to 5 p.m.; Labor Day through October open daily 10 a.m. to 4 p.m.; November open Tuesday through Sunday 10 a.m. to 4 p.m.; December open weekends 10 a.m. to 4 p.m.; closed January through May. Admission $9 adults, $4 youth (Discovery pass available for three museums). (2 hours)

★★ **Fenimore House Museum**—This museum is on an historic site—it was once the Cooper family farm. The magnificent house was built by Edward Clark, heir to the Singer Sewing Machine fortune. Its newest attraction is the most impressive $10-million **American Indian Wing** (donated by Jane Forbes Clark). It was built to house the Eugene and Clare Thaw Collection of American Indian Art, more than 700 objects that include masterworks of extraordinary quality and which represent a broad range of cultures across North America, including Northwest Coast, Alaska, California, Southwest, Plains and Prairie, and Woodlands Indians. Highlights include a rare ledger book of drawings by Black Hawk, a rare and beautiful late-eighteenth-century Montagnais-Naskapi caribou skin coat, and a number of Eskimo masks from the late 1800s.

James Fenimore Cooper, author of 32 novels including the *Leather-stocking Tales*, is the focus of the museum's **Cooper Room**. Portraits of his family include one of his mother sitting on the rocking chair that came with her from New Jersey. Tradition has it that Elizabeth Fenimore Cooper refused to leave New Jersey for the wilds of central New York, saying she "could not face the wilderness." After much pleading to no avail, her husband simply lifted the rocker with his wife in it and placed it in a wagon for the long trip. There's also a remarkable series of bronze life masks of such luminaries as John Adams, Thomas Jefferson, and James Madison. Wheelchair accessible.

Lake Road, Route 80, Cooperstown; (607) 547-1400; June through
Labor Day open daily 9 a.m. to 5 p.m.; Labor Day through October
open daily 10 a.m. to 4 p.m.; November open Tuesday through Sunday
10 a.m. to 4 p.m.; December open weekends 10 a.m. to 4 p.m.; closed
January through May. Admission $9 adults, $4 youth (Discovery pass
available for three museums). (2 hours)

★★ **Howe Caverns**—Father Lester Howe discovered this cavern and
named it after himself when he opened it to the public in 1842. It was
soon heralded as a tourist attraction second only to Niagara Falls. Today
an elevator lowers visitors 156 feet to a subterranean walkway. From
there a guide leads explorers through the cavern, with stalactites and
stalagmites well-lit by spotlights. It is always 52 degrees in the caverns. It
doesn't seem to be the perfect setting for a wedding, but more than 200
couples have tied the knot here, beginning with Howe's daughter, Elgiva,
who was married here as an early marketing stunt. Legend has it that if
you are single and looking, you will be married within the year if you
step on the heart-shaped stone at the Bridal Altar. There are two 22-
passenger boats to carry visitors across the Lake of Venus. Howes Cave;
(518) 296-8990; open daily 9 a.m. to 6 p.m. except Thanksgiving,
Christmas, and New Year's Day. Admission $11.50 adults, $6 children
ages 7–12. (1 hour)

★★ **Iroquois Indian Museum**—This museum is designed in the
shape of an Iroquois longhouse and is in the ancient territory of the
Iroquois, whose confederacy includes the Mohawk, Oneida, Tuscarora,
Onondaga, Cayuga, and Seneca. The children's museum on the lower
level lets youngsters get a glimpse of the Iroquois way of life. They can
play musical instruments, try on clothes, handle tools and furs, and
make some beadwork to take home. An Onondaga storyteller is often
on hand to tell traditional Iroquois tales, and there are musical and
dance performances. The gallery shows works of contemporary Indian
artists. The museum is set in a 45-acre nature preserve with marked
trails and a picnic area. Wheelchair accessible. Caverns Road, Howes
Cave; (518) 296-8949; July through Labor Day open Monday through
Saturday 10 a.m. to 6 p.m., Sunday noon to 6 p.m.; April through May
31 and Labor Day through December open Monday through Saturday
10 a.m. to 5 p.m., Sunday noon to 5 p.m.; closed January through
March. Admission $5.50 adults, $4.50 seniors and students ages 13–17,
$2.50 children ages 5–12. (2 hours)

★ **Corvette-Americana Hall of Fame**—America loves cars, and this museum features Corvettes, of course. But it is also a time-walk through contemporary American culture, from 1953, when Chevrolet introduced its first 'Vette, to the present. Each rare collector's car is built into a dioramic Hollywood set of a famous American landmark such as Mt. Rushmore, Niagara Falls, or the Alamo. The museum features a 1,000-song soundtrack that rocks through more than 40 years of music history. Wheelchair accessible. Route 28, Cooperstown; (607) 547-4135; May through November open daily 10 a.m. to 8 p.m. Admission $8.75 adults, $6.75 youth. (2 hours)

★ **Munson-Williams-Proctor Institute**—This Utica art gallery showcases one of the Northeast's finest collections of eighteenth- to twentieth-century American and European art. Its works include those of Picasso, Dali, Calder, Moore, Pollock, and Burchfield. Also on display are Thomas Cole's allegorical paintings *The Voyage of Life*, depicting childhood, youth, manhood, and old age. The institute includes the museum, a school of art, and Fountain Elms, a restored Victorian mansion. Wheelchair accessible. 310 Genesee Street, Utica; (315) 797-0000; open Tuesday through Saturday 10 a.m. to 5 p.m., Sunday 1 p.m. to 5 p.m. Admission by donation. (2 hours)

★ **Musical Museum**—Visitors are invited to crank, pump, and play restored music boxes, melodeons, nickelodeons, grind organs, and much more. It doesn't matter if your musical tastes run to Paderewski playing Chopin or Elvis singing "You Ain't Nothin' but a Hound Dog," you will be entranced by this wondrous museum. There are 17 rooms in all. Don't miss the giant calliope. There's a picnic area and a gift shop. Wheelchair accessible. Route 12B, Deansboro; (315) 841-8774; April through December open daily 10 a.m. to 4 p.m. Admission $4 adults, $3 seniors and children ages 6–12. (2 hours)

**Herkimer Diamond Mines**—These "diamonds" are, in fact, quartz crystals. Visitors get to keep all the crystals they find. There's a large gem and mineral shop, a museum, a restaurant, and a campground. Route 28, Herkimer; (315) 891-7355; April through December 1 open daily 9 a.m. to 5 p.m. Admission $6 adults, $5 children ages 5–14. (2 hours)

**National Soccer Hall of Fame**—The history of soccer in the U.S. dates back to the 1860s. Much of this history has been preserved and is displayed through photos, trophy exhibits, graphics, uniforms, and other memorabilia. Large screen TVs are available for individual or group viewing of the dozens of historic films on hand in the museum library. 5–11 Ford Avenue, Oneonta; (607) 432-3351; June 1 through September 15 open daily 9 a.m. to 7 p.m.; September 16 through May open Monday through Saturday 10 a.m. to 3 p.m., Sunday noon to 5 p.m. Admission $4 adults, $2 children. (2 hours)

## FITNESS AND RECREATION

The **Clark Sports Center**, on Susquehanna Avenue in Cooperstown, is a world-class facility more likely to be found at a major university than in a small rural village. It includes a complete gymnasium, indoor running track and horizontal climbing wall, bowling alleys, Olympic swimming and diving pools, Nautilus and aerobics rooms, adventure ropes course, and rock climbing wall. A nature trail runs through the 45-acre preserve at the **Iroquois Indian Museum**, in Howes Cave. **Glimmerglass State Park**, in Cooperstown, has hiking trails and nature walks led by park rangers.

## FOOD

In Cooperstown, the **Otesaga Resort Hotel**, Lake Street, (607) 547-9931, open from April 18 through October, offers standard hotel dining and a grand view of the lake. Other popular village restaurants are the **Pepper Mill**, Route 28, Lower Chestnut, (607) 547-8550; **Red Sleigh Restaurant**, Route 80, Lake Road, (607) 547-5581; and **Tunicliff Inn**, 34 Pioneer Street, (607) 547-9611. The **Brae Loch Inn** features Scottish foods at 5 Albany Street, Cazenovia, (315) 655-3431. **Brooks House of Barbecue**, Route 7, East End, Oneonta, (607) 432-1782, is famous for its barbecue, seats 300, and claims to have the largest indoor charcoal pit in the East. **Cathedral Farms**, Route 1, Oneonta, (607) 432-7483, is another popular Oneonta dining establishment.

## LODGING

Rates are generally higher during the busy July and August season, and during the Hall of Fame weekend, it can be very difficult to find a room near Cooperstown. The **Otesaga Resort Hotel**, Lake Street,

Cooperstown, (607) 547-9931 or (800) 348-6222, is a grand old hotel overlooking the lake. It's listed on the National Register of Historic Places. It encompasses the historic 18-hole Leatherstocking Golf Course. The hotel is open from April 18 to November 1. Rates include breakfast and dinner ($260 to $395 for a double). The **Inn at Cooperstown**, built in 1874, 16 Chestnut Street, Cooperstown, (607) 547-5756 or (800) 348 6222, offers warm hospitality in an historic setting in the middle of the village ($89 to $145 for a double). **Lake View Motel & Cottages**, RD2, Cooperstown, (607) 547-9740 or (888) 4-LAKEVIEW, offers free paddle and rowboats, swimming, and fishing ($49 to $122 for a double, $160 for cottages). **Holiday Inn Oneonta**, Route 23, Southside-Oneonta, (607) 433-2250 or (800) 465-4329), has 120 rooms and is just 30 minutes from Cooperstown ($68 to $129 for a double). The village of Cazenovia boasts several lovely historic inns. They include the **Brae Loch Inn**, where the staff wear kilts, 5 Albany Street, (315) 655-3431 ($75 to $125 for a double, includes breakfast); the **Brewster Inn**, 6 Ledyard Avenue, (315) 655-9232 ($70 to $185); and the **Lincklaen House**, 99 Albany Street, (315) 655-3461 ($99 for a double).

## CAMPING

Camping is popular in the Leatherstocking region. There are 39 sites at **Glimmerglass State Park**, R.R. 2, Cooperstown, (607) 547-8662, with swimming and fishing and a beach on Lake Otsego ($10 per night). **Cooperstown Beaver Valley**, Route 28, Cooperstown, (800) 726-7314, has 100 sites, swimming, fishing, and boat rentals ($21 per night). **Cooperstown Shadow Brook Campground**, East Lake Road, Cooperstown, (607) 264-8431, has a pool, fishing pond, and cabin and trailer rentals just minutes from the village ($19 per night). **Herkimer Diamond KOA**, Route 28, Herkimer, (800) 450-5267, has 126 sites and is across the road from the Diamond Mines ($20 per night). **Chenango Valley State Park**, 153 State Park Road, Chenango Forks, (607) 648-5251, has 216 sites, swimming, fishing, and boat rentals ($10 per night).

## NIGHTLIFE

The Oneida Indian Nation operates **Turning Stone Casino**, (315) 361-7711, the state's first and so-far only casino. It offers all manner of

# CENTRAL LEATHERSTOCKING

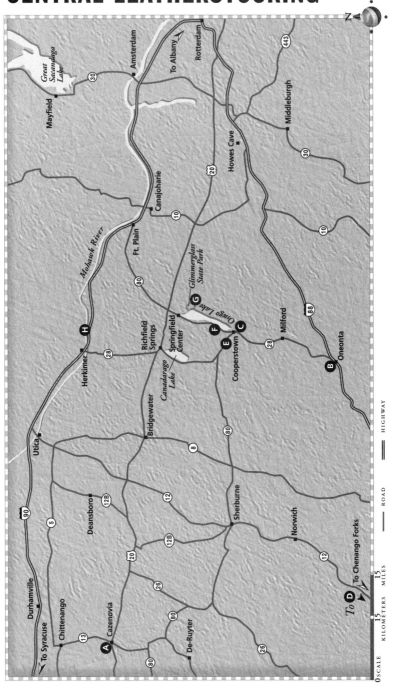

## Food

**A** Brae Loch Inn

**B** Brooks House of Barbecue

**B** Cathedral Farms

**C** Otesaga Resort Hotel

**C** Pepper Mill

**C** Red Sleigh Restaurant

**C** Tunicliff Inn

## Lodging

**A** Brae Loch Inn

**A** Brewster Inn

**B** Holiday Inn Oneonta

## Lodging

**C** Inn at Cooperstown

**C** Lake View Motel & Cottages

**A** Lincklaen House

**C** Otesaga Resort Hotel

## Camping

**D** Chenango Valley State Park

**E** Cooperstown Beaver Valley

**F** Cooperstown Shadow Brook Campground

**G** Glimmerglass State Park

**H** Herkimer Diamond KOA

*Note: Items with the same letter are located in the same town or area.*

casino games, Vegas-style revues, and fine dining. There's also a cultural center and traditional craft store. The casino is open 24 hours a day and is easily accessible ½-mile from Exit 33 of the New York Thruway in Verona. The highly acclaimed **Glimmerglass Opera**, Route 80, 8 miles north of the village of Cooperstown, (607) 547-2255, boasts one of only four American opera houses built especially for opera. Every summer the opera mounts three productions in English in the **Alice Busch Opera Theater**. The theater's side walls roll back, bringing in the beauty of the outdoors. The season runs from July 1 to August 21.

# APPENDIX

## METRIC CONVERSION CHART

1 U.S. gallon = approximately 4 liters
1 liter = about 1 quart
1 Canadian gallon = approximately 4.5 liters

1 pound = approximately $1/2$ kilogram
1 kilogram = about 2 pounds

1 foot = approximately $1/3$ meter
1 meter = about 1 yard
1 yard = a little less than a meter
1 mile = approximately 1.6 kilometers
1 kilometer = about $2/3$ mile

90°F = about 30°C
20°C = approximately 70°F

# Planning Map: New York State

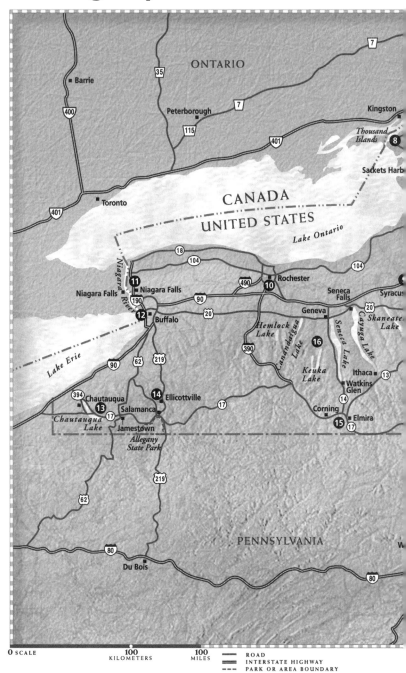

O SCALE

100 KILOMETERS

100 MILES

ROAD
INTERSTATE HIGHWAY
PARK OR AREA BOUNDARY

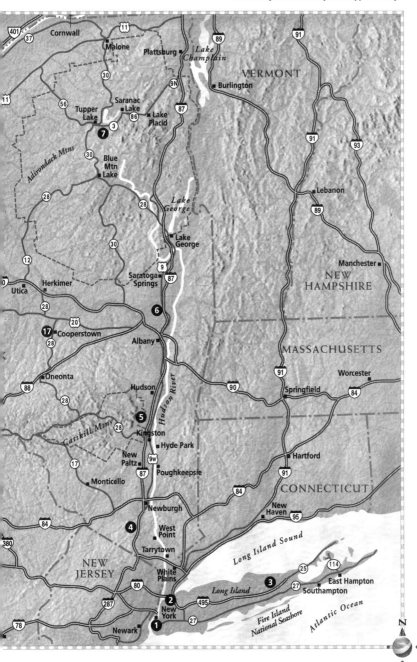

# INDEX

## Map Index

# Books from John Muir Publications

## Rick Steves' Books

**Asia Through the Back Door**, 400 pp., $17.95

**Europe 101: History and Art for the Traveler**, 352 pp., $17.95

**Mona Winks: Self-Guided Tours of Europe's Top Museums**, 432 pp., $18.95

**Rick Steves' Baltics & Russia**, 160 pp., $9.95

**Rick Steves' Europe**, 560 pp., $18.95

**Rick Steves' France, Belgium & the Netherlands**, 304 pp., $15.95

**Rick Steves' Germany, Austria & Switzerland**, 272 pp., $14.95

**Rick Steves' Great Britain & Ireland**, 320 pp., $15.95

**Rick Steves' Italy**, 224 pp., $13.95

**Rick Steves' Scandinavia**, 192 pp., $13.95

**Rick Steves' Spain & Portugal**, 240 pp., $13.95

**Rick Steves' Europe Through the Back Door**, 512 pp., $19.95

**Rick Steves' French Phrase Book**, 192 pp., $5.95

**Rick Steves' German Phrase Book**, 192 pp., $5.95

**Rick Steves' Italian Phrase Book**, 192 pp., $5.95

**Rick Steves' Spanish & Portuguese Phrase Book**, 336 pp., $7.95

**Rick Steves' French/German/Italian Phrase Book**, 320 pp., $7.95

## Adventures in Nature Series

**Belize: Adventures in Nature**, 400 pp., $18.95

**Guatemala: Adventures in Nature**, 400 pp., $18.95

## City•Smart™ Guidebooks

**City•Smart Guidebook: Austin**, 224 pp., $12.95

**City•Smart Guidebook: Cleveland**, 208 pp., $14.95

**City•Smart Guidebook: Denver**, 256 pp., $14.95

**City•Smart Guidebook: Indianapolis**, 224 pp., $12.95

**City•Smart Guidebook: Kansas City**, 248 pp., $12.95

**City•Smart Guidebook: Memphis**, 224 pp., $12.95

**City•Smart Guidebook: Milwaukee**, 224 pp., $12.95

**City•Smart Guidebook: Minneapolis/St. Paul**, 232 pp., $14.95

**City•Smart Guidebook: Nashville**, 256 pp., $14.95

**City•Smart Guidebook: Portland**, 232 pp., $14.95

**City•Smart Guidebook: Tampa/St. Petersburg**, 256 pp., $14.95

## Travel+Smart™ Trip Planners

**American Southwest Travel + Smart Trip Planner**, 256 pp., $14.95

**Colorado Travel + Smart Trip Planner**, 248 pp., $14.95

**Eastern Canada Travel + Smart Trip Planner**, 272 pp., $15.95

**Florida Gulf Coast Travel + Smart Trip Planner**, 224 pp., $14.95

**Hawaii Travel + Smart Trip Planner**, 256 pp., $14.95

**Kentucky/Tennessee Travel + Smart Trip Planner**, 248 pp., $14.95

**Michigan Travel + Smart Trip Planner**, 232 pp., $14.95

**Minnesota/Wisconsin Travel + Smart Trip Planner**, 232 pp., $14.95

**New England Travel + Smart Trip Planner**, 256 pp., $14.95

**New York Travel + Smart Trip Planner**, 256 pp., $15.95

**Northern California Travel + Smart Trip Planner**, 272 pp., $15.95

**Pacific Northwest Travel + Smart Trip Planner**, 240 pp., $14.95

**Southern California Travel + Smart Trip Planner**, 232 pp., $14.95

**South Florida and The Keys Travel + Smart Trip Planner**, 240 pp., $14.95

## Other Terrific Travel Titles

**The 100 Best Small Art Towns in America**, 256 pp., $15.95

**The Big Book of Adventure Travel**, 400 pp., $17.95

**The Birder's Guide to Bed and Breakfasts: U.S. and Canada**, 416 pp., $17.95

**Costa Rica: A Natural Destination**, 416 pp., $18.95

**Indian America**, 480 pp., $18.95

**The People's Guide to Mexico**, 608 pp., $19.95

**Ranch Vacations**, 632 pp., $22.95

**Understanding Europeans**, 272 pp., $14.95

**Watch It Made in the U.S.A.**, 400 pp., $17.95

**The World Awaits**, 280 pp., $16.95

## Automotive Titles

**The Greaseless Guide to Car Care**, 272 pp., $19.95

**How to Keep Your Subaru Alive**, 480 pp., $21.95

**How to Keep Your Toyota Pick-Up Alive**, 392 pp., $21.95

**How to Keep Your VW Alive**, 464 pp., $25.00

## Ordering Information

Please check your local bookstore for our books, or call **1-800-888-7504** to order direct and to receive a complete catalog. A shipping charge will be added to your order total.

Send all inquiries to:
**John Muir Publications**
**P.O. Box 613**
**Santa Fe, NM 87504**

# ABOUT THE AUTHOR

Deborah Williams is a veteran, award-winning travel writer who lives on a 63-acre farm 30 miles south of Buffalo, New York. A member of the Society of American Travel Writers and the American Society of Journalists and Authors, Williams is the author of *Country Roads of New York* (1993) and *Natural Wonders of New York* (1995), both published by Country Roads Press. She has contributed to Fodor's, Insight, Nelles, and Debrett's travel guides on New York, Canada, the Bahamas, and the Caribbean. Previously a reporter and editor for the now closed *Buffalo Courier Express*, she regularly contributes articles to a variety of newspapers and magazines in the United States and Canada. In addition to exploring New York State and the far corners of the globe, she enjoys gardening, sailing on nearby Lake Erie, and scuba diving.